W9-APT-340

Job #: 108554

Author Name:Polkinghorne

Title of Book: Narrative Knowing

ISBN #: 9780887066238

Narrative Knowing and the Human Sciences

SUNY Series in Philosophy of the Social Sciences
Lenore Langsdorf, Editor

Narrative Knowing

AND THE

Human Sciences

Donald E. Polkinghorne

STATE UNIVERSITY OF NEW YORK PRESS

Published by
State University of New York Press, Albany

© 1988   State University of New York

For information, contact State University of New York Press, Albany, NY
www.sunypress.edu

Library of Congress Cataloging-in-Publication Data

Polkinghorne, Donald, 1936-
   Narrative knowing and the human sciences.

   (SUNY series in philosophy of the social sciences)
   Bibliography: p. 215
   Includes index.
   1. Social sciences—Biographical methods.
2. Narration (Rhetoric)   I. Title.
H61.P5875   1988   300'.72   87-17992
ISBN 0-88706-622-4
ISBN 0-88706-623-2 (pbk.)

10   9   8   7   6

To my parents, Elmer and Marge

Language, by naming beings for the first time,
first brings beings to word and to appearance.

Martin Heidegger, *The Origin of the Work of Art*

Contents

Preface

THE impetus for this book came from two nagging concerns about my profession that have intensified for me during the last decade. The first was an unresolved personal conflict between my work as an academic researcher on the one hand and as a practicing psychotherapist on the other. I view my discipline, psychology, as a unified enterprise, and have supported the ideal of the integration of its scientific and professional aspects; yet I have not found the findings of academic research of much help in my work as a clinician, something that I find disconcerting.

My own unsettled feelings about integrating research and practice are not idiosyncratic. The psychology doctoral students I teach express the same feelings of discontinuity between their clinical internship experiences and the research sequence (including the dissertation) that is part of their curriculum. Academics and practitioners seem to be growing increasingly separate, and my discipline's organization, the American Psychological Association, has begun to institutionalize their division. Colleagues in other social sciences, moreover, describe a similar breach in their own disciplines.

The second concern is an apparent devaluation, even loss of faith in the ability of research in the human disciplines to deliver on their original promise of helping to solve human and social problems. In this regard Seymour Sarason's *Psychology Misdirected* made a striking impression on me. He talked about the disenchantment he and others had with the field of psychology because of its lack of progress. Whereas medicine could point to its success in conquering smallpox and polio and in the development of new surgical techniques and medicines, the social sciences could not provide illustrations of similar public accomplishments. Despite the large sums of public funds invested in the human disciplines during the era of the Great Society, little headway was made in solving social problems. The solutions to these problems clearly involve more than just insights from the social sciences; nevertheless, our inability to provide the promised "scientific" knowledge that would contribute to this project is noteworthy. Our advice on how to reduce criminal recidivism or teen pregnancies, or even on how to lose weight, has had little appreciable impact on the problems at hand.

Several personal anecdotes increased my concern. A friend who has been successful in the grantsmanship game was told by a New York City official that they had decided to cut back their funding of social science research because they did not see that the social sciences were being of much help. Another friend reported that the director of a medical center had said that he had decided to shift the center's resources away from psychological research on mental illness because he thought the only significant accomplishments would come from psychopharmacology. And it seemed to me that the indirect message in the severe cutbacks in social science research funding from state and national agencies was that they did not believe they had received value for money. Although an exaggerated picture of the lack of success in social science research has often been drawn, I must concede that the critics do have a point.

The criticism by practitioners and funding agencies of social science research raises the question of the adequacy of its methodological assumptions. Although personally defending the significance of the contributions made by present methods of social science research, I find that our traditional research model, adopted from the natural sciences, is limited when applied in the study of human beings. I do not believe that the solutions to human problems will come from developing even more sophisticated and creative applications of the natural science model, but rather by developing additional, complementary approaches that are especially sensitive to the unique characteristics of human existence.

Despite the general lessening of confidence in the ability of social science *research* to provide useful answers to human problems, people increasingly have been turning for help to the psychotherapists, counselors, and organizational consultants. On the assumption that the *practitioners* have developed a way of understanding that their clients find helpful, I set out to examine what kind of knowledge they used in their practice. The common wisdom has been that the development of research strategies is the province of the academy, who then passed on the results to the practitioners. I decided to turn this wisdom around and look at what could be learned from the practitioners about how research should be done. The idea was that the practitioners, perhaps, are better commonsense epistemologists than academics.

What I found was that practitioners work with narrative knowledge. They are concerned with people's stories: they work with case histories and use narrative explanations to understand why the people they work with behave the way they do. I was encouraged by the fact that other people were starting to reach conclusions similar to mine. I came across the work of Donald Spence and Roy Shafer that looked at the psychoanalytic session as work with narrative information, and heard Jerome Bruner speak on the narrative method at the 1985 convention of the American Psychological Association. William Runyan, whom I met at a seminar on narrative at the University of California, shared with me his work on case histories and psychobiography. The most productive discussions were with my colleague, George Howard, the chair of the department of psychology at the University of Notre Dame. Out of these meetings, in which we spent long hours talking about the implications of narrative understanding for clinical practice, came the outline for this book. Judith Blanton, Theodore Sarbin, and Donald Michael suggested revisions that significantly improved the final product.

The work involved in writing this book has been particularly rewarding in that my nagging concern over the research-practice division has subsided. I still value and use my quantitative research tools for descriptions of large group characteristics. But what I have learned from the practitioner's kind of knowledge is the importance of having research strategies that can work with the narratives people use to understand the human world. Although this perspective presents a problem for the research models to which we have grown accustomed and in which we take pride, it opens up a realm for understanding human beings that will, I believe, make our research considerably more successful and useful.

CHAPTER I

Introduction

EXPERIENCE is meaningful and human behavior is generated from and informed by this meaningfulness. Thus, the study of human behavior needs to include an exploration of the meaning systems that form human experience. This book is an inquiry into narrative, the primary form by which human experience is made meaningful. Narrative meaning is a cognitive process that organizes human experiences into temporally meaningful episodes. Because it is a cognitive process, a mental operation, narrative meaning is not an "object" available to direct observation. However, the individual stories and histories that emerge in the creation of human narratives are available for direct observation. Examples of narrative include personal and social histories, myths, fairy tales, novels, and the everyday stories we use to explain our own and others' actions.

Before beginning the investigation of narrative proper with Chapter 2, I will use this preparatory chapter to describe the general characteristics of human existence. The first section examines human existence as a systemic synthesis of multiple kinds of reality, and identifies narrative meaning as an aspect of one of these realities, the realm of meaning. The second section then investigates the problems inherent in studying narrative meaning and suggests that, given its characteristics, hermeneutic methods provide the most adequate tools for understanding narrative.

The realms of human existence

Human existence consists of a stratified system of differently organized realms of reality—the material realm, the organic realm, and the mental realm. Narrative meaning is one of the processes of the mental realm, and functions to organize elements of awareness into meaningful episodes. The idea of different kinds of reality—in opposition to the popular notion that there is only one basic reality, the material—is explained by the concept of emergence developed in systems theory.[1] This section first describes the theory of the emergence of multiple realities, and then examines in detail the operations of the most evolved of these realities, the mental realm.

Emergence

In the course of human evolution entirely new levels of reality emerge. The regularities of these new levels are autonomous—that is, they are not susceptible to explanation on the basis of theories and laws that account for the phenomena of less complex realms.[2] An often-used example to illustrate this idea is that the theories and laws used to explain the action of hydrogen atoms and oxygen atoms in isolation do not predict or explain the characteristics of their combination—water. The integrated parts perform differently than they do when in isolation, and this difference is attributed to the special influence that comes from the characteristics of their specific organization, structure, and configuration. These establish the emerged properties of the complex.

When these levels of complexity occur with their new organizational patterns, novel and innovative capacities appear in the universe. The prediction of these new structures from the characteristics of previous levels appears to be uncertain. Emergent evolution holds that the development of new structures and properties is an ongoing process and that organizational structures of earlier levels are recombined into still more complex higher-order structures to produce additional novel characteristics. Each level which emerges contains within it earlier levels arranged as strata within the new system. The supervening of this new level on its component parts may engender in those parts, in turn, novel qualities that did not exist in them prior to participation in the new order. Thus, in the human realm the mental subsystem is both affected by and affects the organic subsystem.

Although the process of emergence is cumulative, it reaches certain threshold points of structural complexity where the properties produced by the new organization are dramatically different from earlier ones. The two most dramatic threshold points for the organization of human existence appear at the transition from matter to life and the transition from life to consciousness.[3] (James Miller has a fuller description of threshold points that includes, after the emergence of life, the appearance of the cell followed by the organ, the organism, the group, the organization, the society, and then the supranational system.)[4] The emergence of human beings from life in general to reflective consciousness and language is a threshold change that has brought about a unique level of reality that I will call "the order of meaning."

Because human existence is embedded to various degrees in the material, the organic, and the meaning realms, it includes within itself the three basic structures of reality—matter, life, and consciousness. Although each structure operates according to its own peculiar organizational patterns, the operations of the higher, more recently developed levels (for example, those involved with the deliberative and reflective use of language) is influenced by the peculiar organization of the lower levels. The emergence of the order of meaning, although it possesses unique characteristics, was dependent on the development of an organic complexity, the conglomerate organization of a triune brain, and a highly differentiated neocortex. Jason Brown, writing about the emergence of reflective consciousness in conjunction with the development of three cerebral levels, states:

> These levels are in no sense "separate brains," but rather they are widely distributed systems that develop seriatim out of one another, serving to transform cognition to successively more differentiated states. Moreover, the levels are to some extent arbitrary; each probably comprises several—perhaps innumerable—subsystems. There are not clear transitions from one level to another, since it is not known whether the levels themselves develop as quantal achievements or on a continuum of evolutionary change.[5]

The material, organic, and meaning structures of reality are related to one another in human existence according to a patterned hierarchy.[6] It is the interaction of all these parts that produces the human realm, not merely consciousness and the other unique parts that are newly evolved in the human organism. The existence of the lower levels is the necessary but not sufficient condition for the existence of higher levels: the relationship among the levels is not characterized by a simple pattern of the lower levels' subservience to the higher levels. A vertical binding exists among the strata, such that the higher levels must adjust to the lower, as the lower levels must adjust to the higher. Moreover, patterns developed at various levels can be passed along to both higher and lower levels. For example, thoughts and behaviors originally created by high-level reflective operations can be passed along as habits, sedimented at a lower stratum of the person; genetically given dispositions can be passed through to higher orders as structures of language understanding and meaningful interpretation.

This stratification is not limited to the internal organization of individual persons. It extends to the orders of cultural rules and language systems in which individuals are conjoined in social groups. The unique human capacities of consciousness and language have produced a special stratum of the environment—that is, culture and meaning—in which we exist. This stratum holds traditions and conventions to which individuals are connected in a dialectic manner; they provide individuals with a common symbolic environment that informs their categories of thought and social actions while facilitating human interaction and the accomplishment of group projects.

One of the projects of the mental realm is knowledge of the whole self. The mental realm turns its attention on itself, as well as on its organic and material aspects. The activity of self-study can be carried out in the ordinary and informal manner of self-reflection, or in an organized and formal way following scientific methods. The knowledge produced by the human disciplines, for example, is an organized articulation of one part of the human realm differentiating itself in order to comprehend its own characteristics. But because the various realms are characterized by a peculiar system of organization, no single knowledge system is capable of encompassing the full range of the strata of human existence. I will return to the task of comprehending the various dimensions or structures of human existence in the next chapter.

The realm of meaning

Human beings have a synthetic kind of existence in which the realms of matter, life, and meaning are fused. Although these realms take on a special hue because of their union in human existence, they retain their own integral properties. The matter of human existence shares the properties of nonhuman matter. A person who plunges out of a window will accelerate at the same rate as any other material object. The organic operations within human existence function just as they do in other life forms. The realm of meaning, however, exists only within the particular synthesis that is human existence, although it is always conjoined in interaction with material and organic realms.

Because narrative is one of the operations of the realm of meaning, an explicit examination of this realm will aid in the understanding of narrative. First, the realm of meaning is not a thing or substance, but an activity. For example, the activity of building a house is different from the structure the activity produces, and the activity of the writing of a play is different from the manuscript that is produced. Building and writing are performances, not substances; it is the artifacts they produce that are substances. As an activity the realm of meaning is described by verb forms rather than nouns. The primary dimension of an activity is time, and the sequence in which the parts of an action happen can be decisive in defining what kind of activity it is. Much of the philosophical confusion about the realm of meaning has been related to the attempt to identify it as a substance.[7]

Second, the products of the activity of the realm of meaning are both names of elements and connections or relations among elements.[8] The elements on which the realm of meaning acts to establish or recognize relationships are the contents of awareness. The production of the contents of awareness is the work of the organic realm. Human existence includes the organic realm, and shares with other participants of this realm (for example, dogs and cats) a perceptual openness to the world. Our sensory apparatus and brain structures present a rudimentary experience of objects and activities. The actions of the realm of meaning add to this awareness an additional presence of relationships and connections among these rudimentary perceptions, including: (a) one perception is the *same as* or *not the same* as another, (b) one is *similar* or *dissimilar* to another, (c) one is an *instance* of another, (d) one *stands for* the other, (e) one is a *part* of the other, and (f) one is the *cause* of the other.[9] In the ongoing production of meaning, these various kinds of relationships are combined to construct connections among things.

Examples of these operations include: (a) The perception of a key seen in the lost-and-found box is related to the image of the key that is retrieved from memory through the quality of *sameness*—that is, it is the same key that was lost. The capacity to identify elements as the same is basic for mathematical and formal logic operations.

(b) The way an acquaintance eats reminds one of the way a hog eats, based on the *similarity* of the actions. The ordinary recognition that a perception is linked to a category comes about through assessing the degree of similarity that a specific perception has to a prototype image. A blue jay is recognized as a bird because of its high degree of similarity to one's personal prototype of a bird, perhaps a wren. The notion of similarity is expressed linguistically as a trope or metaphor. This capacity to note and express to another person that one thing is like another thing is basic to human communication and the growth of language systems.[10]

(c) An example of the activity of noting that a rudimentary perception is an *instance* of something has been given by Edmund Husserl.[11] Any one perception presents only a profile of an object; people see only that portion of the object directly facing them. The total object is never directly perceived. It is the work of the realm of meaning to recognize that these various profiles are instances of the same object. Out of the collection of identified instances or partial appearances the realm of meaning constructs a nonperceptual awareness of the object as a whole.

(d) The mental operation of establishing a connection between two things by having one *stand for* the other, or be a sign of something else, underlies the capacity to use symbols and language. In ordinary usage the term "meaning" refers to this particular type of connection. Charles S. Peirce, the American founder of semiotics (the study of signs), distinguished three types of "standing for" based on the degree of similarity between the sign and its referent.[12] The *icon* is a relationship in which the thing stands for the other by resembling it. For example, a diagram or a painting has an iconic relationship to its subject insofar as it resembles it. In the *index,* the relationship is concrete, actual, and usually of a sequential, causal kind. For example, a knock on the door is an index of someone's presence, smoke is an index of fire, and the position of a weathervane is an index of the direction of the wind. In the *symbol,* the relationship is arbitrary. If one person is to signify something to another through an arbitrary symbol, they both have to understand what the signifier stands for. The major manifestation of something standing for another in an arbitrary way is language. There is no similarity between the sound "dog," or the markings (letters of the alphabet) that stand for that sound, and the perceptual image to which it is linked (that is, the actual dog); it is an arbitrary but culturally agreed upon symbol.

The same object can have a number of different other objects stand for it in each of the three types of "standing for." For example, a tree in my back yard can be represented by a painting or photograph (icons), by pointing my finger at it or by observing a leaf from it (indexes), or by uttering or writing the words "the tree (*arbre, Baum, árbol*) in my back yard" (symbols).

(e) and (f) Narrative meaning is created by noting that something is a *part* of some whole and that something is the *cause* of something else. Narrative meaning is focused on those rudimentary aspects of experience that concern human actions or events that affect human beings. For example, the experiences of "feeling an ache in my muscles," "playing three sets of tennis," and "not stretching before playing" can be connected as parts of a whole episode: "I got aching muscles because I didn't stretch before playing tennis." The meaning of each event is produced by the part it plays in the whole episode. The episode needs to include both some end point as well as the contributions that the events and actions made in bringing about or delaying the achievement of that end point.

The question, "What does that mean?", asks how something is related or connected to something else. To ask what a word means is to ask what it stands for. To ask about the meaning or significance of an event is to ask how it contributed to the conclusion of the episode. It is the connections or relationships among events that is their meaning. Meanings are not produced only by individuals who register certain experiences as connected to others. Cultures maintain a system of language and pass on to succeeding generations knowledge of the connections between signifying sounds and the things and notions they signify. Cultures also maintain collections of typical narrative meanings in their myths, fairy tales, histories, and stories. To participate as a member of a culture requires a general knowledge of its full range of accumulated meanings. Cultural stocks of meaning are not static but are added to by new contributions from members, and deleted by lack of use.[13]

In summary, narrative meaning is one type of meaning produced by the mental realm. It principally works to draw together human actions and the events that affect human beings, and not relationships among inanimate objects. Narrative creates its meaning by noting the contributions that actions and events make to a particular outcome and then configures these parts into a whole episode.

The study of narrative meaning

The aim of the study of narrative meaning is to make explicit the operations that produce its particular kind of meaning, and to draw out the implications this meaning has for understanding human existence.

Inherent problems in the study of meaning

Researchers are typically confronted with five problem areas in investigations of aspects of human consciousness.

(1) As mentioned above, the realm of meaning exists in a different form than natural objects do. It is an activity, not a thing. It cannot be picked up and held, nor measured by an impersonal instrument. Robert Romanyshyn suggests that the kind of reality it has is like that of a reflection in a mirror—it presents itself in our consciousness as a fleeting trace or indication; it appears as a wisp. The meanings are continuously being reconstituted as the rudimentary perceptions of consciousness change. The activity of making meaning is not static, and thus it is not easily grasped.

(2) Each of us has direct access to only one realm of meaning: our own. Because it is not available to direct public observation, the region of meaning must be approached through self-reflective recall or introspection in our mental realm. However, the activity of producing and recollecting meaning normally operates outside of awareness, and what is available through self-reflection is only the outcomes of the meaning-making processes, not the processes themselves. A further problem is that in everyday living we are normally busy attending to the world, and meanings express themselves merely in our actions and speech; recognition of their presence requires that we consciously change the focus of awareness to the realm of meaning itself. Yet when we focus on the realm of meaning in self-reflection, the meanings that are available to us can be limited by other mental operations, such as repression.

(3) Study of the realm of meaning requires the use of linguistic data. The problems of direct access to the realm of meaning can be partially overcome by the study of its linguistic expressions. Language is commensurate with meaning. Because in its ordinary use language is able to carry meanings among people, information about other people's realms of meaning can be gathered through the messages they give about their experiences. The structure of language, too, can be studied as an indication of the structure of the realm of meaning.[15] For example, both language and the realm of meaning have hierarchical and layered structures, and both make use of their own creations, such as words or concepts, in the production of more complex meanings. The need to work primarily with linguistic, rather than quantified, data in the study of consciousness does, however, present problems of analysis to the researcher, since linguistic statements are context-sensitive and lose much of their information content when treated in isolation.

(4) The analysis of linguistic data makes use of hermeneutic reasoning. Hermeneutic understanding uses processes such as analogy and pattern recognition to draw conclusions about the meaning content of linguistic messages. Hermeneutic reasoning is used in ordinary experience to interpret what the sound waves of speech or the marks on paper stand for. Hermeneutic reasoning does not produce certain and necessary conclusions, and the sophisticated statistical tools available in the behavioral and social sciences for the treatment of quantified data are of only secondary use in dealing with linguistic data. Because the contours of consciousness correspond more closely with linguistic, instead of mathematical,

structures, the methods for its study are not as precise. Nor do they stand within the tradition of the usual forms of research used by the human disciplines.

(5) The realm of meaning is an integrated ensemble of connections among images and ideas that appear in various modes of presentation, such as perception, remembrance, and imagination. It operates in a complex of interacting strata consisting of various levels of abstraction, awareness, and control. The complex organizational patterns that fold back on one another and link elements through condensation and displacement make the realm of meaning difficult to investigate.

These problem areas confront any attempt to comprehend the operations of the realm of meaning. For this reason, even though meaning is the primary characteristic of humans, it has not been extensively studied by the human disciplines.

History of the study of meaning

In the human disciplines, the study of consciousness has been the project primarily of psychology. Since its origin as a science in the 1870s, psychological research has been based on the ideal that a single scientific method could be used by all disciplines—that is, all reliable knowledge is generated by exactly the same epistemological principles. These principles require that: (a) conclusions must be based on directly available public perceptions; (b) data must be generated by experimentation—that is, an intervention in nature designed to produce changes that can be observed; and (c) general laws, which provide the explanation for why things change as they do, must be the object of science.

The first psychological research is attributed to Wilhelm Wundt's attempt to understand the elements of consciousness. His work took place within the context of the excitement over Mendeleev's publication of the periodic table. Wundt thought that consciousness, like chemical compounds, was composed of elements that combined to produce complex experiences. His research used the design principles consistent with unified science. He developed experiments in which stimuli were presented to the senses (sight, hearing, and touch) of his trained subjects, who were then asked to give detailed descriptions of the ensuing mental elements and operations. Wundt hoped to do for psychology what Medeleev had done for chemistry by developing a periodic table of the mental elements, including the principles of mental synthesis and combination. Wundt's research program was undercut by the notion of imageless thought, that is, that not all mental operations were directly available to self-observation.

During the era of behaviorism, from the 1920s to the 1960s, mainstream psychology abandoned the attempt to study consciousness and limited its data to those available to direct public perception. In the last three decades, however, there has been a "revolutionary" turn in the human disciplines,[16] a change of focus from the study of human beings as objects in the world to the study of the mind or consciousness. This change has centered on the human mental abilities—perceiving, remembering, reasoning, and many others—which are organized into a complex system called cognition. The best-studied topics in cognitive science have been the role of cognitive activity in perception and recognition, in recall and memory, and in language production and reception. Yet despite its centrality for human affairs and cognition, the role of the narrative scheme has only recently come under study in cognitive science.

In the main, cognitive science has approached the study of the actions of consciousness with the same tools of inquiry that were developed to study the objects of the world. Computers have replaced Wundt's use of chemistry as the model for mental processes, based on the suggestion that since computers can be programmed to simulate human responses, the human mind must function like a computer program.[17] Although the first studies using computer analogies of consciousness were heralded as holding great promise, the limits of this approach are now becoming apparent.[18]

Characteristics of the study of meaning

The difficulties inherent in the study of meaning and the use of methods of limited applicability have restricted the success of the human sciences in exploring this region of human existence. However, research into meaning is the most basic of all inquiry. Husserl[19] has pointed out that the whole scientific enterprise is grounded ultimately in the perceptual and meaning-making operations of human consciousness. The understanding of our existence and action requires a knowledge of the structures that produce the experienced or lived realm from which we direct our actions and expressions. The study of the realm of meaning precedes an understanding of the manner in which human beings create knowledge, and thus informs the operations of science itself. The study of the making of meaning is particularly central to the disciplines concerned with explaining human experience.

Because the characteristics of the realm of meaning are different from those of the material realm, its study requires an alteration in the research methods the human disciplines have traditionally used to study consciousness. Although these advanced research procedures have proven very effective in many contexts, they have been of limited usefulness when applied to the study of consciousness. The human disciplines have shared the ideal that all scientific knowledge could be developed through a single and unified approach, an ideal based, however, on the proposition that all reality was of the same type. Instead, approaches must be designed specifically to study all the kinds of reality, since the use of a single approach to knowledge requires a translation of the aspects of one reality into incommensurate categories drawn from another realm. For example, when narrative meaning is translated into categories derived from a description of objects in the material realm, crucial dimensions of the narrative experience are lost, including the experience of temporality that it contains. In addition, translation across realms of existence requires reduction of complexity and loss of information, as, for example, when narrative's intricacy is reduced to only those structures or operations that are recognized in the organic or the material realms.

Although the material realm might best be studied by the use of quantifying procedures and statistical estimates, the realm of meaning is best captured through the qualitative nuances of its expression in ordinary language. The disciplines of history and literary criticism have developed procedures and methods for studying the realm of meaning through its expressions in language. The human disciplines will need to look to those disciplines, rather than to the physical sciences, for a scientific model for inquiry of the region of consciousness.

The goal of research into the production of meaning is to produce clear and accurate descriptions of the structures and forms of the various meaning systems. This type of outcome does not provide information for the prediction and control of behavior; instead, it provides a kind of knowledge that individuals and groups can use to increase the power and control they have over their own actions.[20] This is accomplished by gathering examples of these systems' expressions through self-reflection, interviews, and collections of artifacts; and by drawing conclusions from these data by using the systematic principles of linguistic analysis and hermeneutic techniques.[22]

In order to distinguish this kind of approach from research based on quantified data, some have suggested that we call research using linguistic data "inquiries," "studies," or "investigations," rather than "research." I disagree with this suggestion. "Re-search" implies a systematic attempt to go beyond the cursory view of something in order to generate a greater depth of understanding, and the model of inquiry I have been describing meets this criterion.

In a recent review of the philosophy of psychology, Joseph Margolis reached a similar conclusion. According to Margolis:

> [They] have driven us to concede that the human sciences ... may well be significantly different from the physical sciences, both methodologically and ontologically. Language appears to be *sui generis:* essential to the actual aptitudes of human beings; irreducible to physical processes; inexplicable solely infrapsychologically; real only as embedded in the practices of a historical society; identifiable consensually or only in terms that presuppose consensual practices linking observer and observed; inseparable as far as meaning is concerned from the changing, novel, nonlinguistic experience of a people; incapable of being formulated as a closed system of rules; subject always to the need for improvisational interpretation and, therefore, subject also to ineliminable psychological indeterminacies regarding intention and action.[22]

The plan of the book

The core of the argument I make in this book is that narrative is a scheme by means of which human beings give meaning to their experience of temporality and personal actions. Narrative meaning functions to give form to the understanding of a purpose to life and to join everyday actions and events into episodic units. It provides a framework for understanding the past events of one's life and for planning future actions. It is the primary scheme by means of which human existence is rendered meaningful. Thus, the study of human beings by the human sciences needs to focus on the realm of meaning in general, and on narrative meaning in particular.

Chapter 2 provides a preliminary description of the characteristics of narrative meaning through an examination of the forms in which narrative is expressed linguistically. Because narrative meaning only makes its appearance in the linguistic operations of discourse, considerable attention will be given to the unique strata of meaning communicated through discourse.

Chapters 3 through 5 give accounts of the investigation of narrative by the three disciplines most involved in its study. In recent years narrative has become a central research interest for history and literary criticism, disciplines normally located on the periphery of the core of human disciplines. Research programs aimed at investigation of narrative have also been started in psychology.[23]

Chapter 3 is an investigation of the active debate about the role of narrative in the discipline of history. In discussing the insights and outcomes of this debate, particular attention is given to the special meaning the notions of cause and explanation have as they are used in narrative history and to the recent attempts to clarify the distinction between fictional narrative and "true" or historical narrative.

Chapter 4 examines the approaches to fictive narrative texts, such as fairy tales and novels, of literary critics. These critics have attempted to develop a narrative grammar that would account for the generation of the multitude of surface stories, in a manner analogous to the account of the generation of sentences by deep grammatical structures. The recent work on narrative undertaken by literary critics has emphasized communication theory and the role of the reader.

Chapter 5 describes the early interest of psychology and other human sciences in self-theory and life stories, follows the decline of this interest, and then focuses on the recent renewal of interest in research on narrative as the basis for an understanding of life development and personal identity. Freud developed his theoretical position from patients' case histories and constructed interpretive guidelines for understanding the personal narratives related by his psychoanalytic sessions. Roy Schafer's current reinterpretation of psychoanalysis as a narrative enterprise is examined, along with the implications of narrative for the general field of human science practice.

Chapter 6 draws together the implications the study of narrative meaning has for understanding human existence. The chapter examines the areas of human action, the experience of time, and personal identity from the perspective of narrative meaning.

Finally, chapter 7 examines the role narrative meaning can perform in the work of practitioners and researchers in the human disciplines. The understanding of narrative is especially important for the work of anthropologists, psychotherapists, counselors, and a growing group of people working with meaning systems within organizations.

CHAPTER 11

Narrative Expression

OUR encounter with reality produces a meaningful and understandable flow of experience. What we experience is a consequence of the action of our organizing schemes on the components of our involvement with the world. Narrative is the fundamental scheme for linking individual human actions and events into interrelated aspects of an understandable composite. For example, the action of a narrative scheme joins the two separate events "the father died" and "the son cried" into a single episode, "the son cried when his father died." Seeing the events as connected increases our understanding of them both—the son cares for his father, and the father's death pains the son. Narrative displays the significance that events have for one another. The purpose of this chapter is to investigate the manner in which the narrative scheme operates to produce the particular form and meaning that is human existence. A secondary purpose is to examine the linguistic form through which narrative meaning is expressed.

The term "narrative"

In everyday conversation the term "narrative" is equivocal. The most inclusive meaning of "narrative" refers to any spoken or written presentation. When in a questionnaire, for example, the "narrative" designates that answers are to be given in sentences or paragraphs instead of single words or short phrases. In a written report, the "narrative" portion is that part written in essay form, as distinguished from charts, graphs, or tables. I will not use "narrative" in this generalized, derivative sense,[1] instead, I will confine my use to the more specific meaning of the term, that is, the kind of organizational scheme expressed in story form.

Even this narrowing of the term does not remove all ambiguity, however. "Narrative" can refer to the process of making a story, to the cognitive scheme of the story, or to the result of the process—also called "stories," "tales," or "histories." I will be using "narrative" and its cognates to refer to both the process and the results; the context should clarify which meaning is intended.

As I use it, the term "story" is equivalent to "narrative." The *American Heritage Dictionary* gives the first definition of "story" as, "The narrating or relating of an event or series of events, either true or false." Its next two definitions delimit the meaning of "story" to tales and compositions of fictional events. Although the term "story" can carry the connotation of an unreal or imagined realm generated from pretending and fantasizing, I do not so limit its meaning. I use "story" to refer to any narrative production in general. In fact, I am most interested in "true" stories, such as the "story" of one's life, or the story composed of historical episodes.

The pervasiveness of narratives

The products of narrative schemes are ubiquitous in our lives: they fill our cultural and social environment. We create narrative descriptions for ourselves and for others about our own past actions, and we develop storied accounts that give sense to the behavior of others. We also use the narrative scheme to inform our decisions by constructing imaginative "what if" scenarios. On the receiving end, we are constantly confronted with stories during our conversations and encounters with the written and visual media. We are told fairy tales as children, and read and discuss stories in school. We read novels and watch motion pictures, and take in hours of television dramas. Roland Barthes, one of the most important literary theorists concerned with narrative, opens his "Introduction to the Structural Analysis of the Narrative" with a statement about the centrality of narrative in the lives of people:

> The narratives of the world are without number. In the first place the word "narrative" covers an enormous variety of genres which are themselves divided up between different subjects, as if any material was suitable for the composition of the narrative: the narrative may incorporate articulate language, spoken or written; pictures, still or moving; gestures and the ordered arrangement of all the ingredients: it is present in myth, legend, fable, short story, epic, history, tragedy, comedy, pantomime, painting, . . . stained glass windows, cinema, comic strips, journalism, conversation. In addition, under this almost infinite number of forms, the narrative is present at all times, in all places, in all societies; the history of narrative begins with the history of mankind; there does not exist, and never has existed, a people without narratives.[2]

Barthes believes that narratives perform significant functions. At the individual level, people have a narrative of their own lives which enables them to construe what they are and where they are headed. At the cultural level, narratives serve to give cohesion to shared beliefs and to transmit values.

The stories we encounter carry the values of our culture by providing positive models to emulate and negative models to avoid.[3] In Christian cultures, for instance, the story of Jesus of Nazareth is held to be exemplary, and by imitating his story in one's own life as much as possible it is understood that one will live a life (that is, create a personal story) of the highest value. Our cultural stories also pass on insights about characteristics which are common to all personal histories. The story of Sophocles' Oedipus, for example, demonstrates that our personal histories are significantly constructed by events over which we have no conscious control.[4]

The narrative form can accommodate and generate an almost infinite variety of specific stories. A number of taxonomies has been proposed to identify the basic kinds of stories; these have varied according the type of cross-cut taken through the body of stories.

Two examples will give the flavor of these categorical arrangements. Kenneth and Mary Gergen have developed a design in which stories are classified according to the kind of change the protagonist undergoes in relation to a goal.[5] This design yields three logical types of story: the *stability narrative*, in which the protagonist remains essentially unchanged with respect to the goal; the *progressive narrative*, in which advancement toward the goal occurs; and the *regressive narrative*, in which the protagonist ends up further removed from the goal. Northrup Frye has proposed a different taxonomy based on the characteristics of the protagonist compared to those of the ordinary characters and the environment.[6] His categories are: myth, romance, high mimetic, low mimetic, and ironic. A number of other classificatory projects have been applied to the great variety of stories; these will be discussed in Chapter 3.

Suppositions about human experience

Although I will approach narrative primarily as a cognitive scheme, I am interested in more than merely describing its organizing operations. Rather, I extend the study to ask what contribution the narrative scheme makes to the experience of being human. Having narrative as one of our fundamental structures of comprehension shapes the character of our existence in a particular way. There are three basic suppositions about the human experience (which were previously described in Chapter 1) that I assume to be valid; I shall use them to support the judgments I offer about the function of narrative meaning for human existence.

(1) Human experience is enveloped in a personal and cultural realm of nonmaterial meanings and thoughts. Although this realm is linked to and emerges from the organism that is our body, it has characteristics that are qualitatively different from those of the body itself.[7] The realm of meaning is not static: it is enlarged by the new experiences it is continuously configuring as well as by its own refiguring process, which is carried out through reflection and recollection. This realm is not itself locked within a personal existence: it transcends us as

individuals as we communicate our personal thoughts and experiences to others, and as we, in turn, participate as hearers and viewers of their expressions. Although at times we are driven to action by uncontrolled bodily and environmental forces (when we fall off a chair, for instance) or accede to habitual responses (when we say "fine" when asked how we are), we have the capacity to deliberate and decide how we will act. This deliberation process takes place in the realm of meaning and thought. It retrieves previous experience and imaginatively creates alternate scenarios which anticipate the consequences of possible actions. Human responsiveness thus proceeds from experience, and is not a simple unmediated reaction to the environment.[8]

(2) Human experience is a construction fashioned out of the interaction between a person's organizing cognitive schemes and the impact of the environment on his or her sense apparatus. Experience is an integrated construction, produced by the realm of meaning, which interpretively links recollections, perceptions, and expectations. The structures of cognitive schemes are layered and can undergo modification in the interchange with the linguistic and natural environments. In place prior to any particular perception, these schemes are actively used to organize and interpret a person's encounter with the environment, both internal and external.[9] Most often, they operate outside of conscious awareness and provide awareness with an already constructed meaningful experience. Narrative is one of the cognitive schemes; it presents to awareness a world in which timely human actions are linked together according to their effect on the attainment of human desires and goals.[10]

(3) Human experience is not organized according to the same model we have constructed for the material realm.[11] I envision the primary organizing principles in human experience as more akin to those that construct poetic meaning than to those that construct the proofs of formal logic. Experience makes connections and enlarges itself through the use of metaphoric processes that link together experiences similar but not exactly the same, and it evaluates items according to the positions they hold in relation to larger wholes. The realm of meaning is an open system in which new forms of organization can emerge and new meaning systems can be developed. This description is different from that offered by the structural grammarians. They maintain that the realm of meaning is organized according to innate and unchanging forms that ground the realm and generate all possible combinations of meaning within it. The position is also opposed by those cognitive scientists who picture the realm of meaning as if it were generated by a complex computer governed by binary logic. The realm of meaning has great plasticity, and its processes can be disciplined to perform within self-imposed limits. It can, for example, produce conclusions that conform to the rules of formal logic or mathematics; but I hold that these formal processes are derivative, reduced forms of the linking activities of the meaning realm. Narrative draws on

the metaphorical and polysemous aspects of the original processes as it works to construct experience as meaningful.

Human behavior above the level of reflex is infected with the features of meaning. Human activities, both bodily movements and speech, are expressions and enactments of meaning. Calvin Schrag suggests the term "texture" to describe the basic appearance of human activity as the expression of meaning.[12] He advises against taking either speech (text) or movement as the analogue for the whole fabric of human expressiveness.

> Our middle term, "texture," thus propels us in the direction of neither a primacy of the text, nor a primacy of perception, nor a primacy of action. The texture of communicative praxis gathers the display of meanings with the text of everyday speech and the text of the written word, but it also encompasses the play and display of meanings within the field of perception and the fabric of human action.[13]

The narrative scheme

Cognitive psychologist Jerome Bruner has proposed that narrative understanding is itself one of two basic intelligences or modes of cognitive functioning, together with the logico-scientific mode, which he calls the "paradigmatic" mode. As Bruner puts it:

> There are two modes of cognitive functioning, two modes of thought, each providing distinctive ways of ordering experience, of constructing reality. The two (though complementary) are irreducible to one another. ... Each of the ways of knowing, moreover, has operating principles of its own and its own criteria of well-formedness. They differ radically in their procedures for verification.[14]

Bruner comments that we know "precious little" about how narrative processes work and that this meager knowledge stands in contrast to the extensive knowledge we have of how the paradigmatic processes used in formal science and logical reasoning work. The two processes function differently, and each mode uses a different type of causality to connect events. The paradigmatic mode searches for universal truth conditions, whereas the narrative mode looks for particular connections between events. These types of relationships both involve the connections of sentences in discourse, and will be taken up in the section below on "Narrative as Discourse." The special subject matter of narrative is the "vicissitudes of human intentions"—that is, the changing directions and goals of human action.

The narrative organizational scheme is of particular importance for understanding human activity. It is the scheme that displays purpose and direction in human affairs and makes individual human lives comprehensible as wholes. We conceive our own and others' behavior within the narrative framework, and through it recognize the effects our planned actions can have on desired goals. We can also use the narrative scheme to connect imaginary people (Snow White, for example) to events (the actions in novels) in cohesive stories. Although narrative intelligibility is grounded in the ordinary, everyday actions of human beings, it can be projected by analogy on the behavior of animals (the three bears in Goldilocks, for example) and superhuman characters (such as the Greek god Zeus or the computer Hal in the motion picture 2001).

The registering of relationship by the narrative scheme results from its power to configure a sequence of events into a unified happening. Narrative ordering makes individual events comprehensible by identifying the whole to which they contribute. The ordering process operates by linking diverse happenings along a temporal dimension and by identifying the effect one event has on another, and it serves to cohere human actions and the events that affect human life into a temporal gestalt. As there are a limited number of gestalt operations that produce recognizable perceptual configurations, so there are a limited number of narrative structures that produce coherent stories. By inclusion in a narratively generated story, particular actions take on significance as having contributed to a completed episode. In this sense, narrative can retrospectively alter the meaning of events after the final outcome is known. For example, the significance of an instance of running out of gas can become understood in light of the friendship that subsequently develops with the person who stopped to help. The means by which specific events are made to cohere into a single narrative is the plot or story line. It is the plot which shows the part an individual action contributes to the whole experience. In the example, the plot is the making of a friendship.

In summary, narrative is a meaning structure that organizes events and human actions into a whole, thereby attributing significance to individual actions and events according to their effect on the whole.[15] Thus, narratives are to be differentiated from chronicles, which simply list events according to their place on a time line. Narrative provides a symbolized account of actions that includes a temporal dimension.

Plot

The organizing theme that identifies the significance and the role of the individual events is normally called the "plot" of the narrative. The plot functions to transform a chronicle or listing of events into a schematic whole by highlighting and recognizing the contribution that certain events make to the development and outcome of the story. Without the recognition of significance given by the plot, each event would appear as discontinuous and separate, and its meaning would be limited to its categorical identification or its spatiotemporal location.

A plot is able to weave together a complex of events to make a single story. It is able to take into account the historical and social context in which the events took place and to recognize the significance of unique and novel occurrences. It can draw upon information about physical laws, personal dispositions and character, responses to actions, and the processes of deliberation in reaching decisions. A plot has the capacity to articulate and consolidate complex threads of multiple activities by means of the overlay of subplots.

A plot is constructed in the realm of meaning, recording relationships among perceptions. The recognition or construction of a plot employs the kind of reasoning that Charles Peirce called "abduction," the process of suggesting a hypothesis that can serve to explain some puzzling phenomenon. Abduction produces a conjecture that is tested by fitting it over the "facts." The conjecture may be adjusted to provide a fuller account of the givens.

The reasoning used to construct a plot is similar to that used to develop a hypothesis. Both are interactive activities that take place between a conception that might explain or show a connection among the events and the resistance of the events to fit the construction. Experiments by A.E. Michotte, designed to explore the perception of causality, serendipitously showed the deeply ingrained process of plot construction at work.[16] Observers could see two or more small colored rectangles in motion, and when asked to describe what they saw, they imposed elaborate cause and effect stories on these moving rectangles, using plots to assign meaning to their motions. Similarly, the Thematic Apperception Test presents a set of pictures to subjects who are asked to tell a story about each picture; the subjects are usually able to develop plots relating the various items in the pictures without difficulty.[17] These examples show the capacity of people to create plots imaginatively by forming items into a theme, even when the items are simply moving rectangles or still pictures.

More than one plot can provide a meaningful constellation and integration for the same set of events, and different plot organizations change the meaning of the individual events as their roles are reinterpreted according to their functions in different plots. The meaning and identity of an event is not an isolated phenomenon located in the single event itself. Rather, the meaning of the events in stories is produced by a recognition of how an event and the plot interact, each providing form for the other. Not every plot can order a set of events. An appropriate configuration emerges only after a moving back and forth or tacking procedure compares proposed plot structures with the events and then revises the plot structure according to the principle of "best fit." Thus, emplotment is not the imposition of a ready-made plot structure on an independent set of events; instead, it is a dialectic process that takes place between the events themselves and a theme which discloses their significance and allows them to be grasped together as parts of one story. In addition, the construction of plots is not a completely rule-governed activity. It can generate unique and novel configurations.

Cultural traditions offer a store of plot lines which can be used to configure events into stories. Some of these are passed on as myths (about Athena, for example) and children's tales ("Little Red Riding Hood"). The ordering of events by linking them into a plot comes about through an intermixing of the various elements of the cultural repertoire of sedimented stories and innovations. Plot lines can be used imaginatively as decisions are made about actions in the re-creation of a typical story. For example, a young boy decides to confess his errors to his father in expectation that the plot of George Washington's "I cannot tell a lie" story will apply in the present case and he will be forgiven. Individuals can have typical plots they use to order their own life events. For instance, one can configure the events of one's life as parts of a tragic plot in which the protago-nist (oneself) is defeated and cannot achieve the goals set forth, or, alternatively, as a comedy in which the protagonist achieves the goals and is happy in the end. Two people can, by incorporating the same kind of life events into different types of stories, change the meaning of these events. Psychotherapists have used this property of narrative in their notion of "life-scripts."[18]

The competence for understanding a narrative ordering of events is gradually mastered by children between their second and tenth years. Children learn "to produce and comprehend causally and temporally structured plots that are organ-ized around a variety of themes and involve a myriad of characters."[19] They develop the capacity to tell whether a plot coheres and makes sense, much as one can identify ill-formed sentences that do not conform to syntactic rules. Whether narrative competence is an innate capacity on the order of Noam Chomsky's argu-ment for language competence or a learned skill[20] is unsettled in the cognitive development literature,[21] but, whatever account is given to explain its appear-ance, it is generally agreed that narrative competence appears at an early age and appears in most cultures.

Both the construction and the understanding of plots draw on the human ability to understand human activity as actions. The connecting concepts used in narrative configuration utilize the conceptual network that distinguishes the domain of action from that of physical movement. Key notions here are goals, motives, and agents. The narrative scheme organizes the individual events it addresses using a framework of human purposes and desires, including the limits and opportunities posed by the physical, cultural, and personal environments. The major dimension of human existence is time, and the discourse on human action is pervaded by an awareness of the centrality of time and change. Narrative is always controlled by the concept of time and by the recognition that temporal-ity is the primary dimension of human existence.

Explanation

People ordinarily explain their own actions and the actions of others by means of a plot. In the narrative schema for organizing information, an event is understood to have been explained when its role and significance in relation to a human project is identified. This manner of explanation is different from that favored by logico-mathematical reasoning, where explanation is understood to occur when an event can be identified as an instance of an established law or pattern of relationship among categories. The power of explanation by laws comes from its capacity to abstract events from particular contexts and discover relationships that hold among all the instances belonging to a category, irrespective of the spatial and temporal context. Thus, in principle, one could project backward or forward in time, and the relationship identified by formal logico-mathematic reasoning would hold. But explanation by means of narrative is contextually related and is therefore different in form from formal science explanation.

When a human event is said not to make sense, it is usually not because a person is unable to place it in the proper category. The difficulty stems, instead, from a person's inability to integrate the event into a plot whereby it becomes understandable in the context of what has happened. If a person is asked why he or she has done something, the account given is normally in the narrative mode rather than the categorical mode. To the question "Why did he purchase life insurance?" the answer in a categorical explanation is "Because he is a white male, in the 40-to-50 age category, and those in this category are, in 70 percent of cases, also in the category of people who buy life insurance." The narrative explanation, however, answers such a question by configuring a set of events into a storylike causal nexus. The temporal explanation of why one does something focuses on the events in an individual's life history that have an effect on a particular action, including the projected future goals the action is to achieve. It accepts complex sets of events, including reflective decisions, and explains an event by tracing its intrinsic relations to other events and locating it in its historical context. Thus, narratives *exhibit* an explanation instead of demonstrating it.

In narrative organization, the symmetry between explanation and prediction, characteristic of logico-mathematical reasoning, is broken. Narrative explanation does not subsume events under laws. Instead, it explains by clarifying the significance of events that have occurred on the basis of the outcome that has followed. In this sense, narrative explanation is retroactive.

Communication

The single term "narrative presentation" is used to refer to three different kinds of story presentation. The first is the presentation of the original story to personal

awareness. This story is constructed by the narrative meaning (cognitive) structure and displays a world in which human actions cohere according to plots. The
second kind of story presentation is the representation of the experience in a
language message directed to others. This representation can take various forms,
including speaking, writing, or the making of a drama. The representation can be
the communication of a personally experienced story (as when telling another
about an adventure one has had), a reconstruction of a story about characters in
the past (as in a historical narrative), or an imaginatively constructed story (as in
a novel or drama). The third kind of presentation is involved with the reception—
including interpretation and understanding—of a story by hearing or reading.
Each of these three types of presentation has special characteristics that have
been the focus of research programs.[22]

The three forms of story presentation can be illustrated by a Saturday trip to
the grocery store. The first form appears as a personal experience of a unified
venture composed of a variety of events, such as writing out a list, getting into the
car, driving to the store, selecting items and paying at the store, and returning
home. The second form appears when one is asked what one did in the afternoon,
and the story is represented to the inquirer. The third form comes when the
inquirer hears and interprets the story, perhaps evaluating it as a dull story about
a Saturday afternoon.

In summary, narrative understanding is the comprehension of a complex of
events by seeing the whole in which the parts have participated. Louis Mink,
writing about the historian's work with narrative, says that the problem for the
historian becomes intelligible "if it is seen as an attempt to communicate his experience of seeing-things-together in the necessarily narrative style of one-thing-
after-another."[23] Narrative explanation involves a special kind of understanding
"which converts congeries of events into concatenations, and emphasizes and
increases the scope of synoptic judgment in our reflection on experience."[24]

Narrative and language

Narrative is a function of the relational processes of the realm of meaning. The
interactive connection between meaning and its expression in language has been
a central problem for recent Western philosophy. This section examines alternative positions regarding the meaning-language problem and then proposes that
narrative meaning is most clearly understood from the position that language is a
display, rather than a pure reflection or distortion of meaning.

Human life is not simply an organic unfolding of a physiological plan coded
in genes:[25] it is the product of the interaction between its organic givens and
environment. The nature-nurture issue concerns the extent of the contributions

made by both sides in regard to a particular characteristic. The question of interest in this study is whether the narrative scheme is an innate structure of consciousness, like the grammatical structures suggested by Chomsky, or a learned linguistic form, a cultural product like *haiku* poetry? A second question is whether the narrative form is an accurate description of human reality, or merely an artificial construction projected on our existence. Although definitive answers to these questions may not be possible, we can gain some understanding through analysis of the nature of narrative as linguistic expression: ultimately, the production and understanding of narratives is a function of the capacity of human beings to use language.

The human capacity for language

The human organism is unfinished at birth, and different capacities—including language—do not emerge until certain stages of maturation. Indeed, it appears that if this capacity for language acquisition is not developed during a particular critical period of development, the capacity itself is impaired.[26] It is clear that language use cannot emerge unless an organism has, among other things, a highly complex central nervous system with a very high degree of plasticity. Chomsky holds that particular innate physiological systems are necessary for language acquisition to be possible and that these organic systems set limits on the variations in understandable grammars. Nevertheless, the physiological givens of the human body are only part of what makes up human existence. These givens are transformed into an order of existence that is experienced as meaningful,[27] through interaction with other persons and through the assimilation of such cultural compositions as language, values, and tools. Language is the factor that enables us to express the unique order of existence that is the human realm, because it serves as the medium through which we express the world as meaningful. Language needs to be understood as more than simply a skill for encoding nonlinguistic thoughts into messages that can be understood by others. Language is both the product and the possession of a community.

Language and experience

The traditional empirical model of language describes it as an adjunct to the human sensory apparatus. In this model, the world gives off or reflects energy either in the form of waves or as chemicals. The different senses selectively pick up this energy, and the brain transforms the waves or chemicals into sensual images. For example, the eyes admit a portion of the spectrum of reflected light waves and encode the waves into electrical impulses that are sent to parts of the brain, where they are decoded into visual images. The nose picks up various chemicals from the air, and these chemicals are reconstructed in the brain as smell images. All of these images—or *idées,* as Descartes called them—were understood to be like "inner ghostly snapshots" of the objects in the world. This passive model has been recently amended to include a search-and-seek function, by which a person concerned to locate something scans the field until image is produced that fits the image that is sought. The major portion of the field of discernible energy is passed over or not decoded in consciousness so that objects of concern may be selected and attended to.[28]

Language—words that represent the perceived images—is added in this traditional empirical model after the perception. Language serves as a means for efficiently storing in memory or for thinking about and communicating to another what one has perceived. The first order for language is to describe accurately the image that has appeared in one's awareness. Language should not add its own elements, but it should provide a precise, limited designation for the image. For example, high school science students are given an exercise in which they are asked to describe a burning candle. The required description excludes such interpretive words as "candle" and "flame," which add meaning not in the image itself. The appropriate description is "a cylindrical white object, five inches in height and soft in texture, with an orange, nonsolid light flickering around a limp, woven, small cylindrical object protruding from the top of the cylinder."[29] Ideally, each word is a direct referent to the actual image or idea in one's mind.

This conception of language presupposes that the world undergoing translation into images in awareness has no intrinsic meaning and consists only of energy patterns projected from centers having the appearance of objects. There are no real essences or categories. When we think in terms of general categories and use words to designate these categories, it is understood that we are not describing features of the world, but only mental constructions. We mentally gather our images together into classes and then gather these classes into higher-level units. General ideas are thought to be built up from first-order perceptual ideas. Following this line of thought, then, to know the truth requires that general notions be broken down into their component parts, which are the reflections of reality itself. Indeed, Galileo, Descartes, and Hobbes all held this "resolutive-compositive" process—thinking as the assembling and disassembling of ideas—to be a requirement for knowing and understanding reality.

In this empirical understanding, one needed to be on guard in using language in reasoning, for though language could be helpful in working with ideas and grouping them, it could also mislead and take attention away from the images or ideas themselves. Language was the "great seducer": it tempted people to be satisfied with mere words, when its real function was to ground thought in the ideas to which the words referred. One had to be careful that language did not actually disguise the truth, and maintain constant diligence to keep language transparent. The meanings of words were to be defined such that they would refer directly and consistently to the images of the world and allow one to see through them to the designated objects. The goal of shedding subjectivity from language was to clear the way for access to pure reality.[30]

Although language had the power to disguise reality, if used in a stringently purified way it could—it has been thought traditionally—provide a transparent medium in which reality could be accurately described and known. During the 1920s and 1930s, logical positivists attempted to develop such a transparent language.[31] By limiting language to observational statements of phenomena as they appeared directly to awareness (that is, before anything was inferred about their nature) these investigators hoped to produce an accurate description of real-world objects. An observational report would consist merely of descriptions of experienced colors and shapes (for example, a brown rectangle with four protrusions in each corner) but the object as such would not be classified (as a table). The purpose of the method was to eliminate from scientific observation any contamination by metaphysical assumptions. The proposal was unworkable in practice and was amended by the logical empiricists to include the names of objects in observational reports.

By the late 1950s and early 1960s, the idea that a purified language could be transparent to an external reality, that observational statements could be clear, unproblematic reflections of extralinguistic reality, had come increasingly under attack.[32] Mary Hesse described the arguments developed by philosophers of science that undermined this notion.[33] Because words are learned in empirical situations where the observer is taught to classify certain similarities of individual experiences under single words, information about the dissimilar elements of an experience is lost in all descriptions reporting observations. The particular sectioning of experience into a language of classification is dependent on the theoretical, cultural, and valuing schemes the observer has learned. Moreover, as Gregory Bateson has explained, any experience can be divided or punctuated in various ways. Because two people can link the sequence of events into different chains and create different meaning from the same events, miscommunication and interpersonal conflict can easily arise.[34]

Ferdinand de Saussure's analysis of language undercut the notion that a purified language could accurately reflect the world. He changed the focus of language study from its historical development to the way a single language system distributes meaning.[35] According to Saussure, the relationship between words does not reflect the external relationship among the things the words signify; words evince only the organization internal to a language system. The particular way in which a language breaks down its ideas is arbitrary, the meaning of an idea being determined by the other ideas in the language rather than by external objects. Because various language systems divide the spectrum of conceptual possibilities in different ways, it follows that the categorical expressions of a language are not drawn from or representational of an external, independent objective realm.

A third theory about the inability of language to represent the object realm was presented by Ludwig Wittgenstein in his later writings.[36] He argued that the meanings of words are social constructions, parts of a language game one has learned to play and so linked to the following of rules that allow members of a community to understand one another. Words are not pictures of the world, and they are derived not from private ideas in the mind but from social practice. Thus, there is no neutral language by means of which reality as it is in itself can be described.

The consequence of these developments in the theory of meaning was that, despite the attempt to create an ideal language for formal science, there remains a gap between the categories of any language and those of objective reality. We are, then, caught in the prison-house of language with no way to break through to know extralinguistic reality in itself. These skeptical conclusions have produced a Whorfian position, that experience is an artifact of language rather than reality. Richard Rorty suggests that because language is opaque and prevents our experience from being a "mirror of nature," the philosophic enterprise should turn away from the inquiry into ultimate truths and toward participation in conversation. He writes, "To see keeping a conversation going as a sufficient aim of philosophy, to see wisdom as consisting in the ability to sustain a conversation, is to see human beings as generators of new descriptions rather than beings one hopes to be able to describe [reality] accurately.[37]

Language as display

The skeptical response assumes a dichotomy: either language is transparent and does not stand in the way of our direct experience of reality, or it is a distorting screen which projects experience out of its own categories.[38] Yet a third alternative is possible. Language may be the device that allows reality to show forth in experience. Rather than standing in the way of experience of the real, language may be the lens whose flexibility makes reality appear in sharp focus before experience. This third notion of language as having a positive function in bringing the real to human experience has been developed in the work of Maurice Merleau-Ponty.

In his investigations of the significance of embodiment and language for personal existence, Merleau-Ponty has incorporated many of the developments in modern linguistics. I find his understanding of language the most accomplished and comprehensive in the contemporary literature. In his earliest major work, *The Phenomenology of Perception*,[39] Merleau-Ponty challenged the position that thought and language can be understood as independent of and disconnected from human bodily existence.[40] He also adapted the distinction, first described by Saussure, between language as a system of signs and language as it is spoken by people. Unlike Saussure, though, his interest was on language in everyday speech.

Merleau-Ponty attacks both the traditional empiricist and the intellectualist accounts of language. These accounts sought to find an explanation of the relation between words and thoughts in external causes. They separated words, which were understood to be only so many particular entities, from the meanings the words expressed, and then they looked for ways to overcome the gaps between words and meanings that had been created. The empiricist account (described above) held language to consist of a system of conventional signs that merely denote mental ideas, which are, in turn, mere reflections or generalizations based on physical reality. The ideas to which language refers are essentially independent of the language in which they are expressed. According to this position, speech is just one symbolic system among many, all of which are able to represent pre-existent ideas. Merleau-Ponty describes the situation:

> Men have been talking for a long time on earth, and yet three-quarters of what they say goes unnoticed. *A rose, it is raining, it is fine, man is mortal.* These are paradigms of expression for us. We believe expression is most complete when it points unequivocally to events, to the state of objects, to ideas or relations, for, in these instances, expression leaves nothing more to be desired, contains nothing which it does not reveal, and thus sweeps us toward the object which it designates. In dialogue, narrative, plays on words, trust, promise, prayer, eloquence, literature, we possess a second-order language in which we do not speak of objects and ideas except to reach some person. Words respond to words in this language, which bears away within itself and builds up beyond nature a humming busy world of its own. Yet we still insist on treating this language as simply a variant of the economical forms of making statements about some *thing.*[41]

Merleau-Ponty's criticism of the empiricist account of language is that it understands meaning to be external to words, with words being only pointers to the things that are meant—the ideas, or through ideas, objects, in the natural world. But this understanding does not account for the primary fact of creative language. Merleau-Ponty proposes, instead, that an adequate understanding of language requires that it begin with speech rather than with thoughts. It is in the use of spoken language that new meaning is constructed, he says, as the resources of language are bent to fresh and new usage.

But the focus of Merleau-Ponty's critique in *The Phenomenology of Perception* is not placed primarily on the empiricist position on language, but rather on the intellectualist explanation. His basic concern is with Husserl's phenomenological understanding of language. As in the empiricist account, language was understood by Husserl to be separate from experience. Original experience is prepredicative or prelinguistic—that is, we have experience prior to thinking about it and organizing it according to the categories of language. Husserl claimed that it was possible to discover and display the structure of the original prelinguistic experience without relying on any awareness of the structure of predicative or grammatically organized thought. He believed that the original experience had its own complex structure which is different and quite separate from the structure of thought and language. Husserl's phenomenological method was developed as a means to penetrate through thought and language about experience in order to regain access to original experience.[42] After analyzing the original receptive experience, Husserl then moved on to analyze the structure of linguistically ordered thought and language. "Human thinking is normally done in language," he said, "and all the activities of reason are . . . bound up with speech.[43] Husserl's analysis of thought was based on the structure of a universal grammar in which objects are linked to descriptive predicates.

Husserl believed that human beings employ two separate organizational patterns, one for original experience and one for thinking and talking about this experience. His concern was not only with the independence of these two realms but also with their interrelationships, and he attempted to demonstrate that the objects of the realm of thought are derived from the real objects that appear in original experience.

Merleau-Ponty, however, sees two basic difficulties in Husserl's separation of language from experience. First, he accepts neither the notion that there is a private, inner experience prior to language, nor that, although language comes after experience as a means to think about it, it is not involved in the creation of experience. Second, if there does exist such a prelinguistic realm of experience, Merleau-Ponty questions the idea that we can have direct nonlinguistic access to it through immediate intuition.[44]

Merleau-Ponty's positive contributions to the understanding of language evolved throughout his career and explored three basic questions about the function of language in human existence: the relation between language and perception; the relation between language and silence (the unspoken language system); and the relation between language and truth.

(1) He viewed the structures of perception as the most fundamental for experience, and he believed that other modes of experience, including language, were derived from perceptual structures. His interest in language was limited to the role it plays in the body's constitution of meaningful experience through perception. He held that the primary mode in which we exist is the bodily mode and that language is one of the means we use to give to perceived nature a human signification. It is the body which creates meaning, and speaking is a bodily activity which refines preverbal behaviors of communication, such as gesturing. Merleau-Ponty was particularly interested in the sound of language in relation to the body. He drew attention to the melodies, intonations, and musical contours of various languages and to an untranslatable, primitive level of meaning distinctive to particular languages.

Meaning, he said, is to be found in words themselves. By this he meant that words are not mere pointers to some other realm, such as thought or neural excitation. "Thinking thought" and "speaking speech" are two terms designating a single phenomenon. Speech is not the "sign" of thought as smoke is the "sign" of fire, but its very presence is "in the phenomenal world, and moreover, not its clothing but its token of its body."[45] "Language is ... uncommunicative of anything other than itself, [and] its meaning is inseparable from it."[46] Merleau-Ponty used the analogy of a poem to make his point. The meaning of a poem, he said, does not exist apart from the play of the words that constitute it. Meaning is at one with the speaking of it, and to know an idea is to be able to speak it.

(2) Merleau-Ponty was influenced by the thought of Saussure and by structural linguistics, and he extended the role of language so that it became an expression of the bodily experience of the world. He developed and elaborated a relationship between language and silence. What he meant by silence is the system of linguistic signs that surrounds the speaker and enables speech to be meaningful and understandable. This system he called *la langue,* and though it is itself silent, it is the ground for all speech. The individual speaker does not constitute language; it has its own autonomous existence in which signifiers are related to what they signify because of their place in the whole system of the language. They mean something because they are different from the other signifiers. A system of language, though created by human use, takes on its own determinative reality and is the milieu that provides the meaning structure through which speaking is meaningful. However, the structures of *la langue* are not the same as those that formal science identifies. They are not ahistorical, unchanging laws, somehow definitive of reality, but rather essential or structural laws that participate in the history, contingency, and open-endedness of human experience itself. These structures, which ordinarily lie beneath the threshold of experience, are themselves the structural conditions of linguistic experience.

Merleau-Ponty's idea of flexible linguistic structures provide an alternative to the linguistic science notion of the formal and static structures which were held to govern language. For Merleau-Ponty, linguistic structures are themselves generated by historical, contingent acts of speech, which they serve and which they constitute. They have no prior, ultimate existence in reality itself. They are a means for ordering experience and making it meaningful without having to turn meaning into universal laws.

Merleau-Ponty was interested in the fact that our linguistic ability enables us to descend into the realm of our primary perceptual and emotional experience, to find there a reality susceptible to verbal understanding, and to bring forth a meaningful interpretation of this primary level of our existence. He focused on the manner in which an act of expression enables a speaker to say something new while at the same time participating in the linguistic structure, with its sedimented meanings and syntax. The language system does not determine what is said. Instead, it enables words to be understood in new combinations and in new meanings. It allows the speaker to draw from undifferentiated experience a new meaning and to fix it in a statement that the members of the linguistic community can understand. By finding meaning in experience and then expressing this meaning in words, the speaker enables the community to think about experience and not just live it.

(3) Merleau-Ponty extended his inquiry beyond the project of finding linguistic meaning in the perceptually generated primary experience and attempted to understand perceptual experience through an analogy with linguistic structure. To illustrate: the perception of a color becomes understood not as the experience of a thing that is a particular color but as the experience of a difference between this and other perceptions of color. He came to hold that the structures of perception could be understood as analogues of the structures of language.

The notion that perception is structured like language raised a new issue: is perception really a reflection of the world as it is in itself? The traditional notion of "truth" is that one's experience corresponds to what exists independent of that experience. But Merleau-Ponty proposed that "truth" is not a natural property of the world in itself but that consciousness discovers truth in contact with the world. Truth is inseparable from the expressive operation that says it; it does not precede reflection but is the result of it. In short, truth is a creation within speech that presents itself as adequate.

Merleau-Ponty held that in whatever part of our lived experience that has not yet been spoken of, there is a raw meaning, a "wild logos." This raw meaning calls out for thematic expression. It is "that which . . . summons all things from the depths of language beforehand as nameable. There is that which is to be said, and which is as yet no more than a precise uneasiness in the world of the things-said."[47] Expression is a response to a solicitation from below. "True speech, . . . speech which signifies, . . . frees the meaning captive in the thing."[48] There is no truth that exists ready-made and to which reflection would only have to conform itself, as imagined in the perfectly intelligible world of formal science.

Even though we bring the "call" of reality into language, Merleau-Ponty believed that we are not prisoners of language, making up and projecting ideas on the world. Merleau-Ponty recognized the existence of an inspiration prior to expression. However, he said, this inspiration does not fully exist before it has been interpreted in speech. He insisted that we must reject the notion of "objective" truth. The meaning of the world and of our existence is not given in advance, and the task of knowledge is not merely to discover this given. Rather, the perceived world imposes a task to be accomplished, which is to make out of what is given something meaningful. Just as the meaning of a poem is not to be discovered but is there in raw form to stimulate the reader to interpret it and make it meaningful, the meaning of life is not already there to be discovered. Life presents itself as a raw indication that needs to be finished by interpretation to make it meaningful. This interpretation must be adequate to what is given—it must include the incarnate and temporal dimensions—but it consists ultimately of contributions from both the given and the interpreter.

Merleau-Ponty arrived at the position that is central to my position—namely, that language takes up the contingencies of existence, and the perceptual openness of life to the natural and intersubjective worlds, and molds them into a meaningfulness that is greater than the meaningfulness they originally hold. One of the ways language does this is to configure these givens into a narrative form in which desires and aspirations are used to transform the passing of life into an adventure of significance and drama.

Narrative as discourse

The kind of meaning the narrative conveys about human existence requires the use of discourse, which can be differentiated from the mere collection of words or sentences. A discourse is a unit of utterance: it is something written or spoken that is larger than a sentence. A discourse is an integration of sentences that produces a global meaning that is more than that contained in the sentences viewed independently. There are various kinds of discourses, and each kind links the sentences that compose it according to distinct patterns. James Kinneavy distinguishes five basic discourse forms—referential, expressive, persuasive, narrational, and poetical.[49] A specific discourse—for example, a philosophy article—might consist of a combination of these. Different kinds of discourse require different patterns of comprehension. My primary focus in this section will be on the referential discourse of formal science and on the narrational discourse of stories, both of which produce meaning but by dissimilar organizational patterns.

Words, sentences, and discourse

An analysis of language can be made at various levels—the word, the sentence, the discourse. It is at the level of discourse that language relates the units of understanding given by sentences into meaningful wholes. One theme I want to develop is that language, although it does not simply project a reality of its own, does function to organize human life into meaningful wholes. I will be suggesting that the human disciplines need to attend to the role that language plays in the construction of human meaningfulness and to examine how this construction affects human action.

The disciplines of linguistics[50] and psycholinguistics[51] have moved through stages of development in which the object of study has been consistently enlarging. They have moved from the single sound to the word to the combination of words in sentences and, more recently, to the combination of sentences into discourses.

Certain conventions of discourse organization cover the formation of various kinds of communications. These conventions are similar in function to grammatical rules. Grammatical rules operate at the level of sentences, providing the principles for their formation. Groups of words in a sentence are marked off by punctuation signs or by changes in pitch and breathing, and the grammatical rules designate how groups of words cohere to produce an order of meaning not produced by a simple collection of the words themselves. For example, "You are going" and "Are you going," although composed of the same words, produce different meanings because of the rule in English that indicates that, usually, when the verb appears first in the group, the group of words is meant to ask a question. Additional meaning is given by the organization of the words into a sentence. Moreover, although single words carry some meaning by themselves—"ball," "rubber," "this," and "is," for instance—the combination or composition of single words into a sentence both gives specific meaning to certain kinds of words and produces supplemental meaning beyond the meaning contained in the mere juxtaposition of the words. In the speaking process, the whole thought to be communicated precedes the component words used to express the thought, and thus the same thought can be expressed by various grammatical conventions, such as "John threw the ball" and "The ball was thrown by John."

The same principle that describes the creation of excess meaning by combining words into sentence holds for the creation of additional meaning when individual sentences are combined into discourses. These are often called "texts," even though they may be spoken as well as written. Not every combination of words will produce a meaningful sentence (for example, "Strain blue flute help" is not a meaningful sentence); nor does every combination of sentences produce a meaningful discourse or text. For example, the sentences, "The rain is cold," "Albert fell down the stairs," and "The paint has dried," do not gather themselves into a meaningful discourse. However, the sentences, "Socrates is a man," "All men are mortal," and "Socrates is mortal," produce a logical understanding that is greater than that contained in the individual sentences. The sentences, "Her husband was very ill," "He died," and "She was sad and lonely," produce a discourse of narrative meaning that is greater than the individual sentences alone. Speakers and writers draw on the different principles of discourse formation when they want to produce an order of meaning beyond that possible with individual sentences. Speakers have to translate their whole thoughts into the kinds of connections and order that transform the meaning of their individual sentences, thereby creating discourse forms that communicate their whole thought.

Human expression requires the competency to use the many principles that produce discourse meaning by combining elements into larger units. These principles operate throughout the various levels at which significance is translated into sounds and script. At the first level there are conventions to differentiate the various combinations of sounds and marks so that individual words are produced and distinguished. At the second level there are rules that draw on and transform the individual words into meaning-giving sentences. At the third level there are rules that incorporate the two previous levels and transform them so that the higher-order meaning of discourse is created.

Jakobson's communication theory

Although the communication of narrative meaning requires a message in the form of narrative discourse, the appearance of meaning also requires the presence of a hearer and speaker (or author). The hearer and the speaker draw on communal conventions in a mutual expectation that each member of the communication community symbolizes meaning according to the same set of transforming covenants. The hearer, in the expectation that a speaker's linked sentences are intended as an expression, tries to compose them into a whole so that their meaning can be understood. In conversation, when a series of sentences do not appear to cohere, hearers can ask speakers if the interpretation they have understood is what the speakers have intended.

Roman Jakobson's 1960 essay "Linguistics and Poetry" contributed to the shift from linguistic models of words to communication models of discourse. He sought to expand linguistic concerns to take them beyond the analysis of sentence grammars and move them toward the treatment of whole communicative interactions.[51] In his essay, he outlined his theory of communication:

> [In every speech act] the *addresser* sends a *message* to the *addressee*. To be operative the message requires a *context* referred to, seizable by the addressee, and either verbal or capable of being verbalized; a *code* fully, or at least partially, common to the addresser and the addressee; and finally, a *contact,* a physical channel and psychological connection between the addresser and the addressee, enabling both of them to enter and stay in communication.

Jakobson proposed to study the linguistic function of poetic discourse in the context of verbal messages in general. His theory held that whether we are considering ordinary conversation, a public speech, a letter, a poem, or a narrative, we always find a *message* that proceeds from an addresser or sender to an addressee or receiver. The message communicated is dependent on three factors: a contact, a code, and a context. There can be no communication unless there is contact with the sender's message. Contact occurs through hearing words or seeing them printed on a page. Messages are communicated through a code, which involves more than the connection of meanings with sound or letter combinations, but includes as well the organization pattern of the discourse as a whole. Various codes contribute to a message's meaningfulness—for example, logical codes, hermeneutic codes, and rhetorical codes. The context of the message is the more general subject that the message is about and what the speaker is referring to; it is the broader meaning that is meant to show through in the communication.

When speakers want to send a message to a hearer, they need to organize it into a contact, a code, and a context that will produce the meaning they intend. Jakobson described six functions that messages can perform, and, depending on the function intended, the sender is required to emphasize different aspects of the three elements that produce the message. When the message is to function primarily to point to an external referent, the emphasis is placed on the context (what the message is about) and concentrates on pointing to some object or idea outside the message itself. In contrast to this referential function, in a message that is to perform an emotive function, the context is oriented to the sender and expresses the sender's attitudes. In a conative function the message is aimed at the receiver and, although its message includes extrinsic references, its purpose is to convince or move the receiver to action. Thus it uses a rhetorical code to organize its message. The phatic function is concerned with contact between the sender and receiver, the metalingual function with the communication process itself. When the message is to function poetically (in his essay Jakobson refers primarily to poems), the poetic code is used, in which the patterns of sound, rhyme, and meter serve to organize the message in such a way that the message itself becomes the center of attention, replacing the referent function as primary.

The successful transmission of any message requires competence in the use of the whole system of communication. Prior to Jakobson's theoretical work, the general understanding was that nonreferential speech was either deformed communication or a different kind of language. Jakobson's communication model moved referential speech from its position as linguistic exemplar to one where it became only one of the possible functions of a speech act. Jakobson held that even in referential speech the message does not and cannot supply all the meaning of the transaction, that a good deal of what is communicated derives from the context, the code, and the means of contact. Meaning resides in the total act of communication and, depending on the function of the message, different assessments are required. If the message is intended primarily to convey information, then it should be assessed in terms of the clarity of its formulation and the validity of the information it provides. If, in contrast, a message is to express the emotional condition of the speaker or to engender an attitude in the recipient of the message, then it should be assessed in terms of its performance force.

The paradigmatic and narrative codes

Using Jakobson's descriptions of the various functions of messages, I will focus on two of the codes used to organize messages according to different intended functions, the paradigmatic code and the narrative code. As mentioned above, discourse or text codes operate to form meaningful messages in a manner similar to the way grammatical rules operate to form various kinds of sentences—questions, statements, and exclamations. At the level of discourse, the conventions function to mold the several sentences into a unity—the discourse—and also serve as criteria by which to judge the discourse's "truth of coherence." The conventions are used to evaluate the discourse at a level above the truth of the individual sentences that make up the particular discourse. A single sentence in a discourse can be judged according to the criteria of correspondence; that is, truth, at the level of sentences, can relate to the correspondence of the sentence statement to the state of affairs to which the sentence refers. For instance, the sentence, "The shirt is blue," is true if, in fact, the shirt is blue. It is possible, however, that all the sentences in a discourse can be true by correspondence but that the discourse still does not cohere into a true discourse. The three sentences "Socrates is a man," "Some men are ill," and "Socrates is ill" may each be true by correspondence to actual states of affairs, but the discourse as a whole does not cohere according to the principles of formal logic.

Using Bruner's distinction between the logico-scientific or paradigmatic and narrative rationality,[34] one can clarify the difference between two types of rationality used to collect sentences into meaningful larger units. The term "paradigmatic" is used to refer to those discourses that function to demonstrate or prove a statement by linking it to other statements through connectives of formal logic. The term "narrative" is used for discourses that "demonstrate" by the type of reasoning that understands synoptically the meaning of a whole, seeing it as a dialectic integration of its parts. Narrative comprehension is the kind of acquisition of knowledge which regularly occurs as people understand the written and oral communications produced by others. Some communications, such as ancient and biblical texts, are difficult to understand fully and require special techniques. Access to the meanings of most storied accounts, however, occurs through ordinary narrative understanding.

Coherence entails various principles that are related to the different types of discourse. The coherences of formal logic preside at the formation of paradigmatic discourse, but in narrative discourse principles such as phonetics, rhyme, and metaphoric connections may authorize violations of logical protocols in the interest of producing formal coherences. In the two discourse conventions under consideration, communication can involve the use of *sentences* that truly correspond to some external referent. However, the purposes of the two discourses differ: one is to function as a logical demonstration, and the other is to function as an expression of global meaningfulness. The functional model of discourse presented by Jakobson relegates paradigmatic discourse and narrative discourse to the status of codes that shape and transmit different kinds of messages. The choice of discourse type and its model of coherence depends on the kind of message to be transmitted, either paradigmatic, concerning an extrinsic reference, or narrative, concerning the speaker's experience of a unity. Formal science is a subset of the paradigmatic type of discourse. Demonstrative discourse uses a variety of protocols of formal logic to organize its sentences into a higher order of meaning. Narrative productions, in contrast, organize sentences according to a "narrative logic" which groups sentences according to their contribution to a plot. In this manner, the discourses of narrative and of formal science can be seen to be of different orders, because each communicates a different kind of truth.

Narrative expression

Narrative is a form of "meaning making." It is a complex form which expresses itself by drawing together descriptions of states of affairs contained in individual sentences into a particular type of discourse. This drawing together creates a higher order of meaning that discloses relationships among the states of affair. Narrative recognizes the meaningfulness of individual experiences by noting how they function as parts in a whole. Its particular subject matter is human actions and events that affect human beings, which it configures into wholes according to the roles these actions and events play in bringing about a conclusion. Because narrative is particularly sensitive to the temporal dimension of human existence, it pays special attention to the sequence in which actions and events occur.

Narrative expresses its work of configuration in linguistic productions, oral and written. These productions display the meaningfulness of events for human existence. One's own actions, the actions of others, and chance natural happenings will appear as meaningful contributions, positive as well as negative, toward the fulfillment of a personal or social aim.

The narrative scheme serves as a lens through which the apparently independent and disconnected elements of existence are seen as related parts of a whole. At the level of a single life, the autobiographical narrative shows life as unified and whole. In stories about other lives and in histories of social groups, narrative shows the interconnectedness and significance of seemingly random activities. And in the imaginative creation of stories about fictitious characters, either passed on as part of a cultural heritage or as contemporary artistic creations, narrative displays the extensive variety of ways in which life might be drawn together into a unified adventure.

CHAPTER III

History and Narrative

THE study of history has a long tradition. Its methods and procedures were developed long before the Enlightenment, in contrast to the relatively youthful other human disciplines, which originated a little more than a century ago during the heyday of a fully developed formal science and its particular epistemology. History has been primarily concerned to inquire about the past activities of human agents and about nonrepeatable events, and has employed narrative descriptions and interpretation as the primary form by which it organizes and explains its data. In recent decades it has been argued that history should adopt the methods of formal science and look for laws underlying historical movements.

The first half of this chapter traces the story of the discipline of history during the last century, giving special attention to its responses to the call that it become a formal science. The story begins with the initial responses before the turn of the century, then moves to the covering-law controversy of the 1950s and 1960s, and concludes with the recent French historiographers' deemphasis of the human actor as the subject of history. The second half examines Paul Ricoeur's proposal that historical studies need to be ground by the temporal dimensions constructed by narrative forms.

I too argue that history functions as a human, not a formal, science, and that it provides a model for use in reforming the human disciplines. This idea has previously been proposed in relation to social psychology by Kenneth Gergen,[1] who wrote that "the particular research strategies and sensitivities of the historian could enhance the understanding of social psychology.[2] Gergen's position emphasizes history's sensitivity to causal sequences across time and to altered personal dispositions resulting from cultural changes. He also suggests that historians could benefit from the social psychologist's more rigorous methods and sensitivity to psychological variables.

History and formal science

Although the first comprehensive and systematic historical work in the Western tradition is held to be Herodotus's history of Persian wars,[3] the study of history has its origins in the chronicles of Egypt and Babylon.[4] Western culture has persistently exhibited a concern for the past and has produced historical studies reflecting on the past throughout its span.[5] With the appearance of formal science in the Enlightenment, however, and its claim as the only legitimate approach to knowledge,[6] the discipline of history was called on to defend itself as a rightful form of knowledge.

The early response of historians was to argue for a variety of legitimate epistemological schemes, including the narrative scheme. Johann Droysen wrote in 1868: "According to the object and nature of human thought, there are three possible scientific methods: the speculative (formulated in philosophy and theology), the mathematical or physical, and the historical. Their respective essences are to know, to explain, and to understand."[7] According to Karl-Otto Apel, this is the first time the distinction between explanation and understanding is used to ground the method of the historical sciences. Droysen made the argument that history was an independent and autonomous discipline with a legitimate, alternative form of knowledge. Yet the pressure for history to adopt formal scientific methods continued to gain momentum. By the beginning of the twentieth century the opposition to the integration of history into the unified formal science of nomological explanation had developed three responses: Wilhelm Dilthey's "life philosophy," the neo-Kantian position, and Max Weber's *verstehende* sociology.

Wilhelm Dilthey

Writing in 1883, Dilthey made use of Droysen's distinction between physical explanation and historical understanding as the foundation for distinguishing between the natural and the human sciences.[8] Dilthey stated that the natural sciences have as their objects facts that enter into consciousness from the outside as appearances of objects and individuals, whereas the objects of the human sciences enter consciousness from inside as reality and as living relations. Thus, the connections in nature are derived from inferences, but the connections of psychical life are understood directly as part of conscious experience.[9] Dilthey worked to clarify the method of history by refining the notion of "understanding" as it had been developed in hermeneutics. He emphasized that hermeneutics was not simply a marginal method for use in philological studies, that it was a general method for comprehending all of human expression. He acknowledged the legitimacy of formal science for developing knowledge of the natural realm, but held that the distinctive method of hermeneutics was required for the study of the human realm. Although hermeneutics was indeed a distinct method, Dilthey emphasized that it shared many features with the method of formal science.

Like Kant, who had described the subjective conditions for the development of scientific knowledge (that is, the formal categorical relations), Dilthey sought to describe the special subjective conditions that would produce knowledge of the specific expressive characteristics of human existence. He developed a theory of empathy for understanding an action: the historian would relive, reenact, or rethink the intentions, conceptions, and thoughts of the action's agent. Dilthey's project was to distinguish between the kind of knowledge suitable for the subject-object relation of the natural sciences and the kind of knowledge that takes place when subject knows subject. In his first formulations of subject-subject knowledge, he thought that the discipline of psychology could serve as the base from which the descriptions of human consciousness could be derived.

Under the influence of the neo-Kantians to be discussed below and of the Husserlian critique of psychologism (the idea that the meaning-constructing processes are located solely within the personal mental apparatus), Dilthey abandoned his view that psychology could form the basic science for subject-subject knowledge. Dilthey then turned from the internal mental structures to the forms of figuration maintained in the cultural sphere. Instead of looking inward to understand the rules that construct human experience, he said, one should look outward toward the "objective human spirit"—that is, toward the values, rules, and norms of the culture. There one finds the structures by means of which both the public expressions of human existence and the private, individual experiences of life are constructed. The community of the "objective human spirit" serves as the condition that opens individual "spiritual" subjects to one another, and through that spirit they understand one another's expressions. Dilthey described the communal bond thus formed:

> Each individual life-expression represents something common in the realm of objective spirit. Every word, every sentence, every gesture of form of politeness, every work of art and every political act is intelligible only because a commonality binds those who express themselves through [these forms] with those who understand [the forms]. The individual experiences, thinks, and acts constantly only in such a sphere of commonality, and only in it does he understand.[10]

Dilthey held that the epistemological base of understanding was to be found in the connection between cultural artifacts and one's capacity to create unique and personal elements in one's own life. However, Dilthey's emphasis on the role of culture in human understanding exposed his position to the critique against historicism and relativism, because disparate cultural settings could construct experience according to different patterns.

Dilthey's attempt to establish history and the human sciences as autonomous and distinct from the physical sciences was adopted in modified form by the neo-Kantians and by Max Weber, while criticized by positivists and proponents of formal science. Thus the controversy over explanation and understanding in history that has dominated this century was defined.

Neo-Kantianism

Wilhelm Windelband and Heinrich Rickert were spokesmen for the antipsychological school of neo-Kantianism in Heidelberg. Rickert held that human beings participated in an "irreal" realm of meanings and values, as well as in a physical realm. He also believed, in contrast to Dilthey, that the objects of meaning that existed in the "irreal" realm could be known in the same manner as objects in the physical realm—that is, the same subject-object differentiation could be maintained. The only difference was in the set of concepts used to describe the mental objects. The human realm required the use of individualizing, value-related (ideographic) concepts, while the physical realm required generalizing (nomothetic) concepts. The cost of this solution was the abandonment of Dilthey's position that knowledge of human expression required a form of experience different in kind from that of the natural scientist's observation of sense data. For Rickert, the process of knowing the meaning of a text or a communication from a person and the process of knowing any other aspects of reality differed only in the need for different sets of concepts to use in organizing the observations. By overlooking the difference between the apprehension of meaning and the experience of the physical world, the neo-Kantians moved in the direction of logical positivism's pure logic of science.

Both Dilthey and the neo-Kantians accepted the Kantian notion that all true knowledge, whether of the natural world or of human expressions, should be objectively valid. Consequently, these defenders of a different and autonomous method for history claimed the objective validity of their method of understanding and argued that it did not produce an arbitrary and subjective knowledge solely determined by the historical standpoint of the knower. To this latter end Rickert separated the values that people actually held from the true ideal values that existed independently of people's beliefs or circumstances. Ideal values were suprahistorical and valid in themselves, he argued, like mathematical theorems. Empirical descriptions, he maintained, could be given of the factual history that consisted only of what people believed to be true. Descriptions of the ideal values, however, which he thought also to be the responsibility of historians, required the use of rational philosophical methods. Rickert believed that the ultimate objective validity of the historical sciences rested on the capacity of philosophy to locate these ideal, true values, for they were the ground for grasping the meaning of actual historical practices.

Max Weber

Max Weber, a sociologist, rejected Rickert's plan for the human disciplines, and was the first of the *Verstehen* group to relinquish the presumption that an objectively valid order of values could be rationally founded. Weber recognized the failure of Kant's attempt to found morality on the rationally grounded idea of universality. He believed that reason could not determine the good, and thus that it could not solve conflicts between rival sets of values. Yet although rationality could not determine which values were to be served, it could match the most economical and efficient means to whichever value was chosen.

Dilthey had allowed that valuation was part of the cultural milieu in which people formed their self-understanding, and that values might be relative to a person's culture. In order to overcome the relativist implications of Dilthey's position, the neo-Kantians had separated the descriptive task of history and its methods of investigation from the philosophical task, which was to establish the universal ground of ethics. Weber, in turn, dismissed the second part of the neo-Kantians' understanding of the historians' work while retaining the purely descriptive task. Without an objective order of values, critical judgments about a particular historical event were not possible. Weber developed the idea of value-free understanding—that is, that human expression and action could be understood without the notion of objective values. Weber substituted for the idea of an objectively valid order of values a "polytheism" of values which turned values ultimately into an individual, prerational choice. Weber's reflections resulted in a historicist relativism similar to Dilthey's. However, where Dilthey believed that hermeneutic understanding was appropriate for comprehending all life expressions, Weber defended a dualism of understanding in which the personal decision pertaining to private world-orientations was separated from a scientism or instrumentalism in the sphere of rational, intersubjectively valid information. Weber believed that science was capable of discovering what were the most effective, pragmatic means to achieve a chosen goal.

The idea that individuals make an existential choice about the ends they want to pursue, but that they can call on science to inform them how to accomplish those ends, has led to the notion that science is a separate enterprise from ethics. Through the separation of science and values, Weber became the founder of the Western system in which public scientism and pragmatism are opposed to private decisionism. Alasdair MacIntyre says that "the contemporary vision of the world . . . is predominantly, although not perhaps always in detail, Weberian."[11] In Weber's view, no type of authority can appeal to rational criteria to vindicate itself, except for a kind of bureaucratic authority that appeals to effectiveness rather than to values.

In his early writings Weber proposed that before one could attempt to explain behavior it was necessary to establish the categories people use to organize their actions. To do this, one should employ the method, advocated by Dilthey and Rickert, of "direct observational understanding [*Verstehen*]." What Weber meant by this was an understanding of the historical complexes of cultural values which acting persons employed in giving meaning to their actions. But he thought that this process of understanding was particularly susceptible to the investigator's subjective bias and needed to be supplemented by causal explanation of the kind developed in the natural sciences. Weber used statistical procedures as part of his process of arriving at an adequate understanding or description of phenomena (although not as a separate aspect of the causal analysis itself). He also used the concept of the "ideal type" to facilitate the scientist's understanding. The "ideal type" was a description of an imagined person whose thought and behavior was purely informed by means-end rationality. Although an ideal type was not itself a description of reality, it provided a vocabulary and a grammar for clear descriptions of reality.

The responses of Dilthey, Rickert, and Weber to the demand that history become a formal science were basically defensive, and sought to establish a special and autonomous place in science for history by defining the human realm as one in which there is a unique relationship between the knowing subject and the human subjects of inquiry. They met the challenge of the formal sciences' emphasis on unchanging laws by trying to carve out a piece within reality where the special method of narrative understanding was needed. They tried to argue that because history was concerned with the past actions of human beings it needed a method that could provide access to the medium of cultural values, ideals, and personal concerns—the medium, shared by the knower, in which motives and reasons for personal action were found. The method that could provide access to this human realm was *Verstehen*. The results of research using this method were statements that described the experiences of motivation and morality as well as the decisions and actions derived from them. Thus, history was held to be distinct from the formal sciences, including those human disciplines such as empirical psychology and formal sociology that had adopted the formal science model.

Under the increasingly dominant view that formal science was the only acceptable method for gaining legitimate knowledge, the question changed from whether history was a special science to whether history was a science at all. Frederick J. Teggart, author of leading texts on historical theory in the early decades of this century, recognized in his 1918 *The Processes of History*,[12] a division within the discipline of history between those who "insist upon the conventional aim of reducing all historical facts to narrative" and those who "are reaching out in new directions unknown to the older historiography, directions which are manifestly tentative approximations to a scientific standpoint."[13] Although Teggart favored the move away from narrative, he did not see the imitation of natural science as the appropriate alternative. In 1925 he wrote:

> Until recently, philosophy has asserted that history is not a science . . . A more recent form of the contrast has been that the sciences deal with facts that recur, history with what has once happened and can never be reproduced. The antithesis has lent itself to a wealth of expressions: Nature deals with the typical in the manifold, History separates the manifold from the typical; Nature is the realm of necessity, History in the realm of freedom; Natural Science systematizes and classifies, History individualizes and narrates; Natural Science deals with the abstract and conceptual, History with the actual and concrete.[14]

Teggart retained Dilthey's view that the difference between science and history was in the dissimilarity of methods, that of history being a particular kind having its own particular end. Said Teggart: "The historian views the past as the painter views the landscape, and gives his personal rendering of what has happened in terms of its significance, meaning and value,"[15] and, "History is the narrative statement of happenings in the past."[16] In the final section of this chapter, the question of an enlarged methodology for history will be described which is based on an analogous use of narrative.

The point of this review has been to identify some of the factors in history's early engagement with formal science. Unlike the human disciplines, which began in the latter half of the nineteenth century, when the formal sciences were well developed and fully functioning, the discipline of history had a long tradition prior to the advent of formal science. Thus, it could confront science from a point of view distinct from that of the other human disciplines. Under pressure to conform to the methods and explanatory model of formal science, it examined its traditions and drew from them those features deemed necessary for the study of human actions. Many historians defended their discipline's autonomous status and the use of special procedures for investigating the human realm, although they did accept from formal science those features that appeared useful for historical research. The demands of formal science continued; some historians called for the discipline to give up the notion of *Verstehen* and dependence on the historian's judgment, with its possible subjectivity, and to adopt a completely new formal science paradigm. Other historians continued to defend history as an autonomous discipline with its own methods and procedures.

Analytic philosophy and history

Whether it is possible to perform science and still include other modes of explanation besides the deductive-nomological model has been of central concern for history as recently as two decades ago. The analyses of the difference between formal and narrative explanations, undertaken in regard to history, are especially pertinent for the contemporary struggle of the human disciplines to define themselves as more than imitations of the physical sciences.

The unified idea of explanation

At the beginning of this century, under the influence of Bertrand Russell and G. E. Moore, philosophy turned to the analysis of language.[17] Formal logic was their tool for the study of language; the specific language on which philosophy focused was that used by formal science.

One of the concerns of linguistic philosophers who belonged to the Vienna Circle was to determine the boundary that demarcated the language appropriate to scientific thinking from that used in ordinary subjective and arbitrary thinking. Out of this exploration came a purified understanding of the linguistic and logical structure of scientific explanation—that is, of the truly scientific answer to the question, "Why did it happen?" Members of the Vienna Circle reconstructed a model for scientific explanation which held that explanation occurred when an event could be formally deduced from a general law and a set of initial conditions. From the general law, "If P, then Q," given the condition "P is," the conclusion "Q therefore is" followed. Carl Hempel called this kind of explanation a deductive-nomological explanation because it explained by deducing instances from a law (*nomos*). The conclusion of the analytical examination of scientific statements was that all "true" sciences used this form of explanation.

This construction was developed from investigating the natural sciences and did not originally involve an analysis of historical explanations. In the 1940s, however, analytical philosophers turned the tools of logical analysis on history; Hempel's 1942 article, "The Function of General Laws in History," was the first such attempt.[18] Hempel held that all true sciences used the deductive-nomological model of explanation. History, however, held itself to be a science, yet used other narrative and understanding (*Verstehen*) models. Thus, Hempel's concern was to examine history to see if its alternative forms of explanation were a challenge to his single explanatory view of science.

The first analytic treatments of history were brief, and they held that history posed no real threat to the unified theory of explanation. They said that history was not yet a finished discipline, that as it matured as a science it would conform visibly and in detail to the proposed model of scientific explanation in the way the products of the more mature natural sciences already did. They also assumed that, for history to make progress toward being a real science with explanation by the deductive-nomological standard, it would need to align itself more closely with the formal social sciences.

It was recognized that, in general, the past achievements of the discipline were rife with arbitrary and subjective opinion. Hempel refused to accord any epistemological value to those procedures of understanding or interpretation used by historians. There seemed to be no suggestion that an independent study of the historiographic tradition might be called for. He took it for granted that narrative was simply too elementary a form of discourse even to pretend to satisfy the requirements for scientific deductive-nomological explanation.

Those advocating Hempel's model recognized that the features of history which historians had emphasized in their work, such as the focus on unique events occurring at specific places and times and the concern to describe human actions in terms of goal-seeking agents, did not fit their explanatory scheme.[19] Yet, in an attempt to preserve the unity-of-science notion, they began to look for ways to include some of these features, and to minimize the discrepancies that existed between Hempel's original strong statement for deductive-nomological explanation and the special qualities of historical knowledge. Hempel had opened the way for some diversity in explanation with his notion of "explanatory sketch." This idea allowed the sciences to give a type of deductive-nomological explanation which excluded the mention of certain laws or particular facts that were taken for granted.[20] In working to overcome the incongruity between the explanation model of formal science and the special features of historical research, analytical philosophers encountered the actual work of historians, with a resultant weakening of the deductive-nomological model. They brought to light some features of historical knowledge that did depend upon the model of formal science explanation, but at the same time nothing in the analytic model referred to the nature of narrative, to the narrative status of events, nor to the particular specificity of historical time in contrast to abstract time. The linguistic analysis position held that there was no difference in principle between a historical event and a physical event.

The first major concession to historical practice allowed for an extension in the kind of regularities that could be used in an explanation. In 1952, Patrick Gardiner, focusing on regularities in a person's disposition to act in a certain way in given circumstances, coined the term "*law-like* explanation."[21] The acceptance of this type of explanation opened the way for acceptance not only of the variance and imprecision of these regularities but also of some deviation from the absolute regularity of natural law explanations. Thus, the range of answers the historian might give to the question, "Why did the person do that?", was broadened to include the actor's sedimented attitudes, habits, and inclinations. But this extension stopped quite short of allowing answers based on Dilthey's empathic understanding, which would have allowed the historian to answer a question about why a person did something by imaginative re-construction of an actor's reasons.

A further concession to historical practice was the acknowledgement that historical events were caused by a complex of laws, and therefore could not be explained by a single law. The historian had to weigh the relative importance of the various causal variables and decide which was the principle cause of the event. Unless the various impacts on the event could receive clear statistical description and become available to multiple regression correlation and variance partitioning, the decisions on the relative importance of causes effecting an event could not be decided by mathematical processes but must become dependent on the historian's judgment. The admission of personal judgment into history further extended the process of explanation and carried it still further from the original deductive-nomological position, in which the rules of formal logic remove the subjectivity of personal judgment from historical explanation.

In an essay published in 1957, Charles Frankel continued the modification of the original position, that historical explanation must conform to the deductive-nomological model.[22] He accepted from Hempel the notion that one of the reasons historical explanations did not display a tight deductive-nomological pattern might often be due to the fact that historians offered incomplete explanations. However, he went on to distinguish another kind of explanation not attributable to the notion of incomplete "explanatory sketches." He claimed that historical explanations might fail to be deductive, and therefore lack predictive force, because they stated only certain necessary or essential, but not sufficient, conditions of what occurred. This also happened in other disciplines—for example, in genetic explanations in biology, which were simply a summary of the steps in a process, yet were often used as explanations for development or evolution. Frankel believed that to give such an account, especially as part of tracing the necessary stages in a process, was "one of the stable and accepted meanings of 'explain' "; thus, it would be incorrect to regard such an explanation as incomplete. He said that we should realize "that not all satisfactory explanations supply us with exactly the same type of information, and that not all requests to have something explained are unequivocal requests for a single kind of answer."[23] In short, he supported the general idea that not all explanations needed to be of a single deductive-nomological kind.

Frankel also agreed that interpretation was a necessary component in historical knowing, coming into play when a historian appraised some event, that is, attributed meaning and value to it. He continued to maintain, however, that the basic explanatory model of formal science was necessary, and he held that interpretation should be understood as a preliminary operation separate from the establishment of causal connections between events.

The break-up of the unity of explanation

During the first phase of the analytical attempt to include historical explanation as a species of the deductive-nomological form of explanation and thereby to retain the notion of a single scientific method, narrative was rarely discussed. But during the second phase of the analytical concern with history, narrative became the central focus of the discussion. Two factors operated here: (1) a continued expansion of what was allowed into the deductive-nomological model of explanation for history, reaching the point where the model itself broke apart, and (2) a turn to an interest in narrative by linguistics, not so much for its epistemological value but for the purpose of exploring the kind of thought that is involved when one uses narrative sentences.

Explanation by reasons. William Dray's book, *Laws and Explanations in History,* published in 1957, shattered the attempt advocated by Hempel to limit history to a single, deductive-nomological mode of explanation.[24] Dray expanded the notion of historical explanation to include a variety of acceptable types. He termed Hempel's deductive-nomological proposal the "covering law model," because it alleged that a tie existed between a law and the case it "covered." Dray proposed that when the call for an explanation was answered beginning with the term "because," there was no logical reason why this answer needed to conform to a particular logical structure. The explanations in history constituted "a logically miscellaneous lot," Dray said, and the proposal to take one model of explanation as the exclusive one was wrong.

Dray undertook an analysis of "cause" and demonstrated that "cause" could not be reduced solely to submission under laws. Considering some final state, he stated, causal analysis inquires into why it came into being and what are the necessary and sufficient conditions that produce it.[25] The term "cause" in history is polysemous and has a variety of meanings—for example, "leads to," "sets in motion," "produces," "prevents," "omits," and "stops." When historians undertake a causal analysis to answer the question, "Why did this event occur?", they go through a selective process in which they choose from among the possible explanations the one most likely to account for the event. They submit the choices to two tests, one inductive, the other pragmatic. The inductive test involves thinking through the possible choices to the question, "If this purported causal event had not happened, would the event to be explained have happened?" Historians try to decide, on the basis of what they know about the situation, what difference the nonoccurrence of a suggested cause would have made. If the answer is that it would have made no difference, then it likely was not significant as a cause of the event. The pragmatic test could take a negative or a positive turn. Historians could attempt to explain by judging what should have been done to avoid an occurrence—as when the cause of a war is attributed to a lack of statesmanship—or they could determine what was the catalyst or important contributor to an event—as when a victory is attributed to the leadership of a particular person. The pragmatic test is necessarily incomplete, open-ended, and susceptible to revisions.

The important point in Dray's causal analysis was the idea that the imputation of a cause in regard to some particular event did not necessarily require the application of a causal *law*. Many explanations were the result of judgments rather than the application of deductive logic. The judgments made by historians about causes involved the weighing of opposing arguments and then the rendering of decisions. The judgment about a cause did not require placing a case under a law; it required gathering together scattered pieces of information and inferences and weighing their respective importance in terms of the final result. Historians reached their conclusions through the logic of practical choice, not through scientific deduction.

One of the multiple kinds of explanations that Dray was most concerned to develop was that of "rational explanation." Rational explanation was not applicable to the whole range of events of concern to historians but was limited to those events that are understood as human actions. Dray's account of rational explanation did not use a Dilthey-type direct empathic understanding in which the reasons came to historians when they imaginatively put themselves in the places of the actors. It was a more directed process of reasoning out that involved what actors must have thought in order to have acted the way they did.

For Dray, to give a rational explanation was to show that what was done was "the thing to have done for the reasons given." It was "a reconstruction of the agent's calculations of means to be adopted toward his chosen end in light of the circumstances in which he found himself."[26] The agent's calculations were not limited to a kind of deductive reasoning in propositional form, for they included all levels of conscious deliberation. They included all the reasons the agents would have given for having acted as they did, including their moral criteria, their understanding of the situation, and their emotional and motivational factors.

Historians had to gather inductively the evidence that allowed them to evaluate the problem as the agent saw it. Through the traces left in documents, the historian had to reconstruct the process by which agents came to carry out a particular act. Such reconstruction could be painstaking and could require the inference of details from facts about the environment, about previous actions, and about the agent's understandings of the expected consequences of actions. The notion of explanation by reasons became the alternative model for much of historical inquiry.

Teleological explanation. A further expansion in the variety of explanations recognized as acceptable by logical analysts in the work of historians was provided by George von Wright in his 1971 work, *Explanation and Understanding*.[27] Von Wright constructed a model of explanation that involved the mixing of Dray's expanded notion of multiple causal explanations with teleological explanation. Von Wright proposed the idea of quasi-causal explanation, which was intended to account for the most typical mode of explanation in the human disciplines and in history.

Von Wright added to the realm of natural law two elements of human understanding: (1) the understanding that agents have of their ability to do something—that is, their understanding that they can interfere in the natural flow of events; and (2) the understanding that agents have of their ability to do something *so that* something else happens—that is, their understanding that actions can be intended to accomplish something. This second understanding incorporated the notion of a teleological explanation that was based on an inverted practical syllogism or inference: Persons intend to bring about a result; they consider that they cannot bring about the result unless they carry out a particular action; therefore, they set themselves the task of carrying out that particular action.

By incorporating teleological and causal elements into quasi-causal explanation, von Wright produced a more complex form of historical explanation than had been suggested previously. His idea was more complex than Dray's rational explanation in that it involved more than reconstructing the calculation that actors would have used in explaining why they had done something. Quasi-causal explanations incorporated the sufficient and necessary conditions involved in causal explanations, but they also added the notions of understanding that humans can do something to lead to desired results. For example, an explanation of why the First World War broke out needed to include the whole range of motivations affecting the parties involved; these motivations needed to be understood as leading to intended actions and to be linked to practical inferences; these intended actions then led to certain acts, which in turn changed the circumstances in which new practical inferences were drawn.

Von Wrights's quasi-causal model of explanation linked together various logical types of causes into a complex of schemes to be used in answering why an event occurred, and it restored several specific characteristics of explanation in history. It included human actions in the explanatory scheme by allowing for the idea that humans understand that they can interfere with and affect the world. The acceptance of teleological elements into explanation recognized the significance of actors' intentions for historical investigation. The notion of a complex of explanatory schemes indicated that historians had to include human planning and action with causal accounts of events. Ricoeur has expressed concern that von Wright's recognition of various modes of explanation ended with a scattered complex and did not bring schemes together into a unified explanation. Ricoeur suggests that plot, insofar as it functions to synthesize the heterogeneous, may be the way to integrate the variety of explanatory forms introduced by von Wright into one intelligible whole to include circumstance, goals, interactions, and unintended results.[28]

Narrative explanation. The first statement in favor of a narrativist rather than a causal interpretation of history was formulated within the framework of analytic philosophy by Arthur Danto in his 1965 book, *Analytic Philosophy of History*.[29] Danto's work was aimed at analyzing the kinds of *sentences,* including narrative sentences, used in historical description, rather than at analyzing the combination of sentences in the *discourse* of historical writing.[30] He wrote: "Narration exemplifies one of the basic ways in which we represent the world, and the language of beginnings and endings, of turning points and climaxes, is complicated with the mode of representation to so great a degree that our image of our own lives must be deeply narrational."[31] Danto wanted to understand the way our thinking occurs when we speak in narrative sentences using verbs in the past tense, thus differentiating his concern from empiricism, which, he said, only deals with present-tense verbs as descriptions of present states of affair. Part of the reason for his investigation (as well as for Karl Popper's earlier one)[32] was to critique traditional philosophies of history, such as those of Hegel and Marx, which claimed to have grasped the whole of history, including its future unfolding. Danto held that changes in the past that stemmed from human action could be variously described and that the narrative sentence was one of the forms that could be used. The particular characteristic of narrative sentences was that they referred to at least two time-separated events and that they described the earlier of the events referred to in light of the later event. The example he used for his analysis was this sentence: "In 1717, the author of *Rameu's Nephew* was born." No one in 1717 could have uttered the sentence which redescribed the birth of a child in the light of another later event, the publication of Diderot's famous book. In a historical sentence, Danto said, a first event was redescribed in terms of the second event. Words such as "anticipated," began," "preceded," "provoked," and "gave rise to" appeared only in narrative sentences. Narrative sentences gave significance to prior events by linking them to important following events.

Danto's analysis of narrative sentences had three epistemological implications. First, the notion of cause in narrative sentences is paradoxical in that it appears that a subsequent event transforms a prior one into a cause. Second, in opposition to Dray's rational explanation, in which it is the actor's calculations that explain the action, Danto pointed out that the causal account in history attributes significance to an action that the actor would not have been aware of. It is the historian, and not the actor, who organizes various personal actions into an overall action and who is able to show the significance of even the unintended consequences of an agent's action. Third, narrative sentences are concerned only with what is past, and the symmetry between explanation and prediction required in the deductive-nomological mode is broken in historical statements.

Danto focused on individual narrative sentences rather than on narrative discourse in which a connective structure ties sentences together into a single story. His history resembled a chronicle, a series of narrative sentences of specific causal connections, but lacking a unifing theme. It missed the configuring work of emplotment wherein sentences are linked together into a single story.

W. B. Gallie, in his *Philosophy and the Historical Understanding*, written in 1964, moved closer to a structural description of an entire narrative discourse. He looked at narrative as a form that history shared with fictional literature. Gallie saw that history reports its findings as narratives and that it is the finished products of historical inquiry which are presented to the public, not the methods by means of which the historical past is constituted or known. While previous discussions about the role of narrative in history had been careful to emphasize the difference between history, with its focus on evidence and objective truth, and fiction, Gallie emphasized the continuity between historical and fictional narratives, suggesting that people understand a historical text in the same way that they "follow a [fictional] story":

> Every story describes a sequence of actions and experiences of a number of people, real or imaginary. These people are usually presented in some characteristic human situation, and are then shown either changing it or reacting to changes which affect that situation from outside. As these changes and the characters' reactions to them accumulate, they commonly reveal hitherto hidden aspects of the original situation and of the characters: they also give rise to a predicament, calling for urgent thought and action from one or more of the main characters. The predicament is usually sustained and developed in various ways that bring out its significance for the main characters. Whether or not the main characters respond successfully to the predicament, their response to it, and the effects of their response upon the other people concerned, brings the story to within sight of its conclusion.[33]

A story and an argument use completely different processes. In an argument, the conclusion is compelled to be what it is, and the successful following of an argument necessarily entails the ability to predict its deductive conclusion. In following a story, one has to attend to it all the way to its conclusion, because the ending cannot be deduced or predicted. The story holds surprises, coincidences, and encounters that hold the hearer's attention through to the end. The conclusion of the story needs to have a sense of acceptability or rightness to the reader, not predictability. That is, the story gives a sense of "the main bond of logical continuity, which makes its elements intelligible." In looking back from the end of the story, the reader accepts that the end does follow from the narrated events that have led to it. The kind of intelligence required for following a story, moreover, is different from that required for understanding the lawfulness of a process. It responds to the internal coherence of the story, a coherence that joins together the various chance events and human responses to them. In reading a story, the reader is concerned about the norms of acceptability that have "to be gradually recognized and constantly assessed and reassessed as the story proceeds.[34] The reader expects the story to be composed of existential elements, not logical concepts. Following a story is a temporal process and involves the recognition of a lived time in which unforeseeable disasters can produce fragmentation and discontinuity in the experience of time, although the elements later emerge with a new, altered reintegration.

A further development in the controversy about the nature of historical knowledge and inquiry was undertaken by Louis Mink in two articles written in 1965 and 1974.[35] In the first article Mink reviewed the discrepancies between the prescriptions of the covering law model and the actual understanding displayed by current work in history. He held that these discrepancies could be accounted for only by viewing historical understanding as a different type of understanding from that used in giving logical proofs. He called this type of understanding a "synthetic judgment," in which one "convert[s] an indigestible heap of data into a synoptic judgment by which ... [one] can 'see together' all these facts in a single act of understanding."[36]

Mink reviewed past attempts to clarify the particular characteristics of historical understanding, finding these inadequate. He believed that the idea of synoptic judgment captured the notion toward which previous descriptions of *Verstehen* had pointed. He asked why synoptic judgment had been "so little noted and so much misunderstood," and answered that it was because historians have to set forth their presentations as sequences of events, which gives the impression that their conclusions are inferences from the evidence, when really they are only indicators of the way the evidence has been ordered. Historians have a tendency to divert attention from their reflective act of judgment by presenting their work as a series of statements that are reasons for other statements.

Mink pointed out that the habit of making synoptic judgments and seeing things as a whole is not unique to historians. It is an ordinary thinking process by means of which humans understand and order the world. Mink writes: "This is the same type of synoptic judgment by which a critic 'sees together' the complex of metaphor in a poem, by which the clinical psychologist 'sees together' the responses and history of a patient, or by which the leader of a group 'sees together' the mutually involved abilities, interests, and purposes of its members.[37] He held that historical knowledge is unique not because it deals with an autonomous subject matter nor employs a unique method but because it uses a particular kind of judgment. Historical knowledge is the comprehension of "a complex event by seeing things together in a total and synoptic judgment which cannot be replaced by an analytic technique."[38] Mink accepted that his identification of historical thought with synoptic judgment left unanswered such epistemological problems as whether there are general grounds for preferring one interpretive synthesis to another and whether there are criteria for historical objectivity and truth. Yet he believed that one must first identify the kind of judgments that make up historical inquiry before the epistemological questions can be addressed from a proper perspective.

Mink's 1974 article further clarified his proposal that history is unique because it uses a particular type of understanding.[39] In this article, Mink differentiated three structures of comprehension: theoretical, "categoreal," and configurational.

He held that all three modes of comprehension function to grasp "together in a single mental act things which are not experienced together, or even capable of being so experienced, because they are separated by time, space, or logical kind. And the ability to do this is a necessary (although not a sufficient) condition of *understanding.*"[40] Theoretical comprehension is involved in making a logical or mathematical inference in which we grasp together a complex sequence of inferences and understand it as a whole proof. Categoreal comprehension sees a number of objects as examples of the same category and is used to determine what kind of object a thing is.[41] It uses a system of a priori concepts so that experience, which would otherwise appear chaotic, is organized. In configurational comprehension things are understood as elements in a single and concrete complex of relationships.

In describing the configurational mode of comprehension Mink says:

> Thus a letter I burn may be understood not only as an oxidizable substance but as a link with an old friend. It may have relieved a misunderstanding, raised a question, or changed my plans at a crucial moment. As a letter, it belongs to a kind of story, a narrative of events which would be unintelligible without reference to it. But to explain this, I would not construct a theory of letters or of friendships but would, rather, show how it belongs to a particular configuration of events like a part of a jigsaw puzzle. It is in this *configurational* mode that we see together the complex of imagery in a poem, or the combination of motives, pressures, promises and principles which explain a Senator's vote, or the pattern of words, gestures and actions which constitute our understanding of the personality of a friend.[42]

Mink's contribution to the ongoing engagement of history and formal science was to focus the discussion on the kind of comprehension that is used by narrative history. His proposal, that the difference between a narrative understanding and a formal science understanding is to be found in the varying modes by which information is organized into meaningful wholes, is parallel with the position taken in this study and will be looked at again from the perspective of discourse theory later in this chapter.

This long story of the engagement of history with formal science began by placing understanding (*Verstehen*) in opposition to explanation. The dialogue has moved forward to a clarification of types of comprehension by means of which we organize and make sense of experience and to the identification of historical understanding with configurational comprehension. The final contributor to this story to be discussed here is Hayden White, who, for the first time, assigned the procedures of literary emplotment to the narrative structure of history writing. White's *Metahistory*, written in 1973, followed on Mink's proposal that history and fiction belong to the same mode of comprehension.[43] Because both use narrative structure, White said, the writing of history is linked to the writing of literature. The writing of history is not an afterthought of the historian's work, governed simply by the conventions of the rhetoric of communication, for the writing is itself the historical mode of understanding. Thus White switched the focus of the discussion about history from an exclusive concern about its objectivity and scientific status to the literary form in which it is expressed. This allowed him to consider historical narratives in connection with their literary counterparts and to transfer to history some categories borrowed from literary criticism. In crossing the boundaries of history and literature, White was going against the mainstream concern, not only of historians, but also of literary critics, both of whom had sought to establish a clear boundary between works that deal with representations of the "real" and those that are compositions of the imagination. White says:

> Before the historian can bring to bear upon the data of the historical field the conceptual apparatus he will use to represent and explain it, he must first *prefigure* the field—that is to say, constitute it as an object of mental perception. This poetic act is indistinguishable from the linguistic act in which the field is made ready for interpretation as a domain of a particular kind.[44]

White has fit the events the historian uses into an organizational hierarchy. The first level is the chronicle, the simple listing of events in chronological order. Second is the story line, in which the chronicle is organized in terms of motifs and themes that unify and delineate subsets within the chronicle. Third is emplotment, in which the story line is ordered according to the traditional cultural modes of plot, such as romance, tragedy, comedy, and satire. The historian "is forced to emplot the whole set of stories making up his narrative in one comprehensive or *archetypal* story form";[45] that is, according to one of the basic plot types.

In addition to emplotment, historians argue about the "point of it all" or "what it adds up to," and historians have their own modes of arguing which belong to the narrative domain. But the modes of argument used by historians express their own presuppositions about the nature of the historical field, and so White adopted Stephen Pepper's four root metaphors as the four major modes of argument: the formist, the mechanistic, the organicist, and the contextualist.[46] When one of these modes of argument is improperly treated, as if it were the real essence or content rather than the author's world view, it becomes ideological. White used the combination of the operations of emplotment, argument, and ideology to develop a theory of historiographical style. Although there are elective affinities among the three literary operations, he said, master historians develop their styles from efforts to wed various inconsonant operations.

White also proposed that consciousness itself prefigures areas of experience into a form suitable for analysis and explanation. He was opposed to the Enlightenment belief in language as transparent and able to reflect objects as they are, but he was also opposed to the absolute relativism of the skeptical strategy where the multiple language games each create their own reality. He stated that there are four basic "language games," or means of constructing reality, and he related these to the four stages of cognitive development described by Jean Piaget. All discourse, including the historian's descriptions of the past, are determined by one of the four tropes, he said, or more usually by a particular mixture of the four tropes. The four master tropes, which prefigure the operations of language and which compose understanding according to its particular configuring operation, were identified by White as metaphor, metonymy, synecdoche, and irony. Each trope prefigures the data to be considered for analysis in a unique and fairly exclusive way. Metaphor constitutes reality by means of representation and identity insofar as simlilarity emerges out of an initial perception of difference; metonymy does so by means of contiguity and a reduction characterized by part-to-part relations; synecdoche, by means of an integration characterized by part-to-whole relations; and irony, by means of negation, through a self-conscious awareness of being able to say things about something in alternative ways.

The discussions in this chapter about historical explanation and the role of narrative have ranged in diversity from the position that narrative is a porous, partial, or sketchy version of the deductive-nomological explanations given in the sciences (Hempel's later view) to the notion that narratives give an understanding of the past through techniques, such as configuration, for which there are no counterparts in scientific explanations. Our discussion has been one-sided in its emphasis on the developments leading up to the acceptance of narrative explanation. Many historians are critical of the attempts of philosophers of history to give legitimacy to narrative. For example, Leon Goldstein writes:

> An explicit commitment to narrativism . . . means an explicit rejection of the primacy of history's cognitive function, that is, the task of explaining historical evidence by means of a hypothetical reconstruction of the human past. To my mind, the very formulation of the confrontation to two conceptions [narrative and cognitive] must result in any reasonable man's recognition that the narrativist position cannot be sustained. I cannot believe that anyone would insist upon the narrativist thesis in the face of the claims of history as a way of knowing.[47].

Yet the role of narrative and its relation to historical study have become central issues for any current discussion of the philosophy of history.[48] Sophistication in the analysis of narrative as a form of cognitive explanation has been greatly enhanced by the increasing engagement between history and linguistic analysis. The role of language in shaping human experience and the historical reports of past human action has become apparent. The new view that the question, "Why did it happen?", can be answered in a variety of forms has opened up the concept of explanation to include a variety of conceptual operations by means of which humans organize the events of their experience into meaningful wholes. One of these operations involves the processes of formal logic, and another involves the processes of narrative configuration.[49] There is, in other words, an epistemological break between formal science explanation and narrative understanding.

Narrative and French historiography

While the arguments of the analytical philosophers were concerned to measure explanation in history against models presumed to define scientific knowledge, the arguments of the French school of history were concerned more directly with the profession of the historian. Yet both groups had one goal in common: displacement of narrative understanding from history. The French school held that narrative focused on objects that were inappropriate for true historical investigations; it was concerned only with the events of individual lives, which, they said, are merely the surface perturbations of political history (the plane of events). They called for history to address itself to the social and economic forces underlying the events of individual lives.

The French historiographers also argued against the positivist notion that history could provide a transparent representation of the actual events of the past as they truly occurred. The positivist understanding of history was based on three commonsense ideas that were derived from accepting the notion that historical reports are about what actually happened in the past. (1) A past event—whether physical or historical—differs radically from events that have not yet occurred. What happened in the past is unchangeable and is therefore independent of our present constructions and reconstructions. (2) History is concerned with those past events that people—agents similar to ourselves—have made happen or have undergone. The ordinary definition of history as knowledge of the actions of past human beings reflects this notion. (3) We cannot directly know or communicate with past events. In this sense, past events are strange and different from those which we can directly observe in the present.

Three epistemological features followed from these three commonsense notions about historical events. (1) A past event has happened only once: it is a unique happening, and it is unrepeatable. Therefore, it can be opposed to the universality of a law. Whether the law is a statistical frequency, a causal connection, or a functional relationship, it is not the same as the singular past event. (2) As a human action, a historical event is contingent: it could have happened differently. (3) Because the historical event is over and therefore cannot be known directly, there is a gap between the actual past event and any constructed representation or model of it.

The French group held that belief in the objectivity of historical events, as events that really objectively happened, was in error—as were the three notions that accompanied it. Raymond Aron attacked the reigning positivism of French history of his time, and pointed out that, to the extent that historians are implicated in the understanding and explanation of past events, an actual event is not part of the historical discourse.[50] Understanding—even the understanding of another person in everyday life—is never a direct intuition but always a reconstruction, Aron said. Understanding is always more than Dilthey's simple empathy. No "such thing as a *historical reality* exists ready-made so that science merely has to reproduce it faithfully."[51] The past, conceived of as the sum of what actually happened, is out of the reach of the historian. The lived past can only be postulated by the practicing historian from the documents and traces that are available.

The major text of the French school was Fernand Braudel's *The Mediterranean and the Mediterranean World in the Age of Philip II.*[52] Braudel wanted to overthrow political history (along with narrative, the tool of that approach), with its focus on the individual as the ultimate bearer of change, and proposed rather that the object of history should be the "total social fact" in all of its human dimensions—economic, social, political, cultural, and religious. He held that the history of individuals is the most superficial of historical approaches. Groups, he said—such as social classes, cities, and countries—should become instead the focus of history. History should be concerned with what he called the long time-span—time that flows only slowly—not with a single event that occurs in an instant of time.

History as explanatory discourse

History's function is to describe the events of the real world as they have actually happened and to explain why they have happened. The debate about historical narrative, then, has focused on the legitimacy of narrative discourse as a mode for representing and explaining real past events and their causes. Historical narrative is supposed to be factual—that is, it is supposed to be made up of true sentences that represent actual past events. The sentences of historical discourse are expected to pass a correspondence test based on the evidence of the traces of events left in documents. On both sides of the argument—narrative is or is not an acceptable mode of historical explanation—it has been assumed that the sentences of narrative should refer to actual happenings. The issue, however, is not primarily whether narrative sentences are true but whether narrative functions as demonstrative discourse.

Narrative is a form of discourse or text and can be examined from the perspective of the primary function it is expected to perform. In Chapter 2, "Narrative Expression," two functions of discourse were described, paradigmatic and narrative. It was pointed out that these two functions are not mutually exclusive, and that, in fact, most texts combine a variety of discourse conventions. Nevertheless, it is possible to designate one of the two discourse functions as dominant and to judge the text by the criteria appropriate to that function.

The discussions in the discipline of history regarding the adequacy of narrative have usually assumed that the function of a narrative text is demonstrative; therefore, it should be organized according to the paradigmatic form. As such, the criteria for its acceptability have been thought to be logical protocols, based on logical coherence among statements. Explanatory discourse has been understood to be a type of demonstrative discourse. In a historical explanatory discourse, the minimal logical coherence required is that individual sentences should be logically consistent with each other in regard to the temporal order. For example, an earlier event can be given as the cause for a later event, but not the reverse. It may be allowed, however, that a later event can be given to show the significance of an earlier one, just as the later accomplishments of a person can show the significance of his or her birth.

At the same time, demonstrative discourse is expected to do more than just list events in chronological order. It must also show a logical relationship among them. Hempel held that there was only one acceptable logical protocol for molding sentences into a scientific explanation, the deductive-nomological protocol. It was believed that in scientific discourse individual sentences in the text did not simply correspond to actual references, rather, that the logic by means of which the text was organized was itself a representation of the way the world was organized. In this sense, the whole discourse corresponded to the organization of reality.

Scientific discourse was held to be a special form of demonstrative discourse in which the logical protocols used to make the sentences cohere about states of affairs were the same ones that linked the actual objects of the world into a coherent universe. Thus it was not enough that a narrative discourse used sentences that corresponded to actual past events; it had to link those sentences by means of the deductive-nomological protocol so that they would have a valid external referent.

With the passing of the notion that the deductive-nomological protocol was required for explanation, it was possible to accept the idea that narrative sentences could be organized by other patterns of logic and that the causes attributed to these patterns could be justified by various warrants. Yet it was thought that these more varied protocols still validly represented external referents. The issue remained as to whether a given historical narrative using a varied causal analysis cohered as a whole in a way that corresponded to the coherence of human reality: did human actions actually become configured in the form of plots so that the logic of emplotment was a true representation of them?

For those who understood a narrative discourse to be scientific in form and corresponding to the way history really happened, the form of narrative simply represented reality as it was in itself and did not add any meaning to the events it described. This position held that the narrative form of discourse was simply a medium for the message. Narrative discourse had no more truth-value or information content in it than any other formal structure—a logical syllogism, for instance, or a mathematical equation. It was simply a code that served as a vehicle for transmitting messages about reality, much like the Morse code. Narrative discourse was thought to add no special information or knowledge that could not be conveyed by some other system of encodement—shown by the fact that when the content of a historical narrative account was extracted from the account and represented in demonstrative format it would still meet the same criteria of logical consistency and factual accuracy as other scientific demonstrations. Although it was acknowledged that historians might vary in their artistic descriptions of a particular historical incident, this fact was seen to be nothing more than the equivalent of the way the touch of different telegraphers might be more or less eloquent. To those who held the position that historical narrative discourse was a type of scientific discourse, these differences in expression were understood to be merely ornamental; they had no effect on the actual truth content of the whole narrative. Nevertheless, advocates of the formal science type of demonstrative discourse attempted to purify it of all such narrative elements as purposeful action and metaphoric and analogic links.

History as narrative discourse

Historical narrative has been addressed traditionally as if it were a type of demonstrative discourse. Even though later analytic philosophers, such as Dray and von Wright, accepted historical causes in addition to deductive-nomological causes, they still understood historical narrative discourse to be explanatory because it was a kind of logical representation of actual past causes.

With Dray, and even more with Gallie and Mink, the understanding changed, and narrative came to be viewed as a special kind of discourse that was differently constructed from paradigmatic discourse. These philosophers proposed a radical shift in which historical writing was no longer to be understood as a demonstrative discourse to be assessed by formal logic protocols but rather as a kind of narrative discourse that would be assessed by an alternative form of coherence. They held that narrative was organized according to a configurative protocol whereby units were gathered together into a whole idea. They still understood that narrative represented the real past, but they believed that the organization of the past events into plots was an operation of the discourse itself and that it was the conventions of a narrative discourse that brought the events into a unified whole. White raised the issue of whether historical narrative might be best understood as the construction of a story about reality rather than as a direct representation of it. As the French historiographers had pointed out, there was no way actually to know the past as it was. White believed that, although historical narrative differed from fictional literature in its tie to documents and traces of events, it could best be understood as a literary reconstruction of the past which included the ideological perspective of the author.

This position differs from that developed by the early Anglo-American analytic philosophers in that it proposed that the function of narrative was primarily expressive and that the criteria appropriate for narrative were those of narrative coherence or explication. The key point in the argument presented in this section, that historical writing needs to be understood as narrative rather than as paradigmatic discourse, draws on Jakobson's theory of multiple types of discourse. Narrative discourse includes, in addition to historical writing, such productions as myth, fictional literature, and poetry. Both the paradigmatic and the narrative forms of discourse carry factual information in the sentences that compose them, but each also carries an additional type of information in the form of the coherence they impose on the sentences. The paradigmatic form of discourse was thought to be the only appropriate mode for scientific texts; not only was it believed to be a transparent vehicle for the transmission of information about extrinsic references, but also the logical patterns it uses to relate its sentences to one another were understood to be mere reflections of the actual logical patterns existing in reality. The narrative discourse retains an awareness of the added level of communication that results from its form of organization.[53] For example, in poems, in addition to being related by the ideas they convey, words are consciously related according to patterns of similarity, opposition, and parallelism. In realist prose literature, sentences are linked according to metonymic associations. Thus, the text in narrative discourse shows a density consisting of additional configured meaning, which shows forth in the plot or story type.

Because a particular production is not limited to the use of only one type of coherence, historical narratives retain some logical protocols—for example, adherence to the temporal logic of "before and after." They may also include sections made up of paradigmatic discourse in which explanatory arguments and deductive-nomological causal analyses are given about why things have happened as they have. The sections that draw on the conventions of paradigmatic discourse are usually set forth in the mode of direct address and are easily understood by the reader as a switch in discourse mode. But these sections are more properly considered not as part of, but as a commentary on, the narrative ordering. Although narrative takes advantage of the various protocols of logical argument and scientific demonstration, these protocols by themselves cannot produce the kind of meaning that is distinct to narrative organization. This kind of meaning requires the coherence that is brought about by emplotment.

The historical narrative, like other discourses, is composed of two kinds of referents: (1) a first order of referents, which are the events that make up the story, and (2) a second order of referents, the plot. Just as the reader of a formal science discourse can recognize that the second order of meaning is created by a particular kind of protocol, such as a syllogism or a chronological list, so the reader of a narrative discourse can recognize that it is created by the kind of story type being used to give meaning to events. The types of stories available for configuring the first-order events are drawn from the repertoire of plots available in a particular culture. When the reader of a historical narrative recognizes the type of story being told in a particular account—an epic, a romance, a tragedy, a comedy, or a farce, for instance—the secondary referent has been comprehended.

We see, then, that discourses or texts contain two orders of information. The first consists of the information contained in the sentences, and the second is the information generated by the specific type of coherence used to order the sentences into a discourse. Two different kinds of discourse can take the same set of information contained in the sentences and produce a different second-order meaning, depending on the type of organization used. For example, a set of sentences giving information about events or actions can be ordered within a demonstrative discourse that uses a chronological protocol, producing a chronicle in which each sentence is arranged according to its referent event's situation in time relative to other events. The same set of sentences can be arranged by an encyclopedic protocol, that is according to topics (by countries, for example). Each of these two different logical protocols produces a paradigmatic discourse, but each gives a different second-order meaning to the set of sentences. The narrative discourses, such as historical writing, produce a second-order meaning quite different from that which would be found in a paradigmatic discourse using the same "facts." This distinctive meaning is created by emplotment, and it is lost when narrative discourse is translated into paradigmatic discourse as paraphrase.

Historical narratives are expansions of the type of paradigmatic discourse called the "chronicle." The chronicle is a discourse that uses temporal order as its logical protocol and manifests itself as a list of sentences in which the referent is an event or action. The meaning produced by the chronicle discourse is related to the temporal order of objective time. When the same set of facts found in a chronicle list are emplotted into a narrative, the meaning produced is of a different time order—the historical or recollective order of time.[54]

In order to bring about the transformation in meaning and show the second referent, the events, agents, and agencies referred to in a chronicle must be encoded as story elements. For example, the events in the chronicle, "She graduated in June," "She started a job in August," and "She quit the job in December," need to be extended as elements of specific story types. This the historical narrative does. The second referent, the story type, involves a constructive process through which a given set of first-order references to real events can be emplotted in several ways and can bear the weight of being told as various kinds of stories. Notice that the meaning held in the order of the second referent is a construction and results from the particular kind of plot that is used to draw the first-order events together. The logical coherence of the second referent used in narrative is different from the formal logic used in paradigmatic discourses. Narratives use the logic of plot to help events cohere into meaningful wholes. The kinds of truths with which narrative history deals are of a different order than those generated by the formal logic of scientific paradigmatic discourse. The test of the truth of historical narrative is its capacity to yield a plot from a set of first-order real events. This is the truth of coherence.

In summary, the historical narrative differs from paradigmatic discourse in that it produces as its second order of meaning a coherence of events ordered by narrational or "poetic logic."[55] The narrative code is drawn from the domain of poiesis (making), the paradigmatic code from the domain of noesis (thought).[56] As narrative discourse, historical writing does not use formal logic as its protocol for patterning events into a unified plot; but neither does it use the patterns of sound and meter of formal poetry. Its concern is with the patterns of events as they contribute to a story's plot.

Historical narratives

In addition to historical narrative, there are two other forms of narrative discourse, namely, literature and myth, which also produce meaning through plot structures. The difference among them are that in historical narrative the events in the first order are meant to be real rather than imaginary. History, literature, and myth share the distillates of the historical experience of a people, a group, or a culture. These three modes of narrative discourse are grounded in the actual generalized experiences of a people and are the results of cultural attempts to impose a satisfactory, graspable, humanizing shape on experience. The historical narrative takes the types of plots developed by literature and subjects them to the test of endowing real events with meaning. The knowledge provided by narrative history is what results from the application of the systems of meaning originally elaborated by cultures in their myths and (in some cultures) later refined by their literatures. Historical narratives are a test of the capacity of a culture's fictions to endow real events with the kinds of meaning patterns that its stories have fashioned from imagined events. Thus, historical narratives transform a culture's collection of past happenings (its first-order referents) by shaping them into a second-order pattern of meaning.

The truth of first-order referents is concerned with whether the events have actually happened in the way reported in the sentences of the narratives. Historical facts cannot be established by the "direct observation paradigm" (the idea that direct observation is the only secure foundation for knowledge).[57] The ideal of direct intersubjective observation is the method of testing first-order statements in the formal science mode of demonstrative discourse, but historical narratives' concern with first order statements about the past requires the use of memory, testimony, and other traces to establish the truth of these statements. Thus the statements, "It was raining yesterday" and "It is raining now," require entirely different methods of verification. The discipline of history has developed a full stock of tools for inferring by indirect evidence the truth of its first-order statements about the past.[58]

The truth of second-order referents is established by the principles of coherence that the particular discourse uses. In formal science, the truth of a research report is only partly determined by reference to the accuracy of the first-order observational statements: it requires, in addition, a second-order logical coherence among the statements. Mink describes the difference between establishing the truth of a paradigmatic discourse on the one hand and establishing the truth of a narrative discourse on the other:

> One can regard any text in discourse as a logical conjunction of assertions. The truth value of the text is then simply a logical function of the truth or falsity of the individual assertions taken separately: the conjunction is true if and only if each of the propositions is true. Narrative has in fact been analyzed, especially by philosophers intent on comparing the form of narrative with the form of other theories, as if it were nothing but a logical conjunction of past-referring statements [a paradigmatic discourse]; and on such an analysis there is no problem of *narrative truth*. The difficulty with the model of logical conjunction, however, is that it is not a model of narrative at all. It is rather a model of a chronicle. Logical conjunction serves well enough as a representation of the only ordering relation of chronicles, which is '... and then ... and then ... and then ....' Narratives, however, contain infinitely many ways of *combining* these relations. It is such a combination that we speak of when we speak of the coherence of a narrative.[59]

In historical narrative the truth of the second-order displays itself as a synoptic judgment in which events are seen together in a manner that cannot be replaced by the techniques of analytic logic.[60] Synoptic judgment functions much as Aristotle's *phronesis,* or practical wisdom: in both instances a practical rule or principle is grasped in a way that cannot be explicitly exhibited in a mechanical method.[61]

By the logic of figuration for a narrative, in the transition from the first order of meaning as facts to the second order of meaning as plot, the facts are figured as parts of a plot structure. The truth of narrative, then, is linked to the more general question of the truth of literary coherence, a truth that has been ignored by formal science in favor of logical coherence. Thus, in the approach to narrative explanations by analytic philosophers, the figurative expressions in narrative were held to be either false, ambiguous, or logically inconsistent, and it was thought that they should be translated to conform with the rules of demonstrative discourse. As Hayden White puts it:

> When an element of figurative language turned up in [historical narratives], ... it was treated as only a figure of speech, the content of which was either its literal meaning

or a literalist paraphrase of what appeared to be its grammatically "correct" formulation. But in this process of literalization, what gets left out is precisely those elements of figuration, tropes and figures of thought, as the rhetoricians call them, without which the narrativization of real events, the transformation of a chronicle into a story, could never be effected.[62]

Formal science has been committed to the belief that reality coheres according to the logic used in paradigmatic discourse. The belief has excluded the acceptance of nonformal coherence protocols for use in explaining the facts of reality. The commitment has led most analysts to ignore the specific literary coherence of historical narrative and the type of truth that is conveyed in it. Whatever protocols of coherence actually exist in the physical world, human existence adheres according to protocols that are literary or narrative in character. These protocols show up in the explanations humans give for their actions and in the interpretations they make of the relations among the events of their lives.

Ricoeur on narrative and history

The notion of literary truth has been intensively explored in the hermeneutic tradition of thought.[63] Recent advocates of this tradition as applied to history and narrative are Martin Heidegger, Hans-Georg Gadamer, and Paul Ricoeur. Ricoeur, particularly, has developed the hermeneutic position considerably in his recent study, *Time and Narrative.* He agrees that, in most cases, finding or reconstructing reasons for actions (Dray) and placing them within the configurational whole of a narrative (Gallie and Mink) is more appropriate for explaining individual human actions than the deductive-nomological kind of explanation. But he believes that to identify the historian's work with relating stories about individual human actions is to oversimplify history as it is currently practiced.

Ricoeur takes the French historiographers' concern about long time-spans to be a serious critique of history as merely stories of individual actions. He describes three features of historical inquiry that need to be considered when relating history and narrative.

(1) Historical inquiry is procedural and involves the claim to objectivity. Although historical explanation is not limited to the deductive-nomological mode, it still must authenticate data and justify explanations. When historical events are explained by constructing a narrative, historians are expected to show the superiority of their narrative over alternative accounts of the same events, and they must assure that the narrative coheres with accounts of contiguous events. In a dispute among narrative explanations, historians attempt to prove that one explanation is better than the rest, and they do this by seeking warrants from documen-

tary proof. Where narrative is understood to be "self-explanatory," historians expect the explanation to involve conceptualization, objectivity, and critical reflection.

(2) Current history is usually about groups, peoples, or nations, rather than about individual persons. Traditionally, narrative has been understood to be about individuals, and there has been concern to impute action to particular agents who could be identified. The new history lacks individual characters and replaces the subject of action with entities that are anonymous. If history is no longer about individuals, how can it be said to be essentially made up of narrative stories?

(3) The time scale of current history concerns social entities, not individuals. Narratives are concerned about the time of individual agents–their memories, expectations, and circumspections. The new history either conceives of time as a succession of long-scale intervals or scatters it into a multiplicity of various scales.

These three features set historical inquiry of this sort apart from the activity of constructing followable stories, as Gallie put it. "And yet, Ricoeur says, "despite this triple epistemological break, history cannot, in my opinion, sever every connection with narrative without losing its historical character.[64]

Ricoeur examines these three features of current historical inquiry to show that each maintains a link with narrative in its elementary, storytelling sense:

(1) In regard to its claim to objectivity, history continues to deal with singular events and sequences of singular events instead of seeking general laws. When historians defend their accounts against alternatives, they are in effect exercising the storyteller's imagination by thinking up counterfactual scenarios. No matter what the time scale and the type of objects inquired about, historians' accounts retain a hybrid of explanation and understanding.[65]

(2) Although current history is concerned with such social entities as societies, communities, and states, these entities are composed of individuals and exist by virtue of an individual's sense of belonging to and participating in them. These social entities are not the constructs of the historian's conceptual activity; they have a real existence independent of the historian. In ordinary speech these social entities are given personal characteristics and are taken as genuine subjects of action. In this sense, Ricoeur calls the social entities "quasi-persons" and the chain of singular causal relations in which they are involved "quasi-plots."[66]

(3) Although the French historiographers' distinction between long time-spans and the shorter time-spans of human actions is akin to a distinction between the unchanging and the changing, current historical inquiry is basically still dealing with change, even though the rate of social change is considered to be much slower than change in an individual. The slow movement of a long time-span still involves changes, even turning points, such as the great shift from a Mediterranean civilization to an Atlantic civilization. These slow movements are "quasi-events" (Ricoeur's term) and their temporal configuration, like the events in a story, derive their significance from their place in the whole.[67]

Ricoeur has attempted to demonstrate the narrative character of history in the features of current historical inquiry where the practitioners would deny that their work is narrative in form. He holds that current history, although it is not narrative in the sense of individual stories, is at base analogous to traditional narrative form.

Ricoeur's approach to narrative is different from the approaches of most of those who have defended narrative history. For example, Mink held that narrative was a particular configural mode of comprehension that had as much explanatory power (although different in kind) as the theoretical mode of comprehension. Ricoeur comes to narrative from a concern with the phenomenon of double or hidden meaning,[68] which he believes figure in the most important understandings of human existence—religion, for example, with its language and symbols expressing our ultimate hopes, visions of our destiny, and ideas about our place in the order of things. Hidden meaning is also contained in the language of our dreams and in free associations which are grounded in our deepest desires. If the human disciplines are to understand human existence, they will need to attend to the language of double meaning, and thus, because interpretation is called for, will be required to use hermeneutic understanding. Ricoeur's interest in indirect language has led to his production of a long study on trope and metaphor, *The Rule of Metaphor.*[69]

Ricoeur opens his book on narrative with the statement *"The Rule of Metaphor* and *Time and Narrative* form a pair; published one after the other, these works were conceived together ... The meaning-effects produced by each of them [metaphor and narrative] belong to the same basic phenomenon of semantic innovation."[70] His concern is primarily with heremeneutic language as it operates on the human world, rendering it "habitable." From this perspective he approaches narrative, including historical narrative, as a literary text, and his major interest is the light that narrative throws on the nature of human existence. He asks: What does the existence of these texts and their particular nature reveal about human existence? Metaphor and narrative both use synthesis to produce semantic innovation. The metaphor produces innovation when its words retain the resistance of their ordinary use; the narrative does so by inventing plot, by means of which "goals, causes, and chance are brought together within the temporal unity of a whole and complete action."[71]

While Ricoeur recognizes that historical writing is the outcome of inquiry and research, of the quest for objectivity, his primary interest is in the writings themselves and in their character as texts. The question that engages him is not, What does narrative yield by way of objective knowledge of the past?, but rather, What role does narrative play in the structure of human existence?

This concern sets Ricoeur apart even from Gallie, Mink, and Hayden White, whose work still belongs to the tradition of the critical philosophy of history and its concern with whether or not historical narrative yields objective truth. They are skeptical regarding the representational value of historical narrative. Mink's work leaves one wondering what the cognitive accomplishment of history actually is. Although he stresses its cognitive pretensions as an alternative form of comprehension, he portrays narrative as an inventive, imaginative construction which cannot authenticate its claim to represent the past. White goes even further, moving on to clearly skeptical conclusions. He holds that narrative's value in the representation of reality is nil: "The notion that sequences of real events possess the formal attributes of the stories we tell about imaginary events could only have its origin in wishes, daydreams, reveries."[72] Ricoeur's position is different: "He is neither defending, casting doubt on, nor skeptically debunking the claims of history; he is, to judge by the present work, simply not interested in evaluating these claims at all."[73]

Once historians had put aside the attempts to construct speculative historical systems in the form of a body of laws covering the course of history as a whole, their attention had turned to the epistemological problem of the "truthfulness" of their statements as representations of actual past events. The issue raised by Dilthey and the neo-Kantians and then taken up again by the analytical philosophers was about which methods would produce "real" knowledge. History had been institutionalized in university departments in the nineteenth century, and as a consequence historians were caught up in the overall attempt by the human disciplines to justify their status as legitimate university sciences. Historians sought to ground the objectivity of their findings by establishing an epistemological foundation. The context for the historians' justification was taken from the philosophy of science and, as recounted above, focused on the issue of understanding (*Verstehen*) as a legitimate scientific method. Ricoeur switches the discussion about historical narrative from its legitimacy as an epistemologically sound method to, more generally, what the use of historical narrative reveals about human beings and their relation to the past.

Ricoeur proceeds to deepen the kinds of questions asked about narrative. The use of narratives by historians is possible, he says, because there already exists a general human capacity to construct stories. The historian's use of narrative is one instance of this general capacity, and thus a full understanding of historical narrative requires an awareness of the more general function of narrative in human life. Ricoeur is concerned to examine the epistemological debate in history, then, not in order to take a stand on one side or the other but to draw from it more general implications about the nature of narrative. He identifies two basic notions: (1) narrative is related to the world of human action and (2) narrative is a response to the human experience of feelings of discord and fragmentation in regard to time.

Ricoeur goes on to explore the relationship between narrative description and human experience. The relationship can be defined in any of three ways. The first two ways assume that life, as lived, is independent of narrative description. If this separation is accepted, then one can hold either that narrative gives an accurate description of the way the world really is or that it is descriptively discontinuous with the real world it depicts. The third position, advocated here, is that aspects of experience itself are presented originally as they appear in the narration and that narrative form is not simply imposed on preexistent real experiences but helps to give them form.

David Carr argues that Ricoeur's position is closest to the middle one, where narrative imposes a structure on an original experience that is heterogeneous, unstructured, and confused, composed of scrambled messages that can hardly be spoken of at all.[74] In this, Carr says, Ricoeur is similar to Mink, White, and the structuralists. White says that the world presents itself "as mere sequence without beginning or end or as sequences of beginnings that only terminate and never conclude;"[75] Mink writes that "stories are not lived but told. Life has no beginnings, middles, and ends":[76] it is only in narrative that order is added to make a good story. These theorists use as their model of narrative the written text, in which all is organized and structured and each event (the extraneous clue in a detective story, for example) has some contribution to make to the plot. In contrast to the written story, where all of the threads are tied up, life as lived seems confused and unstructured.

Carr points out that Ricoeur does not propose such a complete separation between life and narrative as White does. According to Ricoeur, experience is originally given form by its own structuring process, which itself calls for narrativization and contains elements that lend themselves to storytelling. "We tell stories because in the last analysis human lives need and merit being narrated."[77] Nevertheless, Carr holds that Ricoeur's "basic scheme seems not to differ fundamentally from that which he subtly corrects."[78] I believe that Carr sees more of a dichotomy in Ricoeur's work—between life as lived and narrative structures—than is present. Ricoeur does hold that there is some, although not complete, overlap between narrative and human action. Without narrative formation, actions would be experienced as inconsistent, and time would be experienced as "confused, unformed and at the limit mute.[79] In the same manner that perception is not originally made up of a confused buzz of isolated sense data but consists of already formed objects, so experience does not originally appear as discrete atoms of experience and then at some later time become organized and patterned.[80] Experience forms and presents itself in awareness as narrative. It is from this original experience that the literary form is derived. I do not argue that the narrative construction of experience is an innate process, but I do argue that it is a process common to all cultures and that it appears in early childhood.[81] Human experience seeks to organize itself into a meaningful unity, and to accomplish this we use not only narrative but also the means-end structure of practical reasoning. Yet even the actions we plan using such reasoning are integrated, finally, through narrative into a complex of many actions.

The narrative structuring of experience is different from the narrative structuring of literature or history. In these narratives, all of the extraneous noise or static is cut out and only those events necessary to move the plot along are related. The equivalent, although not the same, selection occurs in experience through the human capacity for attention. In literature and history, the narrator has control of the story and decides what to include or exclude. In the life narrative, the self is the narrator of its own story. Unlike authors of fictional narratives, however, the self has to integrate the materials that are at hand. Authors of historical and fictional narratives describe events that have already ended, but the self is in the middle of its story and has to revise the plot constantly without knowing how the story will end. Even with these differences, though, there is not a sharp division but a continuity between life—the world of our practical, everyday experience—and the artistic formation of literary and historical narrative.

Returning to the role of narrative in historical inquiry, we see that historians do not work with isolated fragments of past actions which they then construct into a story. Rather, for the most part, they work with materials that are already in story form. Actions have already been lived as stories, at least to the extent that they have entered the experience of historical persons. The traces of past actions are contained in the stories that people have told about their own actions. The historian, having the advantage of hindsight, may tell a story about what has happened that will be different from the various stories told by the past actors. The historian does not narrate past facts but retells past stories from a current perspective.

The discipline of history, whose tradition preceded the development during the Enlightenment of formal science, has been under pressure to justify itself as a science and has had to examine the procedures it has used to recount and explicate past human actions. The discipline has resisted giving up its special forms of understanding and explanation in order to become more like the natural sciences with their commitment to a single deductive-nomological form of explanation. Self-examination has led to a clarification of history's characteristic form of representation, the narrative. The examination has also produced its own skeptical response that is similar to that produced in philosophy by the breakup of the Englightenment's basic model. The response holds that narrative has no epistemological validity and is an artificial construction imposed by historians on the simple sequence of past events. Ricoeur has deepened the examination of narrative and, instead of simply considering narrative as a special historical explanatory mode, has found it to be a life form that has functioned as part of human existence to configure experience into a unified process. For this reason, narrative needs to be included by the human disciplines when they study the human realm.

CHAPTER IV

Literature and Narrative

THE previous chapter looked at narrative as it is used by historians to describe human activity and events of the past. This examination demonstrated that narrative provides a special form of discourse for understanding and explaining human actions, a discourse appropriate for the human sciences in their study of human experience and behavior. In the present chapter the focus will be on narrative as a mode of expression. Literary theorists have examined narrative primarily as it is manifested in spoken and written fictional stories. This chapter will investigate the structural components that produce narrative meaning and the functions of author and reader in the transfer of meaning through a message presented in narrative form. Although literary theorists approach narrative as a literary expression, their insights into narrative form and meaning can be applied by the human sciences in their investigations of human experience and understanding.

Interest in narrative on the part of literary theorists has increased considerably during the last two decades, to the point where it is the discipline currently most engaged in the study of narrative.[1] This study has moved through four phases (1) the acceptance of individual novels into the *oeuvre* worthy of study as literature, (2) the search, begun by Northrup Frye, for common themes in the content of stories, (3) the search by French structuralists for a common deep structure in narrative, and (4) the recent move to study narrative from the perspective of communication models.

The study of narrative by literary theorists has not led to the development of any single or unified theory; it is not a "progressive science" in which old theories are discarded when new ones are developed. Instead, it is a cumulative discipline where new theories are added to the older ones. Wallace Martin writes: "If recent theories are judged on the premise that only one of them can be true, they are likely to prove unsatisfactory. But if judged on the basis of the insights they can provide into particular narratives, their variety is an advantage."[2] In addition to the variety of theoretical approaches, a residue of terms and conceptual schemes derived from earlier traditions of study continues to carry currency in some parts of the discipline.[3]

Until relatively recently the approach literary theorists have used to study narrative has been to focus on its various aspects—the story line, deep structures, the craftsmanship of the author, or the reader of the narrative. As late as 1978, Seymour Chatman noted in *Story and Discourse* that, "Libraries bulge with studies of specific genres" and aspects of narrative theory, but "there are few books in English on the subject of narrative in general."[4] The early literary study of narrative could be located in four identifiable national traditions: (1) Russian formalism, particularly the work of Propp and Schlovsky, (2) the American tradition, (3) French structuralism, and (4) the German writings of Lammert, Stanzl, and Schmid. By the 1960s, however, theorists began to focus less on their own national literary traditions and to engage more in an international discussion of narrative. At the same time, they began to borrow insights from other disciplines, such as linguistics, anthropology, and cognitive science, making narrative an interdisciplinary enterprise. Literary theory abandoned its exclusive focus on the interpretation of individual literary works and began to show a general concern with the kind of comprehension and truth communicated by narrative expression.

The purpose of this chapter is to give an impression of the breadth of work undertaken by literary theorists concerned with narrative. Because the field is too varied to explore in depth in a single chapter, I will attend to some of the methodological issues that have special implications for the construction of a human science equipped to study the human realm of meaning and its expression in oral and written forms. The general plan of the chapter follows the historical development of the exploration of narrative by literary theory, beginning with post–World-War-Two criticism and ending with the current investigations of reception theory.

Prestructural American criticism

New criticism and the novel

Narrative came to the attention of critics in the United States after World War Two in the context of the English "new criticism." In the "new criticism" the focus of attention was an individual text—literally the words that appeared on the page. The literary work was to be approached as an autonomous whole and studied without reference to external contexts, whether biographical, historical, psychoanalytic, or sociological; that is, the "new criticism" maintained that the text was directly accessible to the reader without any need for the accumulated information developed by past studies. The task of the critic was to show how the various parts of the text contributed to the thematic unity, which was then used to justify the work's standing as a literary artifact.[5]

The autonomous texts studied in this way were poetry and drama. Prose narrative, that is, the novel, was given a marginal status because it was not considered worthy of recognition as a major literary genre. Some, however, such as Mark Schorer and Joseph Frank, believed that the novel should be appreciated as a work of art comparable to poetry and drama and added it to the literary curriculum. They tried to show that the techniques used in the novel were as subtle and complex as those used in the other more esteemed works of literature. They pointed to the use novels made of images, metaphors and symbols, and demonstrated how techniques specific to the novel—for example, the author's position in regard to the novel's narrator, the narrator's relationship to the story, and the ways in which access was provided to the minds of characters—could affect the story's message. The focus during this period was not on narrative per se but on one of the forms of narrative, the novel. The task was to gain recognition for the works that used this form and to identify them as art.

The kind of novel that was nominated for inclusion as a recognized literary form was the contemporary realistic novel. The realistic novel represented life as it was and presented it objectively through the use of fictional characters. This kind of representation was understood to be the advanced evolutionary outcome of previous careless "picture book" stories that appeared first as myths and later as romances. In a 1945 essay, "Spatial Form in Modern Literature," Joseph Frank described how authors approached time from both the aesthetic and the representational perspectives and pointed out the relationship between novelistic form and the structures of myth.[6] The interpretation of the realistic novel focused on the content of the individual works. Authors were expected to make the reader aware of the kind of life people lived—for example, what it was like to be a farmer during the Depression and or one of the urban poor. Novels were to represent life as it is and take a stand regarding the ethical issues raised by the representation.

During the period from 1945 until the late 1950s, then, the focus of prose narrative study was on the content of individual novels and on the techniques an author used to produce a work. It was generally understood that the contemporary realistic novel had little to do with previous less developed forms of narrative that depicted godlike figures or unrealistic and idealized romances about human beings.[7] Because the idea of plot was strongly associated with these traditional tales and with the stock devices used in popular fiction, it was little discussed by critics.

The search for a universal plot

Northrup Frye. A major shift in the study of the novel and, consequently, in the study of narrative occurred in the United States toward the end of the 1950s. The shift is identified with the work of Northrup Frye and his 1957 book *The Anatomy of Criticism* in which the focus of attention was changed from contemporary individual works to the whole tradition of prose narrative, beginning with early myths and extending to contemporary works.[8] Frye accused contemporary critics of approaching literature without a conceptual framework. He held that the "new criticism," in which each individual work was to be approached with as few pre-conceptions as possible, led to the false view of literature as a simple aggregate of discrete works. Close examination, he believed, would reveal that literature actually conformed to a system, a system that critics could use to see the themes and modes underlying individual works. For Frye, literature was not simply an educational device to depict current social conditions. Neither was it primarily the expression of individual authors. Rather, it was a vehicle for the expression of the most fundamental human desires.

Frye's review of the variety of content in stories from different historical periods led him to propose that narratives are not simply a creative expression thought up by individual authors. He held that literature contained elements of various modes, genres, symbols, and myths which authors had assimilated into their works without being explicitly aware of the process. Categories forming a general conceptual map through which stories are produced and understood, he said, are constantly at work in the creation of human experience and are reflected in the literary expressions that come out of this experience. One of these categories (as mentioned in the introductory chapter) is the power relationship the protagonist has to other people and the environment. He noted five such relationships, which are reflected in the five modes of literature: (1) power that is superior in kind over other people and over the environment (*myth*), (2) power that is superior in degree over other people and over the environment (romance), (3) power that is superior in degree over other people but not over the environment (*high mimetic*), (4) power that is comparable to that of other people (*low mimetic*), and (5) power that is inferior to that of other people (*ironic*). Moreover, particular power relationships characterize different historical periods, and historical development occurs according to a cyclical pattern in which periods continually devolve from a higher to a lower relationship of the protagonist's power until, finally, the pattern is begun over.

In addition to searching for an evolutionary scheme in the history of literary expression, Frye sought to clean up the taxonomies used in literary criticism. His definitions of genres redirected the critical focus from the realistic novel to the whole of prose writing. With this redirection, narrative was placed in the center of his investigations as the overarching form of prose discourse, with the modern novel becoming only one of all possible narrative expressions.

Frye proposed a further classification based on the way literary works are intended to be presented to an audience. If the work is to be acted before spectators, it is a *drama*. If the work is to be spoken, sung, or chanted to listeners, it is an *epos*. If the work is to be read by a reader, it is *fiction*.[9] The point Frye was making with this division was that the stability of the written word makes it a separate form of communication, something beyond a mere record of the spoken word. Written literature (Frye's "fiction") functions as a communication not of presence but of distance. Another change brought about by Frye's taxonomy was a new conception of fiction as "something made for its own sake," as opposed to "something false that appears true." Within the specific genre of written presentation (fiction), Frye made a further subdivision into four species that were based on the author's perspective. The author may direct his or her view (1) outward to produce a representation of the world *(extroversion)* or (2) inward to produce an imaginative vision *(introversion)*, and the author may apprehend the subject (3) in personal terms or (4) in intellectual terms. The species are mixed in individual works, Frye said, and the resulting mixtures can be used to produce a further typology based on the various combinations. He related these four species of fiction in a symbolic way to the four seasons.

Frye also addressed the issue of the difference between literary expression and scientific expression. He identified two modes of language use, "centrifugal" and "centripetal." The centrifugal discourse, its exemplar being cognitive-scientific discourse, is directed outward from words to things; the centripetal discourse, its exemplar being poetry and literature in general, moves inward toward an inner imaginative realm and the structure of language itself. Frye, then, held that the poetic sentence is objectively false but subjectively true, because it operates according to inward meaning structures. This distinction of Frye's holds promise for distinguishing between the two kinds of investigation in the human disciplines, the external report about the objective realm and the internal report about the realm of human meaning.

Ricoeur has responded to Frye's work, seeing in it an expression of both the significance of the role a story plays in the formation of tradition and the effect tradition has on subsequent story production.[10] According to Ricoeur, Frye's examination of stories in the Western world showed that there is a progression and an order in the development of this tradition, from which the present works emerged. Yet, although the present is linked to the past, this link does not determine what is possible in the present; it merely provides models and plots that can be drawn on to understand and construct the present. For Ricoeur, then, tradition recognizes not only the aspects that produce the continuity of practices but also those that produce changes. To have the character of a tradition, a continuous thread of identity must be evident, which holds the cumulated practices together. A tradition is not simply a continuous repetition of exactly identical happenings, however; it also involves innovation, which produces differences. Thus the making of a tradition involves the mixing together of the continuous and the new, of identity and difference. Ricoeur wants an analysis of narrative to address the role of temporality, and he believes that Frye does this with his notion of tradition as continuity and innovation. Frye did not, like the later French structuralists, look for an atemporal order of logic that precedes all narrative production. Rather, he looked specifically for a pattern of temporal order by means of which narrative could have evolved as part of a cultural tradition.

Frye's work focused on the content level of stories in an effort to find some order in what appeared as a scattered and disconnected hodgepodge of individual tales. He used an inductive method, searching through a large number of stories and drawing out similarities and themes. By laying the stories side by side, he was able to recognize various patterns. Frye's inductive method will later be contrasted with the deductive method, which is used by structural analysts. First, attention will be given to others who followed Frye in investigating the common themes that appear in the individual stories.

Scholes and Kellogg. Frye worked to broaden the critical focus from exclusive concern with the novel to concern for narrative in general. He was also interested in identifying a limited number of symbolic themes that appear and reappear in the variety of narrative expressions. Other American critics followed who sought to do likewise. One of the most significant studies along these lines was *The Nature of Narrative*, published in 1966 by Robert Scholes and Robert Kellogg.[11]

Like Frye, Scholes and Kellogg criticized the prevailing practice of judging all narrative literature by standards appropriate only to the contemporary realistic novel. Their concern was with the elements common to all narrative forms—myth, folktale, epic, romance, allegory, confession, and satire—and they saw the novel as only one of a number of narrative possibilities. They accepted Frye's thesis that Western literature had undergone cyclic evolutions from myth to realism, but they replaced his typology with a unified theory and history of narrative. The epic storytellers were understood by Scholes and Kellogg to be retelling a traditional story and to be primarily concerned with preserving the story itself, not with preserving historical accuracy or with making creative additions to the story. From the epic synthesis two streams separate: the empirical and the fictional. The *empirical* stream has an allegiance to reality and truth, while the *fictional* stream has an allegiance to ideal beauty and goodness. The empirical stream breaks into two further types: the historical and the mimetic. *Historical* narrative is concerned with truthfulness to fact and to the actual past, and it deals with realistic space, time, and causality. *Mimetic* narrative is concerned with true character sketches and autobiography. The streams reunite in the realistic novel, which combines the allegiance to realism with the allegiance to the ideal.

Whereas Frye excluded history and biography from his list of fictions, Scholes and Kellogg included them as kinds of narrative. Like Frye, they believed that the advent of writing significantly altered the development of narrative expression. Within the oral transmission of stories, unique facts that are not locked in place by rhythmic structure or convention are lost. But writing preserves the particular and makes possible the preservation of facts required for the development of historical and other forms of empirical narratives. Scholes and Kellogg noted that personal narratives, which function to interpret one's own experience, most often do not appear in written form. They therefore retain the characteristics of oral transmission—loss of detail and subtle changes—while written autobiographies and personal journals preserve the version of narrative understanding that is held at the time of writing. This distinction has important implications for the psychological studies of self-identity and case histories, and it will be taken up again in the next chapter.

Scholes and Kellogg, like Frye before them, wanted to understand the developmental changes that narrative had undergone through its history and to explain how these changes had led to the primary contemporary expression of the narrative, the realistic novel. They found that changes in narrative subject matter usually occurred only at the level of social topics; the types of characters that authors used to carry the changing subject matter remained relatively stable. These character types consisted of a common repertoire of imaginary figures—the archetypal hero and heroine, the villain, the helper, and so on. Writers drew on this repertoire of archetypal characters and on the ideas and concerns of their contemporary society, and then used their personal imaginative creativity to produce their stories.

Joseph Campbell and Lord Raglan. Scholes and Kellogg and Frye were concerned to describe the evolution of the major forms of narrative (historical, mimetic, romantic, and didactic) and to detail the historical changes in their formation and deformation. Frye had also been interested in discovering the basic story themes that appeared beneath the many surface variations. Two other writers, whose works appeared at about the same time as Frye's, share with him the idea that there was a universal or "archetypal" myth that formed the substructure of modern narratives.

Joseph Campbell argued in his *Hero with a Thousand Faces,* published in 1949, that myths, folktales, and dreams in various cultures display the same essential pattern. He called this pattern the "monomyth." The monomyth is represented by a circular diagram in which there is a movement from departure to return: the hero sets out on a journey and is drawn into an adventure, he encounters a shadow presence at a threshold, which he must overcome; after crossing the threshold, the hero journeys through an unfamiliar world until he is confronted with a supreme ordeal; triumphant, he gains his reward and returns to restore the world.[12] Lord Raglan produced a similar universal plot, but unlike Campbell, he found it in Eastern as well as in Western narratives.[13]

Another summary version of a proposed universal plot was given by anthropologist Robert McAndrews. He described the common story as a hero's journey which moves through the same stages as biological birth. McAndrews writes: "Whether deliberate, non-deliberate, or non-obvious quests, inward emotional/ psychological, outward physical, sacred or secular; whether in literature, mythology, biology, or for spiritual enlightenment, human journeys are found to bear a resemblance to, if not a complete repetition of, the pattern of our ideas about the biological birth process."[14] McAndrews held that the universal plot serves as a metapattern or "template" which organizes human experience.

As Campbell, Lord Raglan, and McAndrews describe it, the same basic story line appears in all cultures. Some who agree with this description have nevertheless suggested that these basic stories are merely the product of oral transmission from travel and migration; however, their explanation is not fully supported by anthropological evidence about cultural transmission. This led those who accept the notion that the same story line appears in all cultures to postulate that this basic story is related to some universal experience—birth or the seasons, perhaps— and that this common core story even informs modern narratives.

These attempts to uncover a single deep plot in all the world's stories are no longer held in esteem in narrative theory. In the end, there is no way to tell whether these investigations are right or wrong, because finding similarities among the surface diversity seems to depend on the imaginative function of the person identifying them. Plot analysis involves the ways that human actions are described. The identification of a clear pattern in the diversity of stories and the description of a developmental sequence from myths through romantic novels to realistic novels give a more orderly picture than actually holds. The tendency to look for an orderly pattern in change is itself evidence of how narratives work: they, too, configure the past into a pattern so that a coherent story can be told about it.

The psychoanalytic story. Despite the efforts to undercover a universal plot amid a multitude of diverse tales, most critics continued to believe that a novel's content was merely a reflection of the individual imagination of each author and that it should deal with the societal changes caused by the same economic and social forces that the social sciences studied. Nevertheless, a further attempt to ground stories in common themes came from psychoanalytic theory. Marthe Robert proposed that stories presented in novels were representations of the common human tension between the ideal and the real and that this tension could be understood using psychoanalytic theory.[15] According to Robert, the evolution of narrative content from stories about mythical characters to the fuller representation of reality in the contemporary novel was simply a move from a lesser to a greater sophistication in creating disguises for intrapsychic tensions. Moreover, she believed, cultures move through stages of psychic development just as the individual person does. As a consequence, the kind of stories produced by a particular culture depends not primarily on the social factors of the outer world but on its stage of psychological development. Stories written under the sway of the pre-Oedipal stage of cultural development contain similar themes, and stories produced in cultures in a later Oedipal stage of development will deal with the psychological conflicts of that stage—for instance, conflicts regarding love, ambition, and misfortune. In Robert's view, the forces at work in the development of the novel's subject matter are the fundamental psychological conflicts that appear at the various stages of psychic development.

Narrative and temporal form

Literary criticism in America then shifted its interest from the search for a universal plot and underlying psychoanalytic themes to the investigation of the general connections between narrative patterns and the human ordering of time. Narratives create temporal meaning by using plots to link events into an orderly sequence that are understandable as total temporal episodes. Human temporal experience consists of drawing out from the continual flow of successive moments episodic patterns by marking off beginning and ending points. In order for readers to comprehend a text, they must understand the particular patterns used in a narrative to separate the flow of time into meaningful episodes. J. Hollis Miller argued that the patterns used to construct temporal episodes are drawn from a culture's concepts of causality, unity, origin, and end.[16]

In *The Sense of an Ending*, Frank Kermode explored the ways narrative gathers up meaningful episodes from the flow of time.[17] He thought that the methods used to make time cohere were drawn from one's culture. He held that in Western culture these methods continue to be drawn from the biblical view of temporality, in spite of nineteenth-century science having replaced the Bible as the major authority for interpreting reality. The biblical notion of time is concerned with beginnings and endings; it is not understood to be an undifferentiated, continuous flow (*chronos*), but broken into periods of significance (*kairos*). The beginning of a period of *kairos* is identified by the occurrence of an event that makes a difference in our lives, and the ending is marked by a resolution and return to a routine. Narrative plots provide the form in which these periods of human drama can be described.[18]

Structuralism and narrative

Thus far our focus has been on the work of American literary criticism before the important change that came with the introduction of structuralism from France. Structuralism in literary criticism is the application of language models to literature. It revolutionized the study of narrative and led to the creation of the new literary science called "narratology." By borrowing research methods from linguistics, literary study was made more rigorous and systematic. These methods provided a way to explain a literary element by its place in a network of relations rather than by its antecedent cause. Thus literary criticism moved to become more rigorous and systematic without having to adopt natural science's cause and effect system of explanation. I will concentrate on structuralism's methodological strategies in the study of narrative.

The method of structural analysis

According to structuralist theory, the hearer and the teller of stories produce and understand narratives without being aware that the narratives are being generated according to a set of mental structures. It was thought that humans possess innate cognitive structures that frame all experience, and that these structures are achronological or atemporal, and located at such a depth that they are not affected or changed by experience. The structuralists' project was to describe these deep mental structures.[19] It was understood that the description would have two parts: functional units and rules by which the units were related.

The methodology used to uncover the structural order lying beneath the surface understanding of narrative had three major features:

(1) Earlier literary study (for example, Frye's inquiry about a universal plot) had used inductive methods. In the inductive method one gathered data (in this case, a sample of various kinds of narratives) and then by comparison and contrast identified regularities in the data. Structuralism, on the other hand, used a hypothetical-deductive method in which a logical order was hypothesized and then tested to see if it could account for the data. The variety of narrative expressions (oral, written, drawn, and acted) and of classes of narrative (myth, folklore, fable, novel, epic, tragedy, drama, film, comic strip, history, conversation, and so on) made it impractical to work inductively from examples to theory. The idea was to hypothesize the features of narrative structure in terms of a formal system and then to examine a sample of narratives to determine if the postulated system could account for their actual characteristics. If it could not, then adjustments to the hypothesis would have to be made. Such an analysis should lead to a hypothesis that posits generative rules to account for the production of any conceivable narrative (of which there are an infinite number), but at the same time the rules should not allow for the production of any incorrect or ill-formed narratives.

(2) The method assumed that narrative structure was like any other linguistic form. Consequently, the axiomatic descriptions of the structures that generate narratives would resemble as closely as possible the descriptions of the structures of other linguistic expressions—for instance, phonemes, words, and sentences. In linguistic theory, it is understood that the code in which a message is communicated can be separated out from the content of the message. The code has functional units, systematically organized, that determine the meaning of an expression. The code can be studied synchronically—that is, it can be isolated from issues

involved with investigating its historical development. To reach an understanding of the code, it is necessary to identify a finite number of functional units underlying innumerable surface appearances and then to establish the set of rules that determine the internal relations among the rules. The resulting structure is depicted as a closed grammatical system with a finite number of units related in a rationally ordered, not random, manner. If one knows the units and the rules, it is possible to predict what any allowable story will look like. As a self-contained system, then, the narrative grammar should be unaffected by and indifferent to any extralinguistic reality. The world interpretation given by narrative form would be based on a representational system that derived not from the external world but from the structures of the mind itself.

Noam Chomsky used this method to describe the linguistical syntax system, which was supposed to generate all possible acceptable sentences. He believed the existence of such rational and content-free structures in the mind made human knowledge and expression possible, that because of these structures much of our knowledge is universal, inborn, and accessible simply by virtue of the fact that we are human. One did not have to be taught how to speak or (in the context of this study) how to tell stories. The structural analysis of narrative by means of linguistic models was an attempt to extend the model of syntax to linguistic entities above the level of the sentence—that is, to develop a grammar for narrative discourses. Roland Barthes summed up the matter: "The narrative is a big sentence, just as every statement is in some sense the outline of a little narrative.[20]

(3) A general notion in semiotic methodology was that the characteristics of a system's operation should be sought through an analysis of the system as a whole (ordered into a hierarchy of levels) rather than through an analysis of the individual units. This third characteristic corresponds to what Ricoeur has called the configurating operation of narrative (although the semiotic structural emphasis was on atemporal, rationally organized rules, neglecting Ricoeur's interest in narrative's temporal quality).

The structuralists' program can be understood as a part of the general movement, which included the formal sciences, to uncover a tightly structured, lawful operation behind the surface appearance of flux, change, and development. However, the structural approach was significantly different from formal science in an important way. It was not making claims about an objective reality that is independent of human mind. Structuralists did not conceive the world to be a lawfully ordered and predictable realm of objects; instead, they thought of it as a space and time continuum without firm and irrevocable boundaries. It is language that divides the world into stable entities, by using its own linguistic structures to encode and create form out of the flux of reality. Dorothy Lee has described this principle of structuralism:

> a member of a given society—who, of course, codifies experienced reality through the use of the specific language and other patterned behavior characteristic of his culture—can actually grasp reality only as it is presented to him in this code. The assumption

is not that reality itself is relative, but that it is differently punctuated and categorized by participants of different cultures, or that different aspects of it are noticed by, or presented to them.[21]

The structuralist's general strategy was to uncover the rules by which humans constructed experience. They assumed the character of the rules to be unchanging and unaffected by experience. Ricoeur has criticized their assumption because it ignores the everyday experience that people have of the centrality of change and temporality for human existence. Bypassing the experience of temporality is especially damaging in regard to narrative, because it is the form in which temporality is expressed. Ricoeur was especially critical of Barthes's declared intention to make narrative logic account for narrative time and to transform the narrative intelligibility of time into a "chronological illusion." He is not opposed to the use of atemporal formal rules in literary criticism (nor unchanging laws in history), but does not believe they can be held to be the ground of reality. In making this point he wrote:

> The situation here [in literary criticism] is the same as in history, where inquiry of a scientific character and ambition was preceded by legends and chronicles . . . What is at stake in the discussion of narratology concerns, in fact, and in a similar manner, the degree of autonomy that should be accorded to the process of logicization and dechronologization in relation to understanding the plot and the time of the plot.[22]

Lévi-Strauss and early French structuralism

Modern French structuralist analysis of narrative began with the pioneering work of structural anthropologist Claude Lévi-Strauss. Building on the work of such earlier linguists as Saussure and Trubetzkoy, Lévi-Strauss looked at apparently different myths and saw them as expressions of a small number of basic structures. In contrast to Lee's acceptance of a variety of language-specific structural creations, he believed that beneath the immense heterogeneity of myths lay certain constant universal structures that were the same for all people and to which any particular myth could be reduced. Myths were a kind of language: they could be broken down into individual units (mythemes), which, like the basic sound units of language (phonemes), acquired meaning only when combined together in particular ways. The rules that governed such combinations could then be seen as a kind of grammar, a set of relations beneath the surface of the narrative which constituted a myth's true meaning. The study of narrative myths was concerned not with the surface of social life as consciously experienced by members of a community but with the elementary rules that generate myths below the level of awareness. In the words of Lévi-Strauss:

> Whether myth is recreated by the individual or borrowed from tradition, it derives its sources—individual or collective . . . —only from the stock of representations with

which it operates. But the structure remains the same, and through it the symbolic function is fulfilled. . . . There are many languages, but very few structural laws which are valid for all languages. A compilation of known tales and myths would fill an imposing number of volumes. But they can be reduced to a small number of simple types if we abstract from among the diversity of characters a few elementary functions.[23]

Lévi-Strauss considered these elementary functions to be inherent in the human mind itself, so that in studying a body of myth one is looking less at its narrative content than at the universal mental operations that structure it. That is, myths are devices to think with: not merely recountings of any particular tale, but ways of classifying and organizing reality. That is their point; they are not descriptions, but models for description (or thinking), logical techniques for resolving basic antinomies in thought and social existence. The mind that does all this thinking is not the mind of the individual subject; myths think themselves through people, rather than vice versa. They have no origin in any particular consciousness, and they have no particular end in view. One result of structuralism, then, is the decentering of the individual subject. The individual is no longer to be regarded as the source or end of meaning. Myths have a quasi-objective collective existence. They unfold their own concrete logic with supreme disregard for the vagaries of individual thought, and they reduce any particular consciousness to a mere function of the structures.

Propp and the structural analysis of narrative

Vladimir Propp, who worked in Russia during the early decades of this century, was interested in uncovering a single plot behind various Russian folk tales.[24] The significance of Propp's work lies not so much in his description of the basic plot of the fairy tale as in his methods of investigation. Instead of attending to the particular story content of the different fairy tales, he looked for a single deep structure underlying the whole body of tales.

Fairy tales with similar features had always been apparent in various cultures. The traditional explanation for this phenomenon had been that the fairy tales were carried by individuals from culture to culture and then amended to produce the stories particular to the different cultures. Propp considered this theory problematic, and so he set out to find a deep structure that would provide an alternative explanation for the tales' similarity. His structural analysis began with the assumption that the recognition of meaning in a fairy tale is similar to the recognition of meaning in a sentence. As humans have the capacity to detect when a group of words do not cohere into a meaningful sentence, they also have the capacity to detect when a group of narrative sentences do not cohere into a meaningful story. A person, when hearing a story, intuitively understands the part an event plays in the story. Propp borrowed from linguistics to explain this understanding of a story: "A living language is a concrete fact—grammar is its abstract substratum. These substrata lie at the base of a great many live phenomena; and it is precisely here that science focuses its attention. Not a single concrete fact can be explained without a study of these abstract bases."[25]

Propp's study can be understood through the analogy of the sentence. A simple sentence, such as, "The bear ran fast," can be divided into three functional units: the subject ("the bear"), the verb ("ran"), and the predicate or adjective ("fast"). Various terms can be substituted in each of these three functional units ("the boy," "the dog," or "the river" as the subject, for instance), and a meaningful sentence will still be produced. The fact that this kind of paradigmatic or vertical substitution can work means that the structural force of the sentence is located in the functional unit itself rather than in any one of the substitutions that can operate in the unit. Propp proposed that, in the narrative, the functional unit was "an act of dramatis personae, which is defined from the point of its significance for the course of action of the tale as a whole."[26] He identified thirty-one functional units that made up the fairy tale—for example, "The villain causes harm or injury to a member of the family, or one member of a family either lacks something or desires to have something"—for which a large number of particular actions could give a surface content: "The banker foreclosed on the farm family's mortgage" or "Mother became very ill."

Propp's proposal to locate one plot beneath all the variations in Russian folk stories culminated in his theory of thirty-one basic units which functioned in narrative much as the syntactical units function in a sentence. Although the units of the story could be filled in with any number of surface characters, these units were always arranged in the same sequence. A functional unit received its determination from its position in the story. Let us use the analogy of the sentence again. In the English sentence, "John shot Bill," the function of a unit is set by its place in the sentence order: the subject is first, the verb second, and the object third—the unit that follows the verb in English receives the action. The unit's position determines the meaning that the surface term will receive. Thus, the same word "John" can receive different meanings depending on whether it is set in the first functional unit ("John shot Bill") or in the third ("Bill shot John").

In Propp's scheme the meaning of a narrative was not to be found in the various surface characters—the king, the superman, the old man, and so on—since these could be substituted for one another or located in different positions in the narrative and still produce a meaningful story. Propp also warned against looking for the meaning of a narrative in symbolic themes that these surface characters might stand for. Rather, the meaning of a narrative was dependent on the deeper-level functional units and their arrangement, and each story was a repetition of these functional units.

Ricoeur is critical of Propp's attempt to produce an archetypal tale by means of structural analysis. Ricoeur writes:

Propp's archetypal tale [does not] coincide with what I have been calling a plot. The archetype reconstructed by Propp is not a tale that is told by anyone to anyone. It is a product of a certain sort of analytic rationality. The fragmentation into functions, the generic defining of these functions, and their placement along a single axis in succession are operations that transform an initial cultural object into a scientific one. This transformation is obvious as soon as the algebraic rewriting of all the functions ... leaves room for only a pure sequence of thirty-one juxtaposed signs.[27]

Ricoeur believes that Propp's notion—that the meaning of a story is given through its functional units—was a misunderstanding of the origin of meaning. Ricoeur's understanding is first of all a grasping of the whole story; only after this has been accomplished can one divide the story into meaningful units. This is because the meaning of a unit is a function of the story of which it is a part and not a function of the kind of unit it is. Its meaning is based on its contribution to the whole story. The finding of function units underlying the variations in stories came as the result of fragmenting what was initially a holistic cultural object. Ricoeur believes that the original understanding of a story involves temporal and teleological conceptions, and these resist any attempt to fit narrative into a taxonomic and mechanical conception of order. Propp's theory was seen to be too limited by the following generation of structuralists and, although they did not move all the way to Ricoeur's idea of grasping the whole, they made the model more flexible.

Extended structural analysis

Narratology consists of generalizing Lévi-Strauss's model and carrying it beyond the unwritten "texts" of tribal mythology to the full range of narrative presentations. The work of Lévi-Strauss and of Propp provided the guiding texts for French structuralism. The myths of Lévi-Strauss's studies and the fairy tale of Propp's investigations rank as the prototypes of all narrative. The particular sequence that Propp noticed in his work with fairy tales, however, was criticized for being "corpus specific" to the highly stylized Russian folk tales that he used and for not holding true for other types of stories. Structural theorists therefore extended his sequence of functional units in order to create an abstract structure that could be actualized in various ways, producing diverse surface structures of stories, just as Chomsky had in dealing with different types of sentences. This extension was closer to the type of analysis that Lévi-Strauss used in his treatments of myths and social practices.

Propp's investigation, as he looked for a structure common to all Russian fairy tales, used an elementary form of "structural analysis." This method was borrowed from the kind of linguistic analysis that involved a search for a single series of basic rules capable of generating all the sequences of words that are recognized as grammatical and complete. The approach drew on the notion that, because people are informed by these rules at a preconscious level, they are able intuitively to recognize which are acceptably formed and meaningful sentences, and which are not; it applied this perspective to the search for the rules that would generate the whole variety of narratives. This is the approach used by other Russian formalists, and it was made available to French structuralism through the translations of Propp's work during the 1950's.

This original method for the structural analysis of a narrative was later extended to incorporate the advances in linguistic method developed in Chomsky's later work. Chomsky's deductive method of analysis attempted to go beyond the simple generation of grammatically correct sentences by uncovering rules capable of accounting for more complex transformation—for example, how varied strings of words could produce the same meaning, how the same sentence could have different meanings, and how different surface structures could have different meanings, and how different surface structures could be developed from a single deep structure. The extended method moved beyond accounting for how sequences of words or action units could be recongized as grammatically well-formed sentences or as completed narratives to an accounting for the generation of variations in meaning of sentences or in narrative form.

Claude Bremond. Claude Bremond has attacked the notion of structure used in Propp's analysis by arguing that every function should open a set of alternative consequences. When reading a novel one has the impression that at any given moment there are various ways in which the story might continue. Bremond says that Propp was working from the point of view of speech acts *(parole)* and had ignored the system of language *(langue):*

> But if we pass from the point of view of speech acts, which use terminal constraints (the end of the sentence determining the choice of first words), to that of the linguistic system (the beginning of the sentence determining its end), the direction of implication is reversed. We should construct our sequences of functions starting with the *terminus a quo*, which in the general language of plots opens a network of possibilities, and not with the *terminus ad quem*, in respect to which the particular speech acts of Russian tales make their selection from among possibilities.[28]

Bremond assumes that in the language system the first word of a sentence, although imposing restrictions on what can follow, leaves open a host of possibilities. But if, as Propp did, one considers a complete utterance, then the first words are seen as chosen in order that the particular end might be reached. Bremond proposes that the basic narrative unit is not the function, as Propp held, but the sequence. A completed narrative, however, long and complex, can be represented as an interweaving of sequences. The basic sequence is a triad in which a choice is presented: to carry out a possibility or not to carry it out. if the choice is to try and actualize the possibility, then it follows that the attempt can be either a success or a failure. Bremond's structure provides for an open sequence in which the ending is not known when the story begins. Alternative possibilities exist at each point in the tale and the story is an actualization of one particular pathway through the choices involved. At each point there are two possibilities—the character acts or does not act, succeeds or fails—and the story branches out like a tree chart. Different plot types emerge from the choices made at each point in the story.

Tzvetan Todorov. Tzvetan Todorov's *Grammaire du Décaméron*, written in 1969, is held to be the most important step forward in basic narratology since Propp.[29] Placing himself squarely outside the general understanding of structuralism, Todorov begins with the assumption that there is a universal grammar that reflects the actual structure of reality: "This universal grammar is the source of all universals and it gives definition even to man himself. Not only all languages but all signifying systems obey the same grammar. It is universal, not only because it informs all the languages of the universe, but because it coincides with the structure of the universe itself."[30] For Todorov, narrative is simply a set of linguistic possibilities that are focused in a particular way by a set of basic structural rules. Because narrative is composed of a limited selection of the total grammatical possibilities, it can be described in terms simpler than are needed for the description of an entire language. Todorov's method is to reduce each narrative to a syntactic summary of its structural features and their combinations; then to operate analytically on this reduction rather than on the language of the text itself.

Todorov has also developed a hierarchy of structural units in which each is built from the units below it. The highest level is the story; below this are sequences that make up a story; then the propositions that make up the sequences; and at the base, the parts of speech. A sequence is a complete system of propositions, a little tale in itself. A story must contain at least one sequence, but it may contain many. The sequence is recognized as completed when a modified repetition of its opening proposition appears. A proposition is a basic narrative sentence and is structurally equivalent to a sentence or independent clause. The basic units out of which a narrative is built are three: the proper noun (a character), the verb (action), and the adjective (attribute). From these basic units a proposition is made by combining either a noun and a verb (a character and an action) or a noun and an adjective (a character given an attribute).

He identified three kinds of adjectives or attributes: a state, which varies on a continuum from happiness to unhappiness; a quality, which varies on a scale from good to evil; and a condition, which includes religious affiliation, maleness or femaleness, and social position. There are also three basic verbs or actions: the principal verb functions "to change or to modify" and is general enough to include the other two verbs; the second verb is "to transgress or to sin"; and the third verb is "to punish." Each of the one hundred stories of the *Décaméron* can be analyzed using these basic units, as an extended sentence developed from a combination of the nouns with the three verbs and the three kinds of adjectives.

Roland Barthes. Roland Barthes also undertakes a structural analysis of narrative in which the smallest units are put together into molecular structures and then integrated at higher levels. Barthes breaks narrative down into units, functions, and indices (indicators of character, atmosphere, and so on). Although in the narrative itself these units follow each other sequentially, the task of the critic is to subsume them into an atemporal frame of explanation. Barthes also opposes Propp's notions that a particular narrative can be read as the manifestation of a single structure and that the elements of narrative can be given fixed definitions. In his *S/Z*, a two-hundred-page study of a thirty page story by Balzac, Barthes writes:

> They say that by virtue of their asceticism certain Buddhists come to see a whole country in a bean. This is just what the first analysts of the *récit* [narrative] wanted to do: to see all the stories in the world … in one single structure. We are going, they thought, to extract from each tale its model, then from these models we will make a great narrative structure, which we will apply (for verification) to any story in existence—an exhausting task … and finally an undesirable one, because the text thereby loses its difference.[31]

Barthes proposes that criticism, instead of viewing a literary text from one model, should espouse an inherent plurality and ambiguity in the text. The elemental functions of a narrative cannot be defined until their interaction with other elements is seen. Each part of the narrative can be categorized in different ways, depending on the relationships being emphasized; these functions link the story together on a time line from beginning to end. Nevertheless, these elements, Barthes believes, are held together by an atemporal formula that generates a display of chronological actions. When the structure has been identified, it will appear as a logical order.

For Barthes, there are two types of unit in a narrative—the function and the indications (indices). The primary unit of a narrative is the "function," which opens or closes with nuclei or kernels, elements that imply each other. "Start feeding the baby" implies "stop feeding the baby"; likewise, "the purchasing of a revolver" has a correlate moment when it will be used. The indications are integrative and may be composed of several references to the same thing—for example, "it was a gray day," "it was overcast," and "the sun was not out." In order to know what purpose indications serve, it is necessary to pass to the level of the actions of the characters or the narration, for it is there that the indication is fulfilled—"the person decided not to go to the beach that day." These two categories of units—functions (actions linking the story surface) and indications (static elements integrated at the thematic level)—are broken down into four subclasses.

There are two kinds of functions: (1) cardinal functions, the sequences that move the plot along and describe choices made by agents, and (2) functional catalyzers or satellites, optional actions not essential to moving the action along that are used to fill space between the cardinal functions. And there are two kinds of indications: (1) indices, which are character traits, thoughts, and atmosphere that require deciphering, and (2) informants, which are minor indices that fix the setting and time.

In addition to developing a set of categories that accounts for all of the units that appear in a narrative, structural theory has to describe the rules that govern the combinations of these categories. For Barthes, the first level of combination integrates the cardinal functions and associated satellites into a sequence. For example, the cardinal functions "receive guests," "dine," "coffee in the drawing room," and "guests depart" are combined into the higher-order sequence of "dinner with guests." Barthes's structural theory also has flexibility: what at one level is a cardinal function can, at the next higher level, become a catalyzer action, filling space. The sequence "having guests for dinner" may fill space in the higher sequence of "getting one of the guests away from their house for the night so that his or her home can be robbed."

The character is at the next higher level of combination. Barthes holds, in contrast to earlier Aristotelian-based theories in which actions were the primary focus, that in modern narrative the character is dominant over the action in the story. In Barthes's theory, the strands of action, information, and personal traits are woven together to form the thread of character. As the story gives more and more information about the characters through the actions they undertake, the ways in which they carry out the actions, and indication about their traits, the reader is led to imagine lines that form a recognizable constellation of character. But each new sequence can lead the reader to reconfigure his or her understanding of the character. The plot and the characters become interdependent: the actions in the plot define the characters, and the development of an understanding of the characters helps the reader realize the significance of the actions in the plot.

The earlier, prestructural notion of character was that it was a static element in narrative, opposed to the dynamic and unfolding progress of the plot. Structuralists changed this idea, making character an integral part of the development of the plot. But for the structuralists the narrative itself is only a working out of a set of linguistic rules. It is not a reflection of reality, not even a fictional reflection. Character, then, is understood to be a collection of verbal statements (physical appearance, thoughts, statements, feelings) that are loosely held together by a proper name. The structuralist position holds that there is a special relationship between words and the world: the images created by words are merely mental constructions generated by a set of logically ordered rules, somewhat like computer programs that follow a set of preprogrammed instructions. Because there is no way to gain access to reality directly, the images are not generated by the world nor are they corrected by reality checks. The persons presented in narrative, then, are conjectural configurations, collections of verbal statements (about a character's physical appearance, thoughts, statements, feelings) held together loosely by a proper name. In this way they are akin to the images of people that are created from bits of gossip: the fragments of verbal reports are pieced together to construct a whole by filling in the blanks with general characterizations that fit with the pieces already in hand.

Yet the characters that the reader of a narrative experiences appear to have a depth that extends beyond the bounds of the story itself. Narrative characters are experienced as selves and, though they are fused with the action of the story, they are not dissolved by it. Wallace Martin, in his *Recent Theories of Narrative,* suggests three explanations for the experience of depth of character by readers of narrative.[32] The first comes from Lacan and holds that we experience the depth and power of the character's desire when the object of desire is hard to define or when achieving what was thought to be the object of desire does not completely satisfy. By facilitating participation in the psychic life of the characters, the narrative allows the reader to feel workings of desire and to see how it motivates and energizes. This "feeling with" the characters arouses the reader's own feelings, and through them the character "comes alive," becoming more than a simple verbal construction disconnected from reality.

The second explanation is that although the actions in the narrative cover only an an episode in a life span, they include recollections of past experiences and anticipations of future episodes extending to the character's death. As Walter Benjamin suggests in "The Storyteller," every narrative, like every life, ends in death.[33]

Martin's third explanation is that the reader moves beyond experiencing the character as a single, whole life to experience the character as a historically situated person. The character is extended to the historical setting in which desires and plans for the future are actualized. The social forces and the historical unfolding show through the character, and thereby give the experience a fullness and a richness regarding the people depicted in the narrative which overflow the limits of the narrative sequences and the internally generated structure.

Jonathan Culler. Jonathan Culler, in *Structuralist Poetics,* published in 1975, systematized the French structuralist approach for American literary critics, and described its literary uses.[34] This analysis is built on the assumption that there is a bare-bones entity called "plot" that remains the same regardless of the particular story being told. Structural analysis requires that a distinction be made between the sequence of actions or events that are referred to in a narrative and the means by which these events are told. Although various terms have been used to designate this difference, the current convention is to use the word "story" to refer to the events, characters, and settings—that is, the content—and the term "discourse" to refer to the form of expression, presentation, or narration of the story.[35] In addition, to make narrative an object of study, it needs to be distinguished from nonnarratives. The problem is to establish the essence of narrative. The story can be represented in various media, and even though each medium has its own characteristics,[36] the basic outline of the story can be recognized as the same story in each medium. The essence of narrative is not the written form, because narratives can also be spoken, acted out as drama, and presented in motion pictures.

Narrative is usually identified as a general form that reports a sequence of events, and these events are identified as something that exists prior to and independently of their narrative presentation. The events need not actually exist outside the imagination of the author, but they appear in the narrative as if they are independent of the particular telling, and they are imagined to have the properties of actual events. Mieke Bal has described the characteristics of story:

'The story consists of the set of events in their chronological order, their spatial location, and their relations with the actors who cause or undergo them ... The events have temporal relations with one another. Each one is either anterior to, simultaneous with, or posterior to every other event.'[37]

The narrative assumes that events do occur in some order and that its description of these events presupposes their prior existence, although fictive. Because the discourse itself is a presentation of these events, the reader and the critic can treat everything in it as a way of interpreting, valuing, and presenting the events. For example, in the story of Oedipus, the sequence of events that constitute the action of the story is as follows: Oedipus is abandoned on Mount Cithaeron; he is rescued by a shepherd; he grows up in Corinth; he kills Laius at the crossroad; he answers the Sphinx's riddle; he marries Jocasta; he seeks the murderer of Laius; he discovers his own guilt; he blinds himself and leaves his country. Treating these events as the story, one can investigate the way in which the discourse interprets and portrays them. The discourse focuses on bringing to light a crucial event which determines the significance of the other events. The play locates the crucial event in what happened when Laius was killed. The event is shaped to impose a meaning on the rest of the events that is more powerful than any intention of the actors in the story and to place an awful guilt on Oedipus.

Culler proposed that narrative operates by incorporating two contradictory logics. The one logic assumes a primacy of events, while the other treats the events as the products of meanings. The force of the Oedipus narrative, then, derives from the interaction of these two logics. Oedipus's guilt is not derived from new evidence that he had killed his father; it is derived from the power of the contrary logic in which the event is not a cause but an effect of the theme. In this contrary logic the event (the killing of the father) is a product of the discourse itself rather than an independent event reported in the story. The present interpretation of the past event, in fact, causes its effects—that is, the effects of events are dependent on their later interpretation. This is contrary to the logic of events that maintains that prior events are the cause of later ones.[38]

Causation requires a narrative structure in which the presence of a cause is first posited and then the effect it produces is given. For Culler, the very notion of plot is based on causation. "The king died, and then the queen died," is not a narrative; but "the king died, and then the queen died of grief," is.[39] This is the story of the causal narrative: first there was cause, and then there was effect. But Culler goes on to restate Nietzsche's proposal that the normal cause-effect sequence is not an aspect of reality but a construct based on a rhetorical operation. First the effect is experienced, then we look for an event we can identify as the cause. A narrative operation then reorders the sequence from effect-cause to cause-effect.[40] Narrative makes use of both these forms of causality. On the level of the actions referred to, ordinary causality is assumed. But on the level of the telling of the story, cause by signification is used.[41]

Culler notes that we still do not appreciate as fully as we ought the important function of narrative schemes and models in all aspects of our lives.[42] He advises that neither choosing the story and its events as primary nor choosing the discourse as primary will provide the critic with an understanding of the full power of narrative. If one thinks of a narrative as fundamentally a presentation of a sequence of events, it will be difficult to account for the sorts of effects of meaning that derive from the logic of discourse. If one thinks of a narrative as only a construction of discourse and the events as simply products, the force of the narrative as an account about something in the world will be missed. Even the most radical fictions depend for their effect on the assumption that they are reporting about events that have features extending beyond those in the discourse. The reader does not normally approach a narrative wondering how the author will disguise the monomyth or will fill in the functional units. Without the notion that the story is about something outside the discourse itself, it would lose its force as a selection from possible events and its power to intrigue us.

The division of narrative processes into story and discourse allows for a distinction to be made between the various times at which a story's events take place. The story time is understood to be an objective time where events are ordered sequentially and where time units are equal—where, for instance, one hour on one day lasts as long as an one hour on a second day. Nevertheless, the narration of the story can play various "games with time,"[43] some chapters covering only one day, perhaps, and others covering years. In any given narration, moreover, the space allotted to different periods of time can vary extensively. One of Chaucer's stories, for example, covers about two weeks, but more than half of it concerns a single morning. Often the narrator will give a summary of events covering a long period of time and then focus in detail on certain scenes.

Gérard Genette has investigated the manner in which time can be represented in the narrative telling of a story.[44] He identifies three categories. First there is *duration*, which involves temporal condensations, such as summary and ellipsis, or the omission of time periods in the telling of the story. The second category is *order*, in which the narrative uses the devices of flashback and flashforward. In flashforward, the narrator lets the reader in on what will happen later, or a character in the story is allowed to imagine the future. Flashback can be used in a complex way, with the order of past events changed around for dramatic effect. For example, the narrative can use a character's memory to report an earlier period, which may evoke still earlier periods or bring us back to the story present. The ordering of time in a narrative may also be emphasized through a combination of order and duration: a period remembered may extend only two hours in length but occupy a full third of the narration. Genette's third category, *frequency*, refers to the number of times an incident is recounted. The use of iteration, or the single description of an event that occurs repeatedly—for example, "they discussed it often," and "the bell tolled every day at that time"—gives the reader an experience of an extended past time.

Genette's descriptions (which are more detailed than outlined here) are representative of his attempt to categorize all aspects of narrative presentation. As Martin has pointed out: "For well over a century, writers have been confusing the categories of the critics ... But we had no convincing analytic account of the traditional categories until Genette pushed them to an Aristotelian extreme by labeling everything. Criticism is a struggle to name that which has never been noticed."[45] It should be noted, however, that actual narratives do not break up into sections merely so that they will fit into these structural categories.

The attempt by structural analysis to dissect stories in order to reduce them to formulas remains alien, if not incomprehensible, to most readers of fiction. The structural theory that individual stories are generated by an underlying set of static, atemporal deep structures has shared the same set of problems that have assailed many deductive theories. For the structuralists, problems arose when they changed from describing the structures that identify what all stories have in common to accounts of how and why stories are different. Moreover, structural theories have tended to overlook the surface ambiguities of stories and to assign only one structural description to stories that have more than one meaning. Ricoeur has argued against the structuralist's notion that narrative is ultimately the product of a set of static rules. Says Ricoeur:

> The chronological dimension was not abolished, but it was deprived of its temporal constitution as a plot. The segmentating and the concatenating of functions thus paved the way for a reduction of the chronological to the logical. And in the subsequent phase of structural analysis, with Greimas and Roland Barthes, the search for the atemporal formula that generates the chronological display of functions transformed the structure of the tale into a machinery whose task it is to compensate for the initial mischief or lack by a final restoration of the disturbed order. Compared to

this logical matrix, the quest [Propp's story line] itself appears as a mere diachronical residue, a retardation of suspension in the epiphany of order.[46]

Ricoeur contends that narrative is an expression ultimately grounded in the human experience of lived time, and receives its order and power from the appeal to this experience in the human reader. He believes that narrative is the retrieval or repetition from the past of a part of human experience and that its form is related to the human activity of recollection, not to an innate grammar. In contrast, it is the contention of the structural theorists that the narrative experience is grounded not in the temporal awareness generated by recollection but rather in a deep set of unchanging logical rules that are located below the human experience of time.

These discussions of the structural analysis of narrative have focused on the generation of plot. As we have seen, a plot can be presented in a variety of forms—as a drama, a motion picture, an oral transmission, or written prose. Moreover, a plot can be transferred back and forth among these forms of presentation and still maintain its identity. The notion of a deep narrative grammar, however, is most applicable to one form of presentation: traditional and orally transmitted tales. These stories take on a stylized form through mnemonic devices and patterns after repeated tellings. Narrative grammars, however, have been less successful with the more complex written narrative. Narrative study in literary criticism has shifted its emphasis from the analysis of deep structure to the study of point of view.

Written narratives and point of view

The emphasis on point of view represents a shift in focus from the underlying plot structure to the devices an author uses to solve problems in the presentation of the thoughts of the novel's characters. This change has involved an emphasis of the communication model of Jakobson (see chapter 1), which links the sender , the message, and the receiver together in a single speech event; and stands opposed to the structuralist view, which emphasizes the linguistic model and the search for formal structures.

The point-of-view theorists have focused on the constructive theory of an author as sender of the message. The author is more than a tool by means of which the grammar constructs a tale: he or she is a creative force in the construction of the story and the source of the devices used in its telling. Significantly, an author's point of view involves a distinctive relationship with the characters in the story. To state the matter in an oversimplified way, authors are allowed only two options regarding the choice of a point of view when they tell a story: they can use either the first person or the third person. The first-person option involves speaking through letters, journals, dialogues, and monologues, and uses the present tense to give the reader a sense of immediate involvement. This approach is termed the "scene" and differs from summary, or "narration," which is always in the past tense. The third-person presentation provides the author with the advantage of being aware of everything and thus able to reveal things not known to any of the characters and to comment on the action. Writers often use both approaches in a novel, combining the presumed accuracy of third-person statements with the feeling of authenticity provided by first-person statements.

Novelists also use a third linguistic form that is called "represented speech and thought." This form does not conform to normal grammatical conventions, but readers understand it without being conscious of the conventions on which it is based. Represented speech combines the present tense of the first-person grammar and the past tense of the third-person grammar and merges the narrator with a character. To illustrate the use of this third form, Martin presents an incident from Katherine Mansfield's *Bliss:* "After Harry has said on the phone that he'll be late, Bertha apparently wants to tell him something: ' "Oh, Harry!" "Yes?" What had she wanted to say? She'd nothing to say.' "[47] Instead of using the first person for Bertha's thoughts, "What had I wanted to say?" the author switches to the third-person narrative form. The represented speech releases the character's consciousness and self from the "I" and allows the reader to experience something outside the range of everyday experience, a subjectivity freed from the boundaries of a body and a voice.

Another issue that has been investigated is the author's use of a character's perspective in telling the story. An author can look through a character so that what the character sees or knows—other characters, for instance—is what is told. This "focalizer" or perceiver, can see things close up or from a distance, in a style similar to the close-up and wide views given in motion pictures. The author might also use more than one focalizer, and shift from one character's view to another.

These investigations of point of view follow a pattern similar to the one seen in the structuralists' investigations. A search is being conducted for dichotomies in the narrative presentation which can be turned into classification schemes. The close analysis of authorial devices comes from an abstracting of particular aspects of the whole presentation. What is lost in the classifications is the effect of the story as a complete configuration as it is experienced by the reader. Usually the reader is not conscious of the author's devices and experiences a direct understanding of the story, an integration of the various parts so that what is gained is a general notion about a character's way of being in the world.

Mikhail Bakhtin, an early Russian critic who had opposed Propp's structuralism, proposed that the novel is basically a presentation of ways of relating to the world. This presentation could not be seen, he said, by breaking language down and looking at its parts in isolation.[48] Bakhtin critized Saussure's concern with the abstract system of language, and proposed that language could be grasped only in terms of its local orientation toward others. Human consciousness and its expression are not components of a sealed interior realm that is divorced from social interaction, Bakhtin argued. People participate in a social field that gives form (an ideology) to ideas and attitudes. Bakhtin showed, for instance, that Dostoevsky used several linguistic approaches to the world (heteroglossia) rather than simply one (monologia), and that he offered a plurality of centers of consciousness engaged in a dialog that reflects those various centers' disagreements and disputes. Bakhtin used the term "ideology" to refer to a particular way of viewing the world—one that strives for social significance—and understood that the language of the narrative presents these ideologies to the reader in a whole form.

Reception theory

Recent critics have attended to the role of the reader in producing meaning in interaction with the written text. The reader performs the functions of fitting motifs together, evaluating characters, and seeking causal connections.[49] Reception theory continues the point-of-view use of the communication model, but it shifts the focus from the sender of the narrative message to the receiver—the reader, who interprets or understands the text. It is this hermeneutic process that is the concern of reception theory. As Wolfgang Iser argues, however, interpretation is not seen to be the process that Dilthey described as an empathic reexperiencing of the author's meaning.[50] Iser opposes what he calls the "referential model," in which the reader is called on to hunt for a truth tucked away in the fold of the textual fabric. He urges that more attention be paid to the process of interpretation than to the result. Meaning is not to be dug out of the text or pieced together from textual clues; it is reached through an interactive process that takes place between the reader and the text. And interpretation does not entail the discovery of a determinate meaning in the text; it is rather in experiencing the work that meaning is created.

The communication of meaning by fictional narrative can be viewed from the perspective of Jakobson's general communication model. To understand a communication event involves an analysis of the entire structure of the transaction among the sender, the message sent, and the receiver. Thus, in addition to the author (the sender) and the text (the message), understanding a novel's communication structure must include "the implied reader" (the receiver). One of the characters produced by an author, along with those described in the text, is a future reader, with his or her expectations and perspectives. The meaning we infer from the text emerges from a productive tension between "the role offered [the implied reader] by the text and the real reader's own disposition.[51] Communication with implied readers is only one of several channels of meaning created by a novel. Meaning also appears through the transactions among characters or when an author makes direct statements to the reader. It is the reader's task to bring about a convergence of perspectives from these various channels.

Interpretations of the same text vary because of the diversity of the receivers, that is, the readers. Each reader brings to a narrative a different set of experiences and expectations. Differences in interpretation can be derived from differences in personal experience and social understanding. Iser says that if we are to read at all we need to be familiar with the literary techniques and conventions a particular work employs; we must have some grasp of its "codes," by which he means the rules that systematically govern the ways the text produces its meanings. As readers we must mobilize our general social knowledge to interpret the meaning of a text. For example, the phrase, "He noticed a lump under his arm pit and started to cry," makes sense because from our general stock of cultural knowledge we are aware that such a lump can be a sign of cancer.

For Norman Holland, individual differences are the result of individual psychic configurations. Holland uses psychoanalytic theory as a way of identifying the psychic condition a reader brings to a work. He says that we each "find in the literary work the kind of thing we characteristically wish or fear most."[52] Whereas earlier psychoanalytic theory held that the psychoanalytic dynamics were displayed in the texts themselves,[53] Holland transfers the dynamics from the text to the reader.

Iser believes that the most effective literary works are those which force readers into new critical awarenesses. Each work, by interrogating and transforming the implicit beliefs we bring to it, by "disconfirming" our routine habits or perceptions, forces us for the first time to acknowledge our perceptions and expectations. The effective work of literature does not merely reinforce our given perceptions; it "violates or transgresses these normative ways of seeing and so teaches us new codes for understanding."[54]

Another reception theorist, Hans Robert Jauss, uses the hermeneutic theory of Hans-Georg Gadamer[55] as a point of departure for his notion of a "horizon of expectations."[56] Gadamer used the label "horizon" to refer to "the range of vision that includes everything that can be seen from a particular vantage point."[57] This is a concept previously introduced by Husserl and Heidegger. Jauss situates a literary work in its historical horizon—that is, in the context of the cultural meanings within which it was produced. He then explores the shifting relations between this situation and the changing horizons of its historical readers. The aim of his theory is to produce a new kind of literary history, one centered not on authors, influences, and literary trends, but on literature as defined and interpreted by its various moments of historical "reception." His point is not that literary works themselves remain constant while interpretations of them change; rather texts and literary traditions are themselves actively altered according to the various historical horizons within which they are received. The text in itself is a kind of skeleton, a set of "schemata" waiting to be concretized in various ways by various readers.[58] Roland Barthes has also addressed the issue of the reader's activity in constructing an understanding of the bare text.[59] The title of a story may be helpful for recalling the story after it has been read, but the title does not give much of an indication of the meaning of a story about to be read. The reading of a story is a temporal activity, according to Barthes, and the process of understanding undergoes changes during the reading process. This process is described by Barthes in terms of five codes that lead to an understanding of the story. (1) The hermeneutic code leads a reader through a series of partial disclosures, delays, and ambiguities as the story moves toward its final disclosures. Barthes compares this process to that of listening to music. The lines of the melody lead forward, interweaving as in a fugue, and adding harmonies and rhythms in recurring patterns. At times the levels of a text may seem to coalesce in a single thematic meaning, "even while the discourse is leading us toward other possibilities." But the meaning skids, each synonym adding to its neighbor some new trait, some new departure."[60] (2) The code of semes, indications which coalesce into a character, has as its locus a person. (3) The referential or cultural code is the stock of knowledge we automatically use in interpreting everyday experience. (4) The code of action, or proairetic code, is the process of collecting actions into groups. This code moves the story along from beginning to end. (5) The code of symbols is based on antitheses—for instance, inside and outside, closed and open, hot and cold, and warm and cool.

Terry Eagleton compares Barthes's approach to Iser's:

> The approach of Barthes's *The Pleasure of the Text* (1973) is about as different from Iser's as one could imagine—the difference, stereotypically speaking, between a French hedonist and a German rationalist. Whereas Iser focuses mainly on the realist work, Barthes offers a sharply contrasting account of reading by taking a modernist text … Such a text demands less a "hermeneutics" than an "erotics": since there is no way to arrest it into determinate sense, the reader simply luxuriates in the tantalizing glide of signs, in the provocative glimpses of meaning which surface only to submerge again.[61]

The theories of reading produced during the past fifteen years have made significant contributions to the understanding of narrative. The reader and the writer have been reinstalled alongside the text itself. Reception theory has revealed that the understanding of a text is a complex process and may vary according to the interests and experiences of the reader at each reading. Readers draw on their experiences with stories in the tradition and with their own narratively preconfigured understanding of their own lives as they approach a narrative. The experience with the narrative then adds to their own breadth of understanding of themselves.

Literary theory has moved through a series of studies of narrative. These have involved concern for underlying story lines and for historically evolved responses to human problems and needs. In its move toward a more "scientific" approach, literary theory borrowed the methods of structural linguistics in an attempt to uncover a narrative grammar that would generate all possible narratives. More recently, literary theory has adopted the communication model, which has broadened the locus of study. Attention is no longer given exclusively to the structure of the text. The writer and the reader now also function as parts in a whole communication event that occurs when the created narrative text is taken up to be understood by different individuals.

CHAPTER V

Psychology and Narrative

U NLIKE the disciplines of history and literature, the human sciences originated after the development of formal science, and were modelled on formal science principles. The interest in narrative by one of the human sciences, psychology, has been chosen for investigation in this chapter. Although a similar investigation of anthropology, sociology, or another human science could have been undertaken, psychology was chosen because of its renewed interest in narrative as a cognitive structure.

Psychology has passed through various phases of interest in narrative during its little more than a century as a separate discipline. During its early development, however, some of its members were concerned about investigating the lives of individuals in addition to factors affecting perception and memory. After 1950, the discipline turned almost exclusively to working within the limits of a positivistic definition of formal science. This meant that attention was given to behaviors and publicly accessible data, and almost all attention to narrative was extinguished. By the 1970's, however, the shortcomings of this approach became apparent, and the discipline opened itself to the investigation of cognitive processes and human experience. It is, in part, because of this renewed attention to human experience that psychology has begun to investigate narrative again.

This chapter begins with a recounting of psychology's early interest in individual psychology, including the role that life story and narrative played in these investigations. It will then turn to the investigations currently being undertaken that treat narrative as a cognitive structure. Self-narrative, narrative competence, and the role of narrative in life-span research will be explored. The chapter will conclude with a look at the Freudian tradition, which is especially concerned with stories and narrative, but which until recently has been excluded from mainstream academic psychology.

The history of narrative study in psychology

Notwithstanding the resistance of advocates of the formal science approach, psychology has made some use of narrative during its history, especially in the investigation of life histories, biographies, and case studies.

For a time, the subdiscipline of "individual psychology"—the study of the individual as a unified totality—represented an ongoing research program with affinities to narrative understanding. Since the early application of formal science principles to the study of the human realm, authors have written about the inability of formal science methods to deal with the problem of human individuality.[1] Even John Stuart Mill, who had called for the application of natural science methods in the study of human beings, wrote in 1851 that character had been left out by the theories of association psychology and that a new science, ethology, should be developed to study character.[2] In 1858 Samuel Bailey also called for the formation of a new discipline, separate and distinct from psychology, to study individual and personal character. In 1867, J.Bahnsen began a study he called "characterology," involving the construction of typologies and theories of human character. Some of Bahsen's typologies were used by L.Klages as the basis for his system of graphology. Wilhelm Wundt, who was identified by Edwin Boring as the father of experimental and formal science psychology, suggested that another, practical psychology be created alongside the study of mental structures. This practical study, which he also called characterology, would investigate the basic and typical forms of individual character, aided by principles derived from a general theoretical psychology.

In 1911, William Stern was the first to give a systematic presentation of the methodological foundations of the study of individuals. He proposed the term "individual psychology" to describe a discipline that would be concerned with all aspects of the psychological life of the individual but would also include more general human psychology. He distinguished "individual psychology" from "differential psychology," which studied the differences between groups and which reduced persons to mere carriers of character traits. Stern at first wanted individual psychology to employ two types of approaches: (1) a nomothetic concentration on the distribution and correlations of characteristics across a population and (2) an ideographic concentration on one or more individuals in whom various characteristics jointly occurred. This second approach would investigate a large number of traits manifested by one individual and analyze their internal relationships. The first proposals generated by individual psychology were generally consistent with the statistical analysis of data favored by formal science. However, Stern was not content with merely noting the multiplicity of traits within a person, and he added the study of personal biographies as a means to understanding the unity of personality.

A few years earlier, Freud had published case studies of his patients to illustrate his theory of the dynamic interactions among the tripartite structure of the psyche. In 1911, the same year that Stern published his proposal regarding individual psychology, Alfred Adler, who had just broken with Freud, published his own theory of individual psychology. Writing several decades later, Adler summarized his basic theory: "The fundamental fact in human development is the dynamic and purposive striving of the psyche. ... The unity of personality is implicit in each human being's existence. Every individual represents both a unity of personality and the individual fashioning of the unity."[3] Adler's theory became so well known that the name "individual psychology" became synonomous with his system, and alternate terms were proposed to designate other approaches to the study of individual lives: "praxiology," for instance (Mercier, 1911), and "personology" (J.C. Smuts, 1926)

Henry A. Murray, director of the Psycholgical Clinic at Harvard, adopted Smuts's term for his work on the individual case, and through his influence on students and colleagues his notion of the organic or whole character of human behavior spread. Murray's 1938 book, *Explorations in Personality*, called for an intensive study of individual subjects.[4] He pointed out the limits of the usual large-scale studies of human behavior in which the findings consisted of group tendencies or overall relations and did not characterize any single individual within the group. Murray proposed that an adequate understanding of behavior could come only from a complete and detailed study of individuals. He had been trained as a physician, and felt that the narrative form of case study, which had been central to the growth of medical science, was also essential for the development of psychology. He held that group studies were important only when accompanied by careful inquiry into subjects who represented exceptions to the group norms. Murray was a pioneer in the interdisciplinary study of the person and the study of normal individuals in natural settings.

Gorden Allport also made significant contributions to the development of a narrative-based study of the individual.[5] Allport supported an idea similar to the one proposed here—that human disciplines should use multiple approaches. He believed that investigators may choose to study the human realm in terms of general principles and universal variables, using a large number of subjects, or they may focus on the individual case, using methods and variables that are adequate to the uniqueness of each person. Allport, who had studied in Europe, borrowed from Wilhelm Windelband the term "nomothetic," to designate universal studies, and the term "ideographic," to designate individual studies. (Later he substituted new terms for these designations, "dimensional" and "morphogenic," respectively.) Allport acknowledged that there was a place for more than one kind of approach, but because American studies had so overwhelmingly emphasized nomothetic or formal science, he felt that a drastic reorientation was necessary.

Allport emphasized the uniqueness of each person and urged the investigator to select methods of study that did not conceal this individuality. As part of his efforts to develop such methods, he proposed the importance of personal documents as information for understanding individuals. Calvin Hall and Gardner Lindzey, in their text on personality theory, stated that Allport "only made a beginning in evolving such methods."[6]

Between approximately 1920 and 1945, there was significant growth in the study of individual lives. In addition to Murray and Allport, Charlotte Bühler and John Dollard made important contributions to the theory of life history as a method of psychological investigation.[7] Along with the developments in psychology during this period, other human disciplines also produced important publications about the case study and life history approaches.[8] In sociology, the single most important work was W. I. Thomas and Florian Znaniecki's 1920 study, *The Polish Peasant in Europe and America*, of which Volume Three was an edited autobiography of Valdek, a Polish immigrant to America.[9] The Chicago school of symbolic interaction supported the notion of the critical use of life history. Its founder, George Herbert Mead, emphasized the importance of symbols and language in the shaping of human behavior. Mead held that individuals were active in shaping their own lives and that to study the events in a person's life required a method that would provide information about the person's own self-interpretation of his or her actions.[10] He believed that such a method would be qualitatively different from the mainstream formal science approach in that it would allow sympathetic introspection as a means for understanding human actions. The symbolic interaction tradition used life history material in its research and produced a number of case studies. Three studies by C. R. Shaw give an indication of the kind of research topics addressed by the approach: *The Jack Roller: A Delinquent Boy's Own Story* (1930), *The Natural History of a Delinquent Career* (1931), and *Brothers in Crime* (1936).

In anthropology, the use of life histories began with the informal life stories of American Indians in the nineteenth century, but in the period we are discussing more methodologically sophisticated studies began to appear. For example, Paul Radin's *Crashing Thunder: The Autobiography of an American Indian* (1926), Walter Dyk's *Son of Old Man Hat: A Navaho Autobiography Recorded by Walter Dyk* (1938), Leo W. Simmon's *Sun Chief: The Autobiography of a Hopi Indian* (1942), and Cora DuBois's *The People of Alor* (1944).[11]

In the period after World War Two the epistemology of formal science became completely dominant in the human disciplines in the United States, and this situation resulted in the virtual disappearance of personality theory and individual psychology from psychology.[12] R. Carlson, after reviewing 226 articles published in the 1968 volumes of two major journals concerned with research on personality, reported: "Although the literature as a whole has elicited a wide range of potentially important information about persons, no single investigation either noted or utilized much information about any individual subject . . . Not a single published study attempted even minimal inquiry into the organization of personality variables within the individual."[13] The goal of studying whole persons, Carlson concluded, had apparently been abandoned. This conclusion is confirmed by a review of *Psychological Abstracts* for the years 1960 to 1978. Only about one percent of the published reports were devoted to the investigation of single persons, and even in these a biography or other such study was rarely a goal in itself. Most articles used case materials merely to illustrate a theory or the use of a therapy technique.[14]

Since the mid-1960s there has been a renewed interest in the study of lives. William Runyan, in his book *Life Histories and Psychobiography*,[15] reviews the enormous amount of work done during this period and notes that scholarly work has been carried out in such areas as normal adult personality development, life history and psychopathology, and life span development. He notes that efforts in this area "share a common concern for studying how life paths are shaped by an interaction of individuals with their social and historical worlds over time."[16] Runyan's book surveys the outcome of this interest and is itself a contribution to the work in the area.[17]

Within the human disciplines, interest in life paths has manifested itself in studies of life span development, with special focuses on adult development and psychohistory studies. A later section of this chapter addresses the use of narrative methods for the study of adult development. Studies in psychohistory have taken two forms: the study of individuals—psychobiography—and the study of the psychohistory of groups.[18] In both these forms, the psychoanalytic view of the person has become something of an orthodoxy. The bond between psychohistory and psychoanalysis has given researchers a perspective other than formal science to interpret the events in individual and group history. Another addition to the literature that recognizes the significance of narrative for psychological understanding, and which was mentioned in previous chapters, is *Actual Minds, Possible Worlds*, by a pioneer in the study of cognition, Jerome Bruner. In this book Bruner focuses on the function of language and narrative, claiming that narrative is one of the two primary knowledge forms, the other being the paradigmatic knowledge of formal science.[19]

Scholarly interest in life stories has passed through phases in which interest and production have waxed and wanted. The decades before World War Two produced a literature that fell into disuse when the human disciplines moved to a stringent formal science behaviorism in the 1950s. This literature remains a rich resource to be reexplored by those concerned with multiple approaches for understanding the human realm. The new awareness of the processes of narrative knowing gives methodological support for the insights contained in this earlier literature.

Self-narrative

One of the areas of interest in psychology's recent attention to narrative has been the role of narrative in establishing personal identity. Two articles in Sarbin's recent collection, *Narrative Psychology* (1986), address the employment of self-narratives and their place in the formation of self-identity.[20] In the first, Karl Scheibe writes about identity and narrative:

Human identities are considered to be evolving constructions; they emerge out of continual social interactions in the course of life. Self-narratives are developed stories that must be told in specific historical terms, using a particular language, reference to a particular stock of working historical conventions and a particular pattern of dominant beliefs and values. The most fundamental narrative forms are universal, but the way these forms are styled and filled with content will depend upon particular historical conventions of time and place.[21]

Scheibe's thesis is that people undertake adventures in order to construct and maintain satisfactory life stories. One's life story needs to include a series of progressive and regressive periods repeating over time—that is, it needs adventures followed by the return to repose. In terms of a psychological biography, a life lived without adventures and on a single plane is insufficient as a story, it does not go anywhere and does not move. It is the variations that provide "the stuff of life story." Scheibe concentrates on the use of sport and gambling to bring adventure to one's life story. These activities of risk provide occasions for the generation and testing of the self in the development of the self-narrative. "Sport provides adventure, a euphoric release from drudgery, tedium, and the gracelessness of ordinary domestic life."[22]

Narrative enrichment occurs when one retrospectively revises, selects, and orders past details in such a way as to create a self-narrative that is coherent and satisfying and that will serve as a justification for one's present condition and situation. The retrospective revision needs to conclude and coincide with the known present. Narrative constructions are the socially derived and expressed product of repeated adventures. Scheibe points out that for some people the stories they have constructed for their lives come to an end before their biological lives do. He quotes Kurt Vonnegut's description of this problem: "If a person survives an ordinary span of sixty years or more, there is every chance that his or her life as a shapely story has ended and all that remains to be experienced is epilogue. Life is not over, but the story is."[23]

The second article, by Stephen Crites, addresses the temporal dimension of story making. Crites argues that appropriating the past and anticipating the future require different narrative strategies.[24] When the strategies are mixed, the resulting self-narrative is confused, inconsistent, and even chaotic. "The self is a kind of aesthetic construct, recollected in and with the life of experience in narrative fashion."[25] One's personal story or personal identity is a recollected self in which the more complete the story that is formed, the more integrated the self will be. Thus, self-knowledge is an appropriation of the past. When this appropriation is not recollective, integrative, and self-discovering, then the person (the "I") experiences unhappiness or a form of despair. Although everyone has a past, one can forget or suppress it, or one can be so intent on a future project that one lets his or her roots grow weak. This results in the loss of identity with no more of a story than a bare chronicle. Identity, recollected out of the past, is the depth dimension of the self that gives the self character. "A self without a story contracts into the thinness of its personal pronoun."[26]

Identity consists not simply of a self-narrative that integrates one's past events into a coherent story, however. It also includes the construction of a future story that continues the "I" of the person. If a person fails to project a hopeful story about the future, he or she undergoes a second kind of unhappiness, a life without hope. Although everyone has a future, it is possible for one to ignore or actively resist its claim and live from day to day without a projective scenario, or to devote all one's energies to protecting and reiterating the identity recollected out of the past. The creation of a future story that imposes on the tightly woven recollective story and attempts to maintain an unchanged self leads to unhappiness with the future. At the same time, treating the past as if it were as indeterminate as the future produces a future story so loose and fragmentary that it resembles a fairy tale or fantasy. There needs to be some continuity between past and future stories. A problem may arise, however, because the past story is a recollection of what has already been, and the future story, although it needs to be a continuation of the past, requires an open and adaptive character.

These studies remind psychologists that people conceive of themselves in terms of stories. Their personal stories are always some version of the general cultural stock of stories about how life proceeds. As narrative forms, these stories draw together and configure the events of one's life into a coherent and basic theme. One's future is projected as a continuation of the story, as yet unfinished.

Before turning to a consideration of the role of narrative in self-identity in the domains of developmental life-span studies, I will review the research on narrative competence and its acquisition.

Narrative competence

The study of narrative competence by mainstream psychology had to await the cognitive turn in psychology during the 1960s.[27] Before that time, academic psychology, under the continuing influence of Watson's vision of a psychological science, had been concentrating its research and theory on behaviors which did not require the examination of internal or mental processes. This research strategy, the stimulus-response (SR) model, could carry out experiments using animals and birds as subjects. Because the theory of the program did not include significant cross-species variation in cognitive processing, it was believed that the learning models it generated from research on animals could be generalized to human behavior. The program limited its investigation to external, publicly observable data, such as the number of times a bird pecked at a colored circle at various rates relative to the timing and schedule for the administration of food pellets.

With the turn to cognitive science, the center of interest changed to internal mental processing, particularly human cognitive functioning. The confrontation between cognitive science and behaviorism came over the theory of language acquisition. The primary spokesperson for behaviorism, B. F. Skinner, believed that the acquisition of language followed the general laws of learning discovered by behavioral research. Noam Chomsky objected to this explanation and proposed that the syntactical core of any language is so complicated and so specific in its form—so unlike other kinds of knowledge—that no child could learn it unless he already had the form of grammar programmed in his mind.[28]

Cognitive psychology was about the acquisition, organization, and use of knowledge. Its research programs were based on the notion that behavior is the result of complex internal or mental processes, and these have to be included if one is to explain and account for the variety of human responses to apparently the same stimulus. Because cognitive psychology understood that the internal cognitive processes within the organism were crucial to understanding human beings, it was called the stimulus-organism-response (S-O-R) model. The topics it dealt with were: recognition of visual and speech patterns, encoding and recall of information from memory, monitoring processes—such as attention, language structure and processing; the structure of categories; and the use of reasoning in problem solving and decision making.

In the cognitive model, stimuli do not affect human knowledge in their original form as energy waves or chemical molecules. Instead, the stimuli are taken in and compared to internal patterns and organized by various mental activities into meaningful and useful information. The information that people experience and use to make decisions is the result of this cognitive processing. Kenneth Gergen describes the epistemological implications that follow from conceiving of experience as a construction by mental processes that match and operate on environmentally generated stimuli:

> What we take to be experience of the world does not in itself dictate the terms by which the world is understood. What we take to be knowledge of the world is not a product of induction, or of the building and testing of general hypotheses. The mounting criticism of the positivist-empiricist conception of knowledge has severely damaged the traditional view that scientific theory serves to reflect or map reality in any direct or decontextualized manner.[29]

Experience is constructed when a person assimilates the stimuli and matches them with his or her existing structural representations of events which are judged to be similar to the input event.

One of the areas of research that has retained a central place in the program of cognitive psychology is the acquisition and understanding of language. The basic model was developed by Chomsky. In the model, people possess an internal understanding of grammar that is used to generate an infinite number of well-formed sentences by means of which they understand the meaning of spoken and written language. Although his particular descriptions of the internal grammars have been challenged, as has his notion that these grammars are innate,[30] the basic conception of an organized cognitive system that generates speech and acts as the interpreter of language continues to hold.

Research programs have now moved beyond individual sentences to groups of sentences that are linked together into discourses and conversations, with particular attention to how grammars for these larger linguistic groups are acquired.[31] One of the discourses that has been of special interest is narrative. The main research questions are: (1) What is the basic structure of narrative discourse? and (2) What is the process by means of which children gain the capacity to tell and understand narratives? Most of the research on narrative skills is in the tradition of experimental psychology and has been aimed at the identification of the mental structures that are used to comprehend written and oral narratives. The research has supported the belief that people assimilate input, particularly textual input, to an acquired, organized internal representation of a narrative grammar.[32] When people who do not have an explicit understanding of story structure are asked to tell stories, they use the common narrative pattern. When people are asked if a set of experimentally prepared episodes make up a story, they can distinguish those that do from those that do not. The research has investigated how this is possible and has sought to determine the precise structure of narrative that operates to inform people about what narrative is.[33]

The investigation of organizing structures in psychology parallels the search for structures in literary theory described in the previous chapter. The two disciplines differ, however, in the topics emphasized. The psychological investigations have attended to the acquisition and use of narrative structures by children and to the effect these structures have on memory and reading skills. Literary theory has emphasized the structure of written prose narratives.

Jean Mandler's work is representative of the approach of cognitive psychology to cognitive structures in general and to narrative structure in particular.[34] Mandler holds that knowledge is not an enumeration of discontinuous facts, rather that it is an organized and structured composition of facts according to particular patterns. She proposes four kinds of structures that organize particular bits of information into knowledge—the categorical or taxonomic, the matrix, the serial, and the schematic. In the *categorical* or *taxonomic* knowledge structure, facts are related according to a shared similarity of form, function, or other aspect; for example, taxonomic knowledge about an individual animal is created by locating it in a particular category, such as feline, through the size and shape it shares with other known members of this category. *Matrix knowledge,* which is related to categorical knowledge, is organized through a matrix structure and is characterized by class intersection. It is formed by overlaying several independent categories; for example, knowledge about tigers or lions would be derived from the intersection of the categories of which they are members, such as ferocious and feline. In *serial knowledge,* items are described in terms of their connection to one another along a unidirectional dimension. The letters of the alphabet and chronologically ordered historical events are forms of serially organized knowledge. *Schematic knowledge* is organized according to a part-whole configuration. For example, a window, a door, a ceiling, and walls are known schematically as parts of a room and are related to one another through being parts of a collection which makes up a whole. Whereas in categorical knowledge each entity is an example of the class through which it is known—a tiger is an example of the class of felines—in a schematic organization, the entity is known through its participation in the collection—the tiger is a part of the jungle scene, not merely an example of the scene. Events or entities can be known in various formats—that is, a particular tiger can be known as a member of the feline category *and* as part of the scene viewed. Mandler uses research on memory and recall to support her fourfold notion of knowledge structures. She understands that the four structures encode and store information according to different formats and that the variations in time required to learn and recall information organized by these formats are the result of distinct strategies of organization.

Formal science uses the first kind of knowledge organization, categorical knowledge, in its approach to elements of information. Formal science generates a set of statements that describe the regularities and relationships existing between and among various categorically arranged data. Categories are organized around either prototypical examples or defining attributes.[35] In a prototypically organized category, particulars are included if they are like the exemplar; for example, objects that resemble a robin are known as birds. Categories organized around prototypes do not have sharply defined boundaries, and thus it is not always possible to determine whether an object should or should not be included in the category. For example, penguins, albatrosses, and ostriches are dissimilar enough from robins to raise questions about their suitability for inclusion with robins in the category of "bird." Because of the lack of clear inclusion-exclusion principles of naturally functioning protoype categories, formal science knowledge often requires the translation of prototypically organized categories into defining attribute categories in which inclusion in the category is determined by a technical definition.

By using closed or operationalized definitions of categories, formal science can make use of the principles of relationship which are described by formal logic and its mathematical expressions. Relationships between categories can be described within principles of logical validity and can yield lawful explanations of past events and a prediction of future interactions under given conditions. By requiring that the subject matter of research be converted into a format of attribute categories so that it can be treated by mathematical and logical operations, formal science removes much information from its consideration. Although this information is often too subtle for scientific treatment of this sort, it can be essential for understanding human experience.

Narrative knowing is able to structure information according to the schematic format. As Mandler has pointed out, schematically organized knowledge can be related either spatially, as when one collects and comes to know the aspects as parts of a spatial whole (such as a whole room, for instance), or temporally, as when one links together various events to make a story or a narrative. The temporal, schematic linking of events as narrative is the kind of knowing that is used to understand personal action and autobiography.[36] It is the format people use to organize their understandings of each other as biographies and case histories. Thus, this format is of particular importance for the human disciplines.

Schematic knowing is different from serial knowing because the schematic strategy contains the notion of a whole or theme that pulls together and configures the bits of information into a systemic relationship: a "scene" in the case of spatial schemas,[37] a "plot" in the case of temporal schemas. The configuring whole is termed a "plot." In the serial ordering of temporally occurring events, by contrast, the information is merely placed along a time line from the earliest to the latest occurrence. The determinative characteristic is the timing of the event, not its significance or its contribution to a plot or a theme. Serial knowing ends with a list or chronicle of events without any relationship to a theme or unifying notion.

Mandler holds that "stories have an underlying, or base structure that remains relatively invariant in spite of gross differences in content from story to story. This structure consists of a number of ordered constituents."[38] She proposes that a story sequence begins with a setting in which the narrator introduces the characters, the location, and the time in which the story takes place. After the setting has been established, the story proceeds with one or more episodes, each of which has a beginning and a development. In an opening episode, the character, reacting to the beginning events, sets a goal and outlines a path to attain the goal. Each episode includes the outcome of the attempts to reach the goal and assumes that the attempts are understood as the causes that bring about the outcome. After the outcome is given, the episode ends, and the ending links the episode to the whole story. After the whole series of episodes has been presented, the narrative includes ending portions which show that the episodes coalesce into one story.

This structure already is available as a cognitive configuring device when people come across a text. They therefore expect the text to conform to the structure, and they assume that it will assemble the elements they hear into a coherent story.

The kind of research used to demonstrate the operation of story structure is similar to that used by psychologists to study language structures. One research program presents participants with a variety of text segments which represent some but not all of the segments that should be present according to the inherent structure. Participants are then asked whether the segments should be classified as a story and are told to indicate on a scale the extent to which they would judge that the collection of segments manifests "storiness." In an investigation of this sort, Stein and Policastro[39] found that the segments must include at least an animate protagonist and some type of causal sequence before they will be considered a story. Those passages with all the parts of an episode were always rated higher than those passages containing permissible deletions of any category information. Other studies of memory processes are used to demonstrate the function of narrative structure. Stories are better retrieved which include material representing all of the properly sequenced parts of the story. It has been noted that readers take more time to process the first sentence of a narrative episode than they do the second sentence of the episode.[40]

The specification of the general ingredients of stories has turned out to be more difficult than was initially supposed by investigators. Stein and Policastro have argued that no single structural definition can account for the wide range of compositions people accept as stories. Their research has showed that, although people can readily distinguish good stories from poor ones, they still accept as stories compositions that are deficient in many of the ways required by the proposed structural models. The researchers cannot establish a "rigid recipe" of what counts as a story. They propose that our concept of story consists of a prototype and its variants. The prototypical story identifies a protagonist and, a predicament, attempts to resolve the predicament, then the outcomes of such attempts, the reactions of the protagonists to the situation, and the causal relationships among each of the elements in the story.[41]

This research shows the importance of narrative for organizing experience into stories. The process of seeing human actions as meaningful sequences of events linked together in a causal chain requires cognitive skill, judgment, and the application of previous experiences. When the story-making process is successful, it provides a coherent and plausible account of how and why something has happened. The story schema can be applied to almost all events in our social life—to any person or incident in the past, present, or future. The reasoning about cause and consequence in this variety of events requires only one kind of structural design and one mode of thought.

The typical person will impose a story structure on a variety of input, and this appears to hold true in widely diverse cultures.[42] Most people can use rudiments of story structure before they are four years old. The story grammar, unlike the syntax of languages, is easily understood by almost any person who speaks a language. Culturally different people experience each other's stories with causal assumptions about human actions that display similar understanding. The widespread capacity to tell and understand stories, together with its appearance at such an early stage of individual and cultural development, has highlighted the issue about how this structure is acquired. Thus, in addition to the study of the general structure and function of narrative, cognitive psychologists have been interested in the acquisition and development of narrative skills by children.

As described in the last chapter, one proposal for how language and narrative structures are acquired was developed by Lévi-Strauss and Chomsky, who held that these structures are developments from deep innate organizing patterns that are part of the human brain structure. This proposal was expanded by R. Fuller to include narrative patterns, when he related the functioning of the story grammar to the evolution and organization of the brain. "If story is the basis of intellectual cohesion," he said, "it could be the engram of our species."[43] However, the more accepted position is that narrative structures, although dependent on basic human capacities, are acquired by abstraction from experiences. According to Mandler: "From an early age we hear a particular class of stories with highly similar structure and we gradually form an abstract representation of that structure."[44] Mancuso proposes that the narrative structure develops epigenetically out of the basic schemata identified by Jean Piaget as the concepts of cause and time.[45]

Susan Kemper has presented a review of previous research on narrative development in children, as well as a report of her own research findings.[46] Kemper proposes that stories serve to function as entertainments and as explanations of actions. They transmit cultural and individual traditions, values, and moral codes, "explicat[ing] observable actions and events in terms of unobservable goals and motives, thought and emotions."[47] She reports that storytelling is one of the first uses of language, a gradually mastered skill that is first developed in the third year and continues to develop gradually in sophistication through the eleventh year. In developing narrative competence, children learn to produce and comprehend causally and temporally structured plots that are organized around a variety of themes and involve a large number of characters.

Kemper has analyzed the development of narrative competence on three dimensions: the content of the stories, the use of patterns in plot structures, and the use of causal structures. The content of children's stories is drawn from their own experiences, but the predominant theme is violence.[47] She reports two stages in the development of plot structure. The first stage, which is completed by age six, is characterized by the mastery of simple stories focused on a dyadic event: something happens and the protagonist responds. The second stage continues until age ten, by which time the basic plot structures have been mastered. Here children elaborate on the basic dyadic event to include additional events which are embedded in the overall theme and provide the background information necessary for understanding and appreciating the story. The use of causal structures begins, primarily, with lists of characters' actions without cause or consequence. Between the ages of two and eight, children gradually master the ability to tell stories of causally connected sequences of events; ultimately they are able to include not only the mental states that initiate actions but also physical states that initiate thoughts, emotions, and cognitions. In order to tell a story, a child has to be able to describe the events in such a way that the listener can follow the chain of causality. This involves explaining a character's motives, the circumstances that make some actions possible and render others impossible, and the consequences of the character's actions. By age ten, children have mastered the ability to tell causally well-formed stories.[49]

Life-span development

Three books published during the later 1970s brought the study of life-span development to public attention. Gail Sheehy's *Passages: Predictable Crisis in Adult Life*[50] was a popularization of the research on adult development and followed along the lines of prior investigations later published by Daniel Levinson and Roger Gould.[51] The life-span perspective in developmental psychology, another relatively recent area of investigation, is an attempt to extend the domain of development psychology to the entire life course. The principles used to study childhood development, however, have not been held to be as useful for understanding adult changes.

The maturational changes of infancy, childhood, and adolescence were thought to occur in a universal ontogenetic sequence paralleled by universal stages in psychological development. For example, it was reasoned that, while there is some variation in the age at which walking or talking begins or the age of first menstruation, both sequence and timing are relatively predictable within broad bounds. Also, in a given culture, it can be expected that children or adolescents will, at any given age, be working at the same set of developmental tasks. These tasks will represent the intersection of biological readiness and social institutions. For example, six-year-olds in one culture may be starting school while six-year-olds in another culture will be learning to hunt.

The life-span perspective recognizes the need to search for a general sequence of change over the entire life course, even though there are no biological maturational markers (the menopause in women is considered the only universal biological maturational change in adulthood)[52] and even though social roles in a pluralistic society are extremely diverse. The developmental sequence is controlled by some givens—for example, one cannot become a parent before puberty or, under our legal system, contract a marriage independent of parental consent before reaching the age of political majority.

Within these very broad bounds, however, there is much possible variation and no single sequence of roles. A first marriage and parenthood may occur at twenty or forty. The peak of a career will occur early for some (professional athletes, musicians, and mathematicians) and later for others (artists, writers, social scientists). Moreover, the sequence of roles can vary: the first marriage may be followed by a second, career peaks may be followed by career changes. Thus, consideration of the entire life cycle is complicated by the absence in adulthood of a biological maturation timetable and by the great variety in social roles.

One of the most influential early works that used the concept of development over the life cycle was Erik Erikson's *Childhood and Society,* published in 1950.[53] Erikson expanded Freud's ontogenetic sequence of childhood stages of development to include the entire life cycle, and offered an explicit recognition of the individual's interaction with the social context. Erikson's description of the stages added new concepts to life-span theory for which there was no Freudian equivalent: identity versus role confusion, when the young adult tries to find a place in society; generativity versus stagnation, when responsibility for the next generation can be taken on; and ego integrity versus despair, when one's own life cycle is completed and the life course can be reviewed.

Despite Erikson's theoretical work, life-span developmental psychology has had difficulty in describing personal continuity across the life course. Predictability of the changes that an adult will move through is very difficult because of the complexity of the variables. Kenneth Gergen has proposed that the attempts to account for stability and ordered change in adult development are unsuccessful because of the role that chance plays in adult changes. Assuming an "aleatoric" perspective, he concludes that "human development trajectories may be virtually infinite in their variegation" and questions the applicability of the tenets of formal science for the investigation of human change over time.[54]

Mark Freeman has proposed that life-span investigations should not attempt to predict what sequences adults will move through so much as explain in retrospect why a particular development would have occurred.[55] Freeman points out that when one looks forward to what will happen, events seem to occur with a kind of stochastic unraveling in time, but when one looks back over the same events, they appear to possess a certain inevitability and seem not to be the result of chance at all.

> That intrinsically different forms of knowledge can be derived retrospectively than is possible prospectively is "just" an ontological fact. Therefore, given the inevitable variability inherent in human development owing to the multiple determination of our intentions, it seems evident that a viable science of the life course must admit the necessity of adopting a fundamentally retrospective perspective for at least a portion of the questions it addresses—a willingness to entertain the possibilities of aposteriority.[56]

The retrospective analysis of life events is the kind of study carried out by historians, and it requires the use of a narrative structure if an analysis is to be an explanation instead of a mere chronological listing. Two critiques of the retrospective approach to life-span investigations have been made. The first critique concerns the temptation not to be content with merely recounting a person's past but to want to systematize life events. Freeman's answer is to point out that aposteriority need not be unsystematic, and for evidence he calls on numerous historical investigations that have systematized past events. Because the life-span researcher is dealing with somewhat more recurrent phenomena than history at large, there is reason to assume that systematization or generalization may be possible. The second critique involves the problem of interpretation and the validity of the generalizations that can be drawn. Freeman sees that this problem is no different from a problem involving prospective research, because the choice of categories used to gather or systematize data is always an interpretive task. In any case, while no one particular systematization of data can be said, ultimately, to be purely objective and correct, one can choose from among the plausible alternatives whatever is most likely. Despite the fact that there can be no certainty, an intersubjective consensus minimizes the likelihood of arbitrariness or even outright falsity in interpretation. Freeman says that it is important to note that "the study of the life course is, of necessity, not only a historical form of inquiry, but one which demands the acknowledgement of its narrative structure . . . It is, in a distinct sense, an ongoing story to be told."[57]

Historical narrative explains by looking back on past events to see a pattern in their unfolding. Although narrative can be used in other ways—for example, to give form to personal identity or to see through the imagination a narrative written in the future about the events one is thinking about carrying out in the present—it is basically retrospective. Its datum is what has happened, and its analysis is the configuration of past events into a meaningful theme. Thus, its approach is different from the approach of formal science, which is primarily interested in explanation and the prediction of future events.[58] In the formal science model, explanation of the past is merely the "turning upside down" of prediction of the future. Just as events will occur because of the lawfulness of behavior, so have they occurred in the past because of this same lawfulness. Narrative explanation, in contrast, comprehends patterns in actions and events that could not have been predicted in advance, and it does this by looking back over what has happened.

Freeman uses an example from Michael Scriven to illustrate the kind of explanation that is uncovered through retrospective narration. Only when a man has murdered his wife do we know something especially significant about him. We may well have detected some instability, maybe even some proclivities toward aggressive action, but we will not necessarily claim that we could have predicted his act, even with the knowledge we have in retrospect. After the act has been committed, however, we are not left completely confused: reasons may be offered, not just as to the immediate cause of the event, but also as to the historical causes. We may appeal to his cruel upbringing, to the fact that he has recently lost his job, and so on. But this historical explanation involves, in addition to establishing the past facts, the necessity of comprehending them in an act of judgment that refers backward and orders the items of evidence, placing them according to their significance into a coherent and acceptable account of how these events have led up to the murder.

In the same manner, we can explain and understand human lives by situating the events that have made them up into a whole pattern of intrinsic relationships. The criterion for historical explanation is its acceptability or intelligibility rather than its predictability. Understanding a narrative explanation is like following a story, where the themes and patterns are retroactively detected among arrays of contingencies.

Freeman addresses the matter of the kind of cause used by narrative as retroactive explanation. He notes that having a good reason for expecting an event is not the same thing as explaining why it happens according to law. The process of "singling out" historical connections requires examining their rational (but not lawlike) necessity within some situation or context, as a sequence of related events that are delimited by the field of expected action. In a narrative reconstruction one can understand that it is reasonable that things have happened the way they did: given the circumstances, one can see why the events occurred. Freeman refers to Mandelbaum's proposal to do away with the Humean version of cause where events are isolated and bounded (pool ball model).[59] Narrative explanation does not focus on how one event is predicted or deduced from another, but on how change from "beginning" to "end" takes place. Life-span events are parts of an ongoing process which culminates in the "effect" to be explained. Although the reason why the life event has occurred does not flow from a deduction of formal logic, the perception of the patterned totality described by narrative brings with it the experience of causal "power." The subjective need to know why something has happened is satisfied when all the events leading up to the occurrence are gathered together in a narrative statement.

If life-span development is to be explored by postdictive or retrodictive study, how are information gathered and conclusions reached? To construct a narrative explanation, one needs to know to which later events certain actions are related. The actor cannot describe these at the time of an action; he or she can only say what is expected to occur and what consequences are hoped for. But the complexities of the situation and the unanticipated consequences enter into the final narrative explanation. Freeman recognizes the problems that arise from using the information that people give from memory. Recollection frequently represents less the actual reproduction of the lived past than an imaginative reconstruction that includes distortion, wishful thinking, and "outcome interference." He poses two options: one is a "depth hermeneutics"—psychoanalysis, for instance— and the other is the juxtaposition of the data of a person's immediate experience with the data of his/her recollection. The first option attempts to unmask the self-deception of recollection through communication laid bare in free association. Freeman, however, believes that this approach has theoretical and practical problems for life-span investigators, and he himself supports the second option. He describes its use as a dialectic between a person's narrative story—how that person has moved through the past to arrive at his/her present position—and that person's best attempts at recalling the actual events of the past.

A life-span psychology based on a retrospective narrative understanding of individuals' pasts could lead to some systematic understanding of the general patterns through which people have passed. This knowledge would not, however, produce predictive laws that would determine how life would be for everyone. As Freeman puts it:

Although narration moves inescapably backward in its concern with the understanding of the past-in-the-present, the view of development that derives from it can retain a focus on the forward movement that is rendered in the texts provided. Thus, perhaps, paradoxically, it is out of retrospection that a project, an approximation toward desired ends, can be revealed. The shape that emerges out of the past extends itself into the future. It is this temporal dialogue which can lay the foundation for a new conceptualization of life-span developmental knowledge.[60]

Two exemplary studies related to life-span narrative by Kenneth and Mary Gergen demonstrate investigative strategies. The first study explored how members of two American subcultures, namely, adolescents and the elderly, characterize their life histories.[61] Twenty-nine youths between the ages of 19 and 21 were asked to chart their life history along a general evaluative dimension, and seventy-two persons ranging in age from 63 to 93 were interviewed about their general sense of well-being during various periods of life. Analysis of the data showed that the set of young adults reported a romantic story line for their lives, that is, "on the average these young adults tend to view their lives as happy at an early age, then beset with difficulty during the adolescent years, but now on an upward swing that promises well for the future." In contrast, the typical narrative of the older person was an inverted rainbow, that is, "the young adult years were difficult, but a progressive narrative enabled a peak of well-being to be achieved somewhere between the ages of 50-60"; however, they reported that since that time their lives had regressed. Gergen and Gergen are cautious in their interpretation, pointing out that the findings parallel the typical narrative formations given in our society for these ages.

The second study addressed the issue of the social embedding of self-narrative.[62] The Gergens' position is: "Although the object of self-narrative is the single self, it would be a mistake to view such constructions as the product or possession of single selves." As a test of their thesis Gergen and Gergen carried out a project analyzing conversations which began with one person expressing an emotion (for example, "I am angry at you"). Gergen and Gergen found that the ensuing mutually constructed story at each choice point followed a typical pattern of a choice among three intelligible alternatives—remorse, reframing, and anger. If remorse was chosen, it led to a compassionate or cautious response; if reframing, the scenario usually continued; if anger, hostility was escalated. Gergen and Gergen's investigation sought to identify the socially given patterns that inform the stories that people produce together. Their general findings about lived narrative as relational scenarios were:

First, we found that the actor's capacities for intelligibility are embedded within a socio-historical context; in the telling of a story the actor is relying on certain features of a pre-existing social order. In this sense it would be plausible to say that the culture is speaking through the actor, using the actor to reproduce itself. Further, we found that self-narratives depend on the mutual sharing of symbols, socially acceptable performances, and continued negotiation. Finally, we found that narratives typically require the interweaving of identities, and thus, the support of others within the social sphere of interaction.[63]

People use self-stories to interpret and account for their lives. The basic dimension of human existence is temporality, and narrative transforms the mere passing away of time into a meaningful unity, the self. The study of a person's own experience of her or his life-span requires attending to the operations of the narrative form and to how this life story is related to the stories of others.

Freudian psychoanalysis and narrative

We have seen earlier how psychoanalytic theory has been introduced into the study of literary narrative. It has been used to account for the basic story lines of novels as representing psychoanalytic developmental stages (Marthe Robert), and it has been used to interpret wishes and fears expressed in narratives through reception theory (Norman Holland). My concern here is to note the important contribution Freud made to narrative theory. Donald Spence opens his book *Narrative Truth and Historical Truth,* with this statement:

> [Freud] was a master at taking pieces of the patient's associations, dreams, and memories and weaving them into a coherent pattern that is compelling, persuasive, and seemingly complete, a pattern that allows us to make important discoveries about the patient's life and to make sense out of previously random happenings. Freud's most impressive achievements ... are lasting accomplishments of innovative synthesis ... Freud made us aware of the persuasive power of a coherent narrative—in particular, of the way in which an aptly chosen reconstruction can fill the gap between two apparently unrelated events and, in the process, make sense out of non-sense. There seems no doubt but that a well-constructed story possesses a kind of narrative truth that is real and immediate and carries an important significance for the process of therapeutic change.[64]

Freud and the early generations of his students accepted a close kinship between psychoanalysis and literature, and they drew from literature both stimulation and confirmation. And Freud often presented his theories through case studies in narrative form.

Roy Schafer has described psychoanalysts as "people who listen to the narrations of analysands and help them to transform these narrations into others that are more complete, coherent, convincing, and adaptively useful than those they have been accustomed to constructing."⁶⁵ Freud has contributed two important conclusions about narrative that are of general significance. The first, which is in accord with a point made by the historians, is that the meaning of an event can be radically dependent on what happens later. It may be true that an event was meaningless and inconsequential when it occurred, and it may also be true that it later became all-important. The second conclusion is an extension of the first. A crucial experience in a patient's life, which the psychoanalyst only with difficulty may succeed in eliciting, may not even have occurred; this does not, however, alter its crucial importance. In view of the retrospective character of all narrative and the inseparability of the self from its story, the event is a necessary hypothesis for understanding, regardless of whether it is factual or fictional.

Schafer argues that, in general, Freudian theory makes narrative the preferred mode of explanation. He says that Freud's "major misconception was that psychoanalysis is a new natural science,"⁶⁶ that psychoanalysis is not primarily about scientific laws of the form "if X, then Y." Psychoanalytic understanding involves reconstructing a story, tracing a phenomenon to its origins, and seeing how one thing leads to another. Freud's case histories were narratives with reconstructed plots. Each one presented a sequence in the patient's life, but the episodes of that life were presented in the order in which they appeared in Freud's conduct of the case. A case study, like a narrative, leads to the revelation of a decisive event in a patient's life which, when placed in the true sequence of events, can be seen as the (narrative) cause of the patient's present situation.

One of Freud's more dramatic cases is that of the Wolfman.⁶⁷ Through his analysis of key dreams and associations, Freud was led to the conclusion that at the age of one and a half years the child awakened to witness his parents copulating. Freud reconstructed a sequence of events that began with the decisive "primal scene" and included the transformation of the memory into a trauma at age four. Although Freud had constructed the event from the patient's discourse, he argued that the event must actually have taken place in order for it to have caused the neurosis. "It must therefore be left at this (I can see no other possibility): either the analysis based on the neurosis in his childhood is all a piece of nonsense from start to finish, or else everything took place just as I have described it above."⁶⁸ Freud held to the priority of the events and their causal efficacy. He was committed to the notion that there must be an intelligible and motivated pattern that is eventually accessible to human detection. If something is happening in the present, it must be possible to go back and recover the event that has set things in motion.

Later, though, Freud came to see that perhaps an actual primal event need not have happened. Brooks calls this admission "one of the most daring moments of Freud's thought, and one of his most heroic gestures as a writer."[69] In place of the event we would have a primal fantasy, the product of meanings. To account for the present feelings of guilt, the narrative constructs an event in the past to explain why the guilt is present. The importance of the past becomes dependent on the present situation. For example, present guilt attributes a signficance and causal efficacy to possible early sexual experiences, even though they would have occurred before there was any understanding of sex and meant nothing at the time. In light of the present guilt feelings, the possible incidents are reinterpreted and become so painful that they are repressed. Brooks recognizes the significance of Freud's acknowledgement of the possibility of fantasy events:

> We have at this crucial moment of the case history an apparent evacuation of the problem of origins, substituting for a founding event a phantasy or fiction on which is conferred all the authority and force of prime mover, and the evocation of a possible infinite regress in the unconsciousness of the race. This "solution" might appear irresponsible, an abandonment of all distinction between the fictional and the nonfictional, might indeed appear to build into Freud's explanatory account a kind of self-destruct mechanism.[70]

Jonathan Culler understands that the tension Freud uncovered between the deed and the word had the effect of deconstructing the notion that actual facts have precedence over the meaning attached to them. This tension brings into question the assumption that prior events cause succeeding events. The order of understanding has been inverted: the past is now understood as meaningful because of the present, and the concept of cause appears as a rhetorical imposition. The narrative operates to find causes for present conditions, or for experienced pain or guilt. Freud did not abandon the notion of the primacy of the event in producing the effect, but neither did he abandon the idea that the present operates to reinterpret meaningless past events in order to give them a force of causation they did not originally have. He maintained that the two logics—one which insists on the causal efficacy of origins and the other which treats events as the products of meanings—must exist side by side.

A person in the present can differ from his or her previous manifestations, and an early experience can now have a different meaning than it had when it occurred. The change in meaning comes from a reconfiguration that is possible in the narrative process. Freud's conclusions support the notion of the power of the realm of meaning in human existence. Human beings are not simply constructions based on past events; they are also products of narrative structures. They exist in narrative creations and are powerfully affected by them. The implications of these insights from Freud will be treated again in the chapter "Practice and Narrative," and their use in psychotherapy will be considered.

Organizational consultation

Increased interest has recently been shown by organizational consultants in the realm of meaning and in the symbolic aspects of organized settings.[71] Narrative structures operate to give significance and unity to group events in a manner similar to the way they operate in the lives of persons. Linda Smircich, a developer of the idea of organizations as cultures, described culture as a network of meanings: "The emergence of social organization depends on the emergence of shared interpretive schemes, expressed in language and other symbolic constructions that develop through social interaction. Such schemes provide the basis for shared systems of meaning that allow day-to-day activities to become routinized or taken for granted."[72] The notion of organizational change or transformation is linked to the concept of change in an association's realm of meaning, that is, its culture, which is expressed through the particular narratives that carry and create the meaning that informs the group.[73] The narratives—also called organizational myths, stories, sagas, and legends—function to help members to interpret and signify the purpose of the organization and the role of its individual members. The group narrative provides information about norms and values, and it fulfills a number of functions within an association—reduction of tension, concealment of power plays, the mediation of contradictions between theory and practice and between group and individual needs, and building of bridges between the past and the present.

Seven forms of narrative have been identified as occurring in a wide variety of organizations:[74] (1) a story about rule breaking in which a high-status manager breaks a rule which a low-ranking employee must then enforce; (2) a story concerning the amount of humanity and respect the boss displays in relationships with lower-status employees; (3) a story about the possibility of a deserving employee being rewarded by promotion within the company; (4) stories about how an organization responds when faced with the possibility of firing or laying off employees; (5) stories dealing with the question of how much help an organization will provide for its employees when they have to move often; (6) stories about how the boss reacts to mistakes; and (7) stories about how the organization deals with obstacles. Each story has positive and negative versions, which invariably express the tensions that arise from a conflict between organizational needs and the values of individual employees. These tensions concern the issues of equality versus inequality in the organization (the use of hierarchical power), security versus insecurity, and control versus lack of control.

When these stories or episodes become linked together in a more inclusive narrative, the organization's basic theme or identity is established. This basic narrative organizes episodes and events into a primary interpretive scheme for the organization. In a recent issue of the *Administrative Quarterly Review*, devoted to organizational culture, a number of organizational consultants described methods they have developed for clarifying the interpretive schemes that operate at deeper levels of an organization.[75] As an aid to problem solving and planning, for example, Mitroff and Killman had managers tell stories about an ideal organization; they then clustered the managers according to four Jungian-based personality styles.[76] Managers with similar personality scores were introduced and asked to conceptualize the "problem" from their perspectives. Afterward, the four groups met, presented their points of view, and worked toward an integrated solution. The process helped the managers to become more sensitive to "other ways of perceiving and analyzing organizational disturbances and problems."

Narratives can promote the work of an organization by providing a common understanding of its values and purposes. Because of its temporal quality, the narrative retains the organization's continuity and consistency in times of ambiguity and change; but it can also be maladaptive over time. Narratives appropriate for new and struggling organizations are not as effective in giving coherence during later developmental stages. Because of the continuity they provide, organizational narratives are difficult to change. An organizational consultant cannot bring about a change in a narrative simply by pointing out how it no longer fits the actual operation of the organization itself. The consultant can assist, however, in the emergence of a new narrative that is more integrative and that addresses the tensions of the organization better than the old one.

This brief section gives only a hint of recent developments in understanding and working with organizations. Research strategies are being explored which address the meaning schemes through which organizations configure their "existence."[77] The narrative is a basic form of coherence for an organization's realm of meaning, just as it is for a person's realm of meaning. Organizational consultants are turning their attention to the power and importance of the narratives for the groups with which they work. The understanding of narrative structures and configurational processes can assist in this work.

The human disciplines had only peripheral interest in the study of narrative before the 1960s debates in history about the nature of narrative explanation. In the 1970s, literary criticism came to the fore with its interest in structure and communication theory. With the 1980s, psychology along with other human sciences, has begun to turn its attention to narrative. Psychological studies are taking place in the context of a general interest in cognitive contributions to the construction of experience. Narrative is the primary scheme by which human beings take form. Thus, in the understanding of human existence—both individual lives and organizational "lives"—narrative has a central role. The human sciences (the behavioral and social sciences), with their tradition of quantitative research, are not yet comfortable with dealing directly with the linguistic rationality by which narrative operates. However, for the human sciences to gain a full appreciation and comprehension of human experience and behavior, narrative approaches will be required.

CHAPTER VI

Human Existence and Narrative

T HE three previous chapters have reviewed the treatment of narrative by the disciplines of history, literary theory, and psychology. This chapter, on theory, and the next, on practice, pull together the themes developed in those earlier chapters and supplements them with Heidegger's investigations. The purpose is to assemble a narrative theory for the practice of the human disciplines.

According to a narrative theory of human existence, a study needs to focus its attention on existence as it is lived, experienced, and interpreted by the human person. This interpretation finally involves the processes of language, as well as the order of meaning, which interacts with and brings to language the physical and organic orders.

Heidegger has proposed that human experience in its original form is hermeneutically meaningful.[1] Narrative is a primary scheme by means of which hermeneutical meaningfulness is manifested. A theory of human existence that can inform the practice of the human sciences will need to make explicit the centrality of narrative in human experience and existence. The first section of the chapter attends to the function of narrative in levels of temporality as they appear in human experience, and the second section develops an understanding of human action as it is configured in the temporal order by narrative. The final section deals with the role of narrative in the definition of self and personal identity.

The object of inquiry for the human disciplines is the human being, and in order for these disciplines to function properly as generators of knowledge about their subject, they must have knowledge tools that can respond to the particular characteristics of human beings. The development of formal science during the Enlightenment was based on the notion that reality, including human beings, was ultimately located on a plane consisting of objects whose actions and reactions were governed by stable laws: In this perspective, human existence was considered to be simply one object among others—a corrective to the revelatory notion that the nature of human existence was primarily spiritual and was governed by a relationship to God rather than by the laws of nature. Yet the Enlightenment definition of human existence was overly reductive. It neglected the significance of language for the understanding the human realm. In order to be cogent, the human sciences need to develop a theory that attends to all the strata of human existence.

As mentioned in Chapter 1, Maurice Merleau-Ponty and Stephan Strasser have claimed that human existence is made up of interacting layers of reality that extend from the objective plane of the physical realm to the linguistic plane of expression. Integration of these various layers is part of the expressive activity and is ordered according to linguistic characteristics. The linguistic realm is not a place; it is a kind of activity. It is the ongoing process of creating meaning for existence—a process similar to the creation of meaning that is reflected when a person speaks a sentence or writes a poem. Thus, being human is more a type of meaning-generating activity than a kind of object. It is an incarnated or embodied making of meaning—that is, it is primarily an expressive form of being.

Narrative is one of the forms of expressiveness through which life events are conjoined into coherent, meaningful, unified themes. From one perspective human existence manifests itself as simply an ongoing sequence of activities linked together into a single life. Yet these activities are marked according to different segments of time. Short-time-span activities, which are identified as separate events, are understood to be the result of conscious or unconscious purposes; they include such events as thinking, feeling, and moving the body. Other activities are marked according to long segments of personal time; these include such developmental changes as the move from childhood into adulthood. The temporality of human experience is punctuated not only according to one's own life (for example, one's fiftieth birthday) but also according to one's place within the long-time-spans of history and social evolution (e.g., the 1980s). Narrative is the mode of meaning construction that displays these various experiences of time.

Narrative and temporality

In the objective view of reality constructed by the formal science or the Enlightenment, the world was pictured as space filled with meaningless objects that moved through a time plane which made up the present moment. By abstracting objective time and space from the original human experience of the world, one could, it was thought, derive a more accurate depiction of the world as it really is. Thus the hierarchical organization of original experience was torn down and reorganized to fit a grid of formal logic, and meaning was shorn off the appearance of objects in awareness. According to Merleau-Ponty and Heidegger original human experience is multilayered, hermeneutically organized, and abundantly meaningful, and the reduction of this original experience to create an Enlightenment image of how reality actually is, independent of human experience, has produced a representation of time that is extremely thin compared to the thick and varied appearance of time in human experience.

The sources of the temporal features of reality as experienced are found in the temporalizing activity of human beings, namely, narrative production.[2] It is the purpose of this section to explore the role of narrative in producing the human experience of time. This will be attempted in three steps: first, by showing that the human experience of time does not conform to the objective notion of time as a series of instants along a line; second, through a discussion of Heidegger's extensive analysis of a multilayered time experience; third, by presenting the place of narrative in the production and reproduction of the multilayered human experience of time.

Time as a series of moments

The experience and interpretation of time is a basic and dominant theme of human reality. Narrative is able to structure and organize time according to hermeneutic principles and to present time through multiple levels of interpretation. Paul Ricoeur's two-volume work on time and narrative provides a thorough investigation of the way the narrative form organizes language to reflect the human experience of time.[3] It is Ricoeur's basic hypothesis that "between the activity of narrating a story and the temporal character of human experience there exists a correlation that is not merely accidental but that presents a transcultural form of necessity."[4] Time becomes human as it is articulated through narrative. Narrative, he says, attains its full meaning when it becomes a condition of temporal experience.

Before Ricoeur's exploration of human temporality and narrativity is described, however, we must look at several earlier attempts to understand the human experience of time. Time is one of the fundamental and most pervasive phenomena of our lives. Yet, unlike a thing, it cannot be tasted, seen, smelled, heard, or touched. It has remained a perplexing and problematic phenomenon for human understanding.

Tradition has used a thinglike analogy for time, picturing it as instantaneous moments advancing along a geometric line.[5] Time is viewed, in this analogy, as a medium which exists entirely on its own, independent of human awareness. There is a conception that the biological organism has an "internal time clock" which signals various changes in glandular secretions, but this bodily awareness is not part of conscious awareness. The traditional representation presents time as a serial order and as a succession of "nows" that measure the movements of objects across space. Clocks and chronological instruments are used to locate the length of time between events on the time line. This conception, however, neglects the significance of time as a dimension within which human existence takes place. People simply do not experience time as a succession of instants.

William James could not locate the instantaneous present in the process of human experience, so he suggested the notion of the "specious present."[6] James wanted to account for the phenomenon that occurs when one hears a series of sounds as a melody or as a whole sentence. The specious present is not a knife-edge which a present moment passes through. It is a period of breadth or thickness of time (six to twelve seconds) in which experience unites previous moments of awareness with anticipated moments of awareness.

Edmund Husserl, acknowledging his debt to James, produced a full phenomenological investigation of inner time experience. Like James, he insisted that the experience of time is not limited to a momentary now. He saw the consciousness of time as a primal impression of a streaming present surrounded by an awareness of immediate "retention" of the past and immediate "protention" of the future. He identified "retention" as the active recollection of memories and "protention" as the active expectation of imagined results. Husserl presented a diagram that showed the awareness of a previous present moment sinking steadily out of awareness over time until it becomes sedimented and accessible only through acts of recollection.[7]

Another philosopher of the same period who challenged the notion of time as a series of instantaneous "nows" was Henri Bergson. Bergson believed that reality is continuous and that dividing it, as the Enlightenment did, into categories, falsifies it. Bergson held that there are two different ways of knowing—objectification and intuition. Objectification is the process of knowledge acquisition that is used by formal science. Intuition, in contrast, is a way of knowing through direct experience without concepts, through a kind of "intellectual sympathy" where the object of inquiry is experienced in its uniqueness before it is located and given a name within a category. When one uses intuition to become aware of one's experience, one does not find an awareness filled with objects that change; one finds "duration," or the experience of change itself, in which the past infiltrates the present. Bergson said that becoming intuitively aware of duration is difficult, and at best it is only momentary. The experience is also wholly private and incommunicable through a language of concepts. Nevertheless Bergson attempted to write about the experience of duration: "Duration is the continuous progress of the past which gnaws into the future and which swells as it advances. . . . Memories, messengers from the unconscious, remind us of what we are dragging behind us unawares. . . . Doubtless we think with only a small part of our past, but it is with our entire past, including the original bent of our soul, that we desire, will and act."[8] Bergson understood that the self is duration, a flowing, creative, and productive process. Time is not located in an instantaneous moment. Time is a forceful movement that retains its past as it produces a new future.

James, Husserl, and Bergson all sought to explain the difference that exists between the ordinary representation of time, as a line linking mathematical points, and the human experience of time as extended awareness. Augustine had identified a similar difference between measured and experienced time in Book Eleven of his *Confessions*. According to Augustine, the ordinary representation of time was sufficient for defining the time when something happens, for deciding what comes earlier or later, and for knowing how long a certain event has lasted. But it does not take into account the centrality of the present as the actual now in experience, the primacy of the future expectation that exists in the present as the orientation of human desire, or the capacity for recollecting the past in the present. Augustine's suggestion, which was later accepted by Heidegger, was that the present is not singular notion; it is a threefold notion that includes a present about the future—expectation; a present about the past—memory; and a present about the present—attention. Time is constituted not by the movement of objects but by the multiple structure of the threefold present, a structure of human experience. The representation of time in the threefold present retains the notion of time as linear succession, but now it appears as an aspect within experience.

Augustine also introduced two other problems. The first was that time is sometimes experienced as a concordant whole and at other times as splintered and discordant fragments. When time is experienced harmoniously, the three dimensions hold together in a whole—as in the recitation of a poem, where we experience the whole poem despite the fact that part of it is still ahead and another part is already past, and only a phase of the whole is present. But time is not always experienced in such an integrated fashion, with a harmonious interplay of past, present, and future. At times it is a discordant experience, as when we think of the past with regret or nostalgia, making present what can no longer be changed or returned to. By the same token, the future can appear in the present as fearful or hopeful, and the present can appear as a frail, fleeting moment. Augustine's second problem of time for human existence was that the disharmony of time experience is not something that can be overcome. The knowledge is inherent in human awareness that our existence stretches along from birth to death. We cannot step out of time or keep the future from becoming the past. We are radically temporal.

Ricoeur believes that the exploration of narrative can provide a still deeper understanding of the human experience of time and also deal with the problems identified by Augustine. He says that the reciprocal relationship between temporality and narrative is often overlooked by those writing about narrative—both those concerned with the epistemology of history[9] and those concerned with the literary criticism of fictional narrative—because they have taken for granted narrative's place within a temporal framework that represents time by the ordinary conception, as a linear succession of abstract "nows." He acknowledges Husserl's investigation of inner time consciousness but calls it limited because it has overlooked the privileged access that narrative provides for understanding the way we articulate our experience of time.

Multiple experiences of time

Ricoeur uses Heidegger's analysis of human time experience to introduce a description of the way narrative functions in ordering human temporality.[10] Heidegger's important work, *Being and Time,* was a study of the phenomenon of time and its importance to life.[11] Heidegger's primary insight was that experience is organized into strata analogous to a symphony made up of several melodies, each going on at the same time. One of these melodies is the highest or core theme of the symphony, below which the others lie at various distances. Heidegger distinguishes three levels or thematic centers in human consciousness, ranged according to how far they stand out from the plane of ordinary objects and time. In each level of experience, our interaction with the world is interpreted differently, and time receives a particular organization that is related to the level of interpretation. The first level is closest to everyday awareness, but the other two are more deeply hidden in consciousness and require reflection to bring them to awareness.

Heidegger's first level is defined by human presence among the world of objects and is based on the interaction of one's self with objects and with the assignment of significance and importance to some of those objects. At this first level of standing out from the objective plane, we reckon with time, calculate how much time is available to us to do something, and set a time to meet someone, employing such expressions as "have time to," "take the time to," and "to lose time." The ordinary use of verbal tenses and temporal adverbs—such as "then," "after," "later," "earlier," and so on—are oriented toward the datable and public character of this level of time preoccupation.[12] However, this organization of time in experience is merely borrowed from the ordinary representation of time as linear. It is focused on the personal need to get around in the world, and it is organized from that perspective rather than from a neutral, nonperspectival point of view. Even at this first level of temporal experience, there is some notion of our own movement through time: it is already something other than the ordinary representation of time as measurable intervals along a geometric line.

In the next higher level of standing out from the merely objective realm, which he calls "historicality," Heidegger locates an organization of time that still retains some of the notions of time as linear, but they are fewer than at the first level. In this organization, human experience moves from the day-to-day occupation with accomplishing things by a certain time to an awareness of oneself as a being with a past who is existing through time. Three features are emphasized in the experience of time as one's own history: (1) the awareness of the extension of time between birth and death, with its concern with getting things done, (2) the change of emphasis in experience, from the present to the past, looking back, and (3) repetition, which permits the recollection and recovery of past events.

At Heidegger's highest level, that of "temporality," the unique human experience of time is most apparent. Here we become aware of time from the perspective of personal finitude. Understanding that existence has a beginning and an ending, we recognize the self as an expression marked off from the nothingness from which we came and into which we will disappear. We come to see that existence is a unity and that past, present, and future are aspects of our one existence. I am that existence which includes what I have done, what I am doing, and what I will do, and each moment is part of the whole that I am.

Time in narrative

In applying Heidegger's conception of the levels of temporal experience to the analysis of narrativity, Ricoeur first points to the significance of plot in narrative. Plot can be isolated from judgments about the *reference* and content of a story, and to be viewed instead as the *sense* of narrative.[13] And although plot is a structure common to both historical narratives which claim to be true, and fictional stories which are not necessarily grounded on true events, this is often overlooked by writers on history and literature.

As described in Chapter 2, "Narrative Expression", plot refers to the theme of a story that governs and gives significance to the succession of its events. "A plot is a way of connecting event and story. A story is *made out of* events, to the extent that plot makes events *into* a story."[14] To be temporal, an event must be more than a singular occurrence; it must be located in relation to other events that have preceded it or will come after it. The first level of connection is a mere listing of events one after the other, as in a chronicle. This listing reflects the ordinary representation of time as one moment following the other in a linear fashion. By gathering these events together into the unity of a story, the plot makes them stand out from the plane of linear time by giving them significance in relation to other events. Plot combines two dimensions—one chronological, the other nonchronological. The chronological dimension characterizes the story and shows that it is made up of events along the line of time. The nonchronological dimension lifts the events into a configuration so that, scattered though they may be, they form a significant whole. Ricoeur uses Louis Mink's notion of "grasping together" as a description of the configurational act. The act of the plot is to elicit a pattern from a succession, and it involves a kind of reasoning that tacks back and forth from the events to the plot until a plot forms that both respects the events and encompasses them in a whole. The "humblest" narrative is always more than a chronological series of events: it is a gathering together of events into a meaningful story.

Introducing the significance of plot structure in narrative allows Ricoeur to test his hypothesis that the language structure of narrative has temporality as its ultimate reference, and that temporality, as a form of life, reaches expression in narrativity. He is concerned to investigate whether narrative provides models for articulating in a symbolic way the various levels of the human experience of time. He carries out his investigation by relating the analysis of narrative to the different levels of time experience introduced by Heidegger.

a. The *first level* of time experience, which Heidegger called "within-time-ness," involves temporality in relation to: (1) a shift from the abstract; (2) our need to reckon with time in our public interactions; and (3) the context in which we get things done.

(1) The concern with time as present in experience is a shift from the abstract representation of time as a series of "nows," instants that exist along a time line. In our experience at this level, time is gathered around our place in the world and relates to the tasks we want to accomplish. The first function of narrative, then, is to raise time experience from the abstract succession of events to the level of Heidegger's "within-time-ness." When someone starts recounting events in story form, whether as history or as fiction, there is a first-level understanding of time that parallels Heidegger's first level, and it has three characteristics: reckoning with time; public time; and the emphasis on the "now" characteristic.

The art of storytelling places the narrative "in" time. Rather than being reflections on time, stories assume an experience of time. The heroes of stories reckon with time: they have or do not have time for this or for that. The time of the hero is not derived from instruments that measure the progress of time in nature; it is connected instead to personal activity, to the actions of the characters. It is time reflected in the preoccupation with how temporality impinges on the lives and actions of the protagonists and the supporting cast with respect to their accomplishing their goals and purposes.

(2) The second characteristic of within-time-ness is the sense that one person's time for getting things done is a shared time to which others are connected. In narrative, time matters to people acting *together.* Characters agree to get together at a certain time, and their actions are woven together in a common time. Usually the narrative involves more than one character. There is interaction between and among protagonist and antagonists and helpers, and the actions of others in time can affect the success or failure of the quest. This side of public time in the narrative is internal to the story, but the time of the audience that hears or reads the the story is also addressed. This audience is not an anonymous "they" of pure objectivity, for the audience is lifted out of objectivity into significance as the invisible audience. The story is not told to just anyone, but to an audience.

(3) The final trait of within-time-ness is the primacy of the present in the preoccupation with getting things done, a "now" that stands out from the mere movements of serial moments.. Narratives invite a similar lifting out of the "now" into meaningfulness. By emphasizing the notion of heroic quest and the phenomenon of intervention, the narrative medium becomes a discursive expression of the preoccupation to get things done. Ricoeur writes: "These narratives, in fact, represent a person acting, who orients him- or herself in circumstances he or she has not created, and who produces consequences he or she has not intended. This is indeed the time of the 'now that . . . ,' wherein a person is both abandoned and responsible at the same time."[15]

In the story, there is an interplay between the fact that a character is able to act and the fact that he or she is bound to an objective order. At the instant of acting, the character seizes hold of the surrounding circumstances and inserts his or her action into the objective course of things. Narrative describes the phenomenon of intervention, in which a character's power to act is linked to the objective order and its serial time. It is in intervention that the characteristic of within-time-ness, the intersection of the personal and objective orders, is displayed. Thus, the first level of time interpretation telling a story lifts the understanding of time from abstract representation and moves it to an existential understanding of within-time-ness, thereby establishing the notion that time is involved with human actions and passions.

b. The *second level* of Heidegger's descriptions of the human experiences of time, historicity, is also examined by Ricoeur. He again proposes that this level of time experience is related to narrative with its power of emplotment. By configuring episodes into a whole, we can translate the story into one "thought." In this context, thought may assume various meanings, such as the theme of a story, the point of the tale, or the explanation of what a narrative is about.[16] The plot's configuration also imposes "the sense of an ending"[17] in place of the notion of an infinite succession of instants in abstract time representation. Events are pulled out of mere succession into an adventure with a beginning, a middle, and an end. "The flux of time coagulates at certain points, and where it has hardened, has congealed, it is seized by language and takes on literary form."[18] The gathering together of events in a plot does not remove them from time but places them in a higher, historical, understanding of time. In the second hearing of a story, the ending is already known, and the hearer understands the beginning in light of the ending. This is a reversal of the ordinary experience of time of the past flowing into the future. Time is experienced as the recapitulation of what has already happened and as something that has stretched along between a beginning and an end. In this way, narrative not only establishes human action in time, as in Heidegger's first level of understanding, but also draws from the memory of past actions, the feature of the second level of time experience. In Heidegger's analysis of historicity, experience focuses on the notion of "repetition" or "retrievability." The past is not over, because it can be retrieved in memory. The going back into the past is not a mechanical reproduction of what has been; rather, it is a fetching back of the possibilities that have passed by in order to make them real again in the present.

c. At its *third* and utmost level of standing out of the objective plane, however, our experience is governed by the recognition of the singularity of our existence in the face of death. Death is the most personal of possibilities and cannot be shared. Although the understanding of time as historical can involve the recollection of the past and the destiny of the community of which one is a member, the power of the awareness that it is "I" who will die focuses the remembrance on one's own past and one's own fate. Heidegger's emphasis on the awareness of the singularity of one's own existence and its relationship to death gives individual existence priority in his philosophy. It makes one's past nontransferable to others and places individual personal recollection above the communal tradition.

Ricoeur holds that narrative calls Heidegger's primacy of individual existence into question and acts as a corrective to Heidegger's analysis of experience of time remembered. Says Ricoeur: "Narrativity, from the outset, establishes repetition on the plane of being-with-others."[19] Narrative opens the experience of history and moves it beyond personal history to create a communal history. Narrative is a communication not just between contemporaries but also between predecessors and successors, and the common destiny is more fundamental to it than any individual fate. Through the transmission of past possibilities to present hearers, the tradition of a historical community's common destiny is repeated or retrieved. Thus, narrative enlarges Heidegger's analysis of the experience of time, and his personal memory is expanded to a communal memory.[20]

In Heidegger's analysis of temporal experience, the most profound level of understanding is the realization that one's personal existence is coming to an end. This realization elevates the experience of personal time to a unity in which the past, the present, and the future of one's existence are seen as a whole, a single episode. This experience, which Heidegger calls "temporality," is most distant from the plane of objectivity and is akin to that ascribed to God's experience of time: above the movement of time, He can see all of time at once. Heidegger's emphasis is different to the extent that the experience of temporality is limited to the vision of one's personal existence as a whole. One says: "I am that which I have been, am now, and am coming to be. I am this temporality which began and will end."

Ricoeur has doubts that the narrative experience of time penetrates to Heidegger's level of "temporality." Ricoeur says: "The question is whether the theory of narrative has anything to say concerning the return from historicality [the second level] to this deep temporality."[21] He offers three possibilities: (1) Narrative is incapable of the radical movement to the height of temporality because of its tight link to within-time-ness and historicality. (2) Narrative may be a more accurate reflection of the two-level organization of human temporality and thus may serve to call into question Heidegger's analysis of a level of "temporality" (much as narrative has served as a corrective to Heidegger's emphasis on personal tradition in place of communal tradition). (3) There may be in narrative analysis the uncovering of a level in which the awareness of death precedes and makes possible the awareness of history and the memory of dead heroes.[22]

Ricoeur proposes that narrative discourse is the linguistic, hermeneutically reasoned expression of the human experience of time. By telling stories and writing history, we provide a public shape for what ordinarily remains "chaotic, obscure, and mute," lying outside the daily focus on getting things done. The contents and particular referents of histories and fictional stories are set in the temporal understanding of existence that is inherent in narrative structure. The form of narrative shapes our experience of time, regardless of the real or fictional quality of the characters and events in any one of its expressions. The retrieval of the past in narrative form is an expression of our historical structure of understanding. Ricoeur concludes: "The reasons for which we tell stories are rooted in the same temporal structure that connects our 'élan' towards the future, our attention to the present and our capacity to emphasize and to recollect the past."[23] Life is lived above the objective plane and its instantaneous "nows." Temporal existence draws the past and its possibilities into the present through tales and histories, and it imaginatively anticipates the future consequences of activity by seeing them as reenactments of its repertoire of stories.

Action and narrative

Humans use the socially given linguistic domain to understand themselves, others, and the world as meaningful.[24] The linguistic domain and the human order of meaning are organized according to a hermeneutic rationality and aligned on various interactive levels. On this basis, humans make decisions about what they want and what they need to do to satisfy these wants. We retrieve stories about our own and the community's past, and these provide models of how actions and consequences are linked. Using these retrieved models, we plan our strategies and actions and interpret the intentions of other actors. Narrative is the discourse structure in which human action receives its form and through which it is meaningful. The Enlightenment separated the subject from its body and its movements, viewing the knower-subject not as part of the known world but as a spectator. Formal science accepted this separation, and it has consequently found problematic an explanation of human action made in terms of agents and decisions. In a recent article in *American Psychologist,* Martin Packer reported: "Recent writers have noted that psychology lacks a method for studying the structure or organization of human action."

Physical movement and action

The Enlightenment strategy was to abstract content from the human experiential realm and fasten it to a grid of formal logic, thus creating a diagram of a flat plane of objective reality external to human experience. Experience itself was not conceived as a participant in the world, but as a spectator of it, and the diagram of the world was drawn by reconstructing from the distortions of experience what the world was really like in itself. The strategy produced a representation of reality that filled pure space with colorless objects and provided a pure time made up of serial instants passing along a geometric line. The objects in this pure space—including human bodies—reacted to each other according to unchanging laws that conformed to the rules of formal logic.

In contrast to this abstracted picture of reality, the representation of the world in original human experience is given in terms of hermeneutic expressiveness and includes human existence within it. In original human experience, the world does not appear as a reality separate from the experience of it. Instead, experience is part of the world itself, and it is conceived as the world folding back on itself and providing a clearing in which it can display itself and so be made meaningful. The world includes, within its being, processes of self-reflection by means of which it can appear to itself. Thus, in the portrait of reality given in human experience, the hermeneutic and linguistic structures are understood to be that aspect of reality which gives meaning to reality's self-display.

The attempt by formal science to account for human action as an aspect of the diagram of objectivity has had limited success. The model of physical action-reaction, analogous to a pool ball moving when struck by another pool ball, has been reshaped into a stimulus-reaction framework by the human sciences. Yet human action fits into the model with difficulty; there has been little success in uncovering determinative laws predictive of human movement.[26] In the model, changes in one part of the physical environment were supposed to produce law-governed changes or movements in the human body, conceived of as another part of the physical environment. The treatment of the human body as a mere object in the plane of objectivity, rather than as an expression of an integrated, incarnate person, underlay early behaviorism as well as Western medical practice.[27]

The extension of this approach to include mental states—as if they were things in an objective realm—still did not produce determinative laws. Although this extension moved beyond the limits of the understanding that all physical action is caused by other physical events, it retained the idea that actions are reactions to other events.[28] Alvin Goldman was a proponent of the model in which mental events—a thought containing a reason, for instance, or the mental state of tiredness—could cause human action.[29] Even though his view kept the nucleus of the notion of physical cause as the explanation for all physical movement, it was criticized because it did not meet the formal science criteria for the determination of laws: for example, that it must have a formal and undirectional connection, its cause must be completely independent of the effect and it must have the capacity to predict future movements given the same mental cause. The whole notion of using the model of physical cause to account for human action has fallen into disrepute. It failed according to its own goal of prediction and explanation by covering law, and it failed philosophically by representing human experience as composed of "objectlike" mental states. Nevertheless, the physical cause model, in which movement is reckoned with as if it were a manifestation of physical law, has been retained by the mainstream human sciences as their preferred approach.[30]

Action as rule governed

The approach to understanding human action proposed here entails conceiving of actions as rule-following activities. Action as a performance manifesting a set of instructions can be viewed from different perspectives. Three traditions reflecting the notion that action can be understood as conformity to rules will be discussed: (a) Max Weber's position that actions can be structured according to an ideal means-end rationality; (b) the structuralists' notion that action is directed by a static set of innate, logically organized rules and (c) the language-game position that action follows socially generated rules. Then the position advocated in this study, that action is an expression of narratively understood projects, will be described.

Weber's means-end rationality. Weber understood that human action could, in the ideal, be understood as the manifestation of purposeful rationality *(Zweckrational)*. Weber retained the distinction created by formal science between a mental subject and the subject's body but accepted the idea that in human action the body is guided by the subject and not merely by biological responses to environmental events. He thought that the object of inquiry for the human disciplines ought to be the meaning an action has for the actor. In Weber's view, human actions are undertaken in four basic ways: the first two involve reflective calculation or committed awareness; the second two do not. (1) Actions are rationally selected according to the contribution they make toward attaining a particular end. (2) Actions are undertaken not as a means to a particular end but because the actor believes that the acts themselves are intrinsically meaningful. (3) Actions are engaged in out of habit or social tradition. (4) Actions are pure emotional expression without any reflective deliberation. A particular actual action usually includes a mixture of these various meanings, and so the categories should be recognized as abstractions made for the purpose of theoretical analysis.

Weber focused his investigations on the first type of action as the appropriate mode. By retaining the idea of the body/mind separation, Weber was provided with a way to account for the fact that human action is not always an expression of means-end rationality. He believed that the mechanical and biological aspects of the body become mixed with the rational aspects so that the outcome is an action of mixed lineage. On the one side is pure reason, on the other is the organism. Thus, an ideal description of means-end rationality must be abstracted from the goings-on of daily life, cleansed of the distortions of irrational factors, such as emotion and tradition, that are involved in the other types of action. Weber did not hold that the ideal type of purposeful action is a description of actual human action. He believed that it is a description of how humans would act if they were to act completely in accord with rationality.[31]

Of interest for this study is Weber's description of the logic of means-end rationality. This is not the same as the logic of categorical relations used by formal science to describe the order of objective reality. Means-end rationality consists essentially of establishing an imagined valued end or desired state of affairs. One constructs in the imagination different courses of events with their probable consequences, then compares the consequences of the possible courses of events with an imagined goal. This rationality follows the logic of the practical syllogism and is teleological, in that the validity of the conclusion is determined by the judgment of which events will produce consequences closest to the designed end. The valid answer to the pragmatic question, "What should be done?", is which course of activity is most likely to produce the valued future state of affairs. (The role that narrative performs in providing a set of imagined courses of activity with their consequent productions will be described later in this section.) Weber's position holds that knowledge from formal science is limited to providing information about only the most efficient and appropriate means to a given end. But the determination of that end cannot be undertaken by either the formal logic of science or means-end logic, for both of these logics are useful only after a goal has been chosen.

Weber's separation of values from the plane of objectivity is derived from Immanuel Kant's separation of knowledge into three compartments: science (the theoretical realm), ethics (the practical), and aesthetics.[32] In this scheme, the knowledge of the theoretical realm, provided by formal science practices, was limited to the objective world of space and time. Questions about morality and values were concerned with practical judgments or ethical action and required a different kind of knowledge based on principles of universal application. Questions about beauty were to be answered by the third kind of knowledge, derived from the experience of pleasure. The separation of ethical and aesthetic inquiry from scientific inquiry was a retreat from the earlier Enlightenment notion that all aspects of reality, including the ethical, could be understood through formal science. Kant believed, nevertheless, that formal logic could be used to answer moral questions, and he proposed the logic principle of the "categorical imperative" as a means to provide ethical knowledge.[33]

Denying ethics and aesthetics access to formal science reasoning developed over time into the denial that ethical statements could contain meaningful content; rather, they remained the emotive expression of personal preference.[34] By extension, this led to the denial that true—that is, objective—knowledge of values could exist. Aesthetic judgments were also relegated to statements of mere personal preference without basis in objective reality. The elimination of these spheres from the enterprise of formal science permitted the drawing of the strange conclusion that, if the realm of objects in space and time is the only area that yields objective knowledge, then reality must be made up only of objects in space and time. This study has emphasized hermeneutic reasoning and has claimed that it is the primary form of rationality by means of which humans organize their experience. Kant did suggest, it should be noted, that aesthetic (hermeneutic) reasoning may provide an integration of thought about space and time on the one hand and morality on the other.[35]

Structuralism and human action. Structuralists have generally understood action to be the activity of a person rather than merely a physical movement caused by either physical or mental events. They believe that action is organized according to formal structures that underlie and generate experience. This commitment to a formal and logical organization at the base of human existence differs from the understanding of a flexible and changing narrative organization (described later in this chapter). Structuralists hold that experience is created through logically related categories, rules, concepts, and principles. Human existence in its linguistic and thought forms is believed to conform to formal structures, where logical rules operate to generate specific expressions. In opposition to the Enlightenment discourse, structuralists maintain that thought and language are not reflections of an external objective plane of reality but instead are the result of innate reasoning principles that produce and organize experience into systematic patterns.

Structuralism can be traced back to Saussure's analysis of language as a formally organized system. According to Saussure, the rules governing the way meaning is manifested in language have no material existence. They are like the rules of a chess game, in which a piece is determined to be a knight not by its material or even its shape but by identification with the rules governing a knight's moves. Any material piece can count as a knight as long as the value of knightness is attributed to it. In the same manner, sounds are determined to have meaning not by their particular pitch but by the value the language system attributes to them. Language does not assign meaning in isolation; meaning is derived from the divisions established by the whole system. For example, if the language system does not differentiate between a stream, a creek, and a brook, if it differentiates only between a stream and a river, then a particular flow of water will receive only the meaning of "river" or "stream." By extension, human experience is created by the action of the linguistic system in attributing meaning to particular events in the continuum of events.

Claude Lévi-Strauss drew on the principles of structural linguistics to describe a structural system that lies below consciousness and that organizes human action into meaningful piece units. He and those who followed him differed from Saussure in that they located the source of logical structures in the person as a psychological given (called psychologism), whereas Saussure located the source of structuration in the language system, which operates independently of personal psychological makeup. Lévi-Strauss viewed such various actions as the preparation of food, the telling of myths, and responses to incest taboos as manifestations of a formal structural system that followed the logic of binary oppositions and differences (e.g., "for and against," "good and bad," "ordinary and non-ordinary"). For example, the incest taboo is a structure that classifies relatives as either "acceptable" or "not acceptable" as marriage partners. The determination of which people are acceptable as partners results from the divisions ordered in the meaning system and not from a characteristic of people in the world.[36]

A second version of structuralism was developed by Jean Piaget, who studied the development of thought in human experience. He maintained that this development is governed by an inherent pattern which generates the growth of the mental schemes children use to organize their experience. By these schemes children interpret the environment as a meaningful order, adapting—accommodating and assimilating—experience into categories ultimately usable in reasoning. In Piaget's descriptions, the innate schemes unfold into higher-order schemes as a child matures.[37]

Noam Chomsky, too, has developed a model of language acquisition based on a structuralist approach. He holds that there are innate grammatical structures that allow people to make or generate correct sentences. He shares the general structuralist notion that the mind operates in terms of rules or principles that organize experience and generate expression.[38]

Structuralism maintains that human action is an expression of human experience but that this experience is constructed by deep, innate rules. Because these rules are formal and function according to the tenets of logic, they produce a logically organized human experience. The rules are not the result of learning from interaction with the environment, nor are they context-dependent. They are unchanging and static, just like those rules postulated by formal science concerning the motions of the objective realm. Although the structuralists treated action as if it had a meaningful linguistic structure, their notion of linguistic structure is very different from the open and fluid notions of narrative structuring described in our second chapter. Ultimately, they have failed to bridge the gap between their descriptions of formal structures and actual expressive human activity, in all its variety and "illogic."[39] The structuralist position stands within the philosophical tradition of rationalism, which has tried by means of a logically ordered system to give form to human experience. This tradition includes Descartes's study of the properties and organization of the mind, Kant's reflectively understood categories, and Husserl's ideas of consciousness.[40]

Language games and action. Peter Winch shares with the structuralists the notion that action is the manifestation of rules, and he shows a similar lack of concern with history. However, Winch's understanding of the origin and organization of the rules is very different. Winch draws on Wittgenstein's concept of language games instead of on Saussure's concept of a language system. The structuralist position has tended to hold that the system of language and thought rules is the necessary result of the inherent characteristics of language (Saussure) or theoretical thinking (Piaget), and some structuralists have even located the necessity for the organization in the "hard wiring" of the human brain (Lévi-Strauss and Chomsky). Winch maintains, in opposition to this syntactically or logically necessary organizational pattern, that the rules of behavior are socially generated and exist merely as the sedimented agreements developed over time within a social organization. The rules that generate action are like the rules of playground games, which are made up by the players as new situations arise. For example, players would lose their ball if it went over the fence surrounding their playing field, and so they make up a rule that the ball has to be bounced into the goal. After several summers of play, during which members of the group that originally made up the rules have stopped playing and a higher fence has been built, players continue to act according to the rule and continue to bounce the ball at the goal. Rules of this sort are not like either the logically necessary laws of formal science or the systematic linguistic rules. They have developed in a somewhat haphazard way in response to personal and social needs.[41]

The difference between the structuralist approach and the language game approach can be found in their contrasting understandings of the origin of the rules that arrange human actions. In the structuralist approach, the rules originate in and are ordered by the characteristics of formal closed systems. In the language game approach, the rules are grounded and maintained by sedimented social agreements. Wittgenstein's later work was concerned with language's production of meaning as a function of socially agreed-upon rules in which particular signs and sounds were accepted as having particular meanings. In Wittgenstein's view, to understand a language required learning the rules of the language game. Winch extended this theory to the understanding of action in general. He held that action is understood and explained when one knows the rule it is following. Thus, to understand the meaning of conduct is to grasp the rules that actors follow in doing what they do. Likewise, because meaningful action is activity oriented to rules, knowledge of those rules provides the actors with "reasons" for their conduct.

What is "reasonable" is a function of the particular language game, and does not rest on a universal or innate sense of rationality. For structuralism, rationality is transcendent, that is, it is a universal given for all human beings. Translation among languages and understanding across cultures is possible because one basic logically organized rationality is manifest in all surface expressions. The Wittgensteinian language position denies such an underlying transcultural logic. There, what is reasonable and sensible is a function of the context of each particular language game. Language games are not commensurate, and meaning cannot be translated across games.[42] We are all boxed in by the rules of the games in which we participate. We have no way to get outside a game in order to understand, for understanding is created only within a game.[43]

There is an alternative to the three positions presented here, that is (a) purposeful action is the result of a means-end calculation to achieve personal ends, (b) action is the enactment of transcendent and logically ordered rules, and (c) action is behavior conforming to socially agreed upon rules. The concept of narrative action provides the basis for an alternative.

Narrative action

The concept of human action proposed by a narrative approach is that action is an expression of existence and that its organization manifests the narrative organization of human experience. Acting is like writing a story, and the understanding of action is like arriving at an interpretation of a story. In this conception, there is no notion of distance between the movements of the body and the person as agent; there is no need to account for something that pushes or pulls the body to make it move. Instead, a unified being expresses itself directly in bodily movement. The idea of cause is completely changed from physical cause to expressive cause.[44] Expressive cause is linked to the process in which alphabetical letters on a page "cause" the reader to understand meaning in them or to the process in which the spoken words of a poem "cause" the reader to "hear" them as meaning something. Human action is the physical texture of an embodied agent's meaningful statement, and bodily movement is "caused" by the meaning to be expressed.

Human action, understood to be more than mere physical movement, but as the result of the human competence to comprehend particular movements as the acts of agents, can be refigured or represented symbolically in the acts of speaking or writing. The bodily movements of the hand when holding a pen and writing a note or of the tongue and larynx when speaking to someone make no sense when explained as mechanical movements of organic pulleys and bellows: they are aspects of an integrated person giving expression. In a similar way, one's movement across a room or the focusing of the eyes to see something small are expressive of a personal involvement with the world.

As described previously, narrative involves the gathering together of events into a plot in which signification is given to the events as they relate to the theme of the story. The plot configures the events into a whole, and the events are transformed from merely serial, independent happenings into meaningful happenings that contribute to the whole theme. As the meaning and function of an individual word becomes clear when the sentence of which it is a part is understood, so the significance of an individual event becomes apparent when one knows the plot of which it is a part. Because the creation of a meaningful plot from a set of events uses the same processes of hermeneutic reasoning that are involved in the creation of a meaningful sentence from a set of words, examples drawn from sentences are not merely analogous but illustrative of the narrative process.

The meaning of a sentence is not simply imposed on the individual words that make it up. Rather, the composite of the words gives the sentence its particular meaning. It is possible that the same group of words can make up several meaningful sentences. For example, the words, "Flying planes can be dangerous," can be made meaningful in two ways, and depending on which understanding is held, the significance of the word "flying" changes. Similarly, the same set of events can be gathered together in different plots, thus changing the meaning of particular events. However, just as groups of words are not open to interpretations that produce just any meaning, and only sometimes allow multiple interpretations, so sets of events can be emplotted only sometimes in multiple ways. As in sentences, the temporal order of the events is crucial if they are to contribute to the meaningful whole of the plot. The two sentences, "The mouse chased the cat" and "The cat chased the mouse," although composed of the same words, produce different meanings because of the change in the word order. Moreover, not just any group of words will produce a meaningful sentence. For example, the sentence, "Colorless green ideas sleep furiously," although grammatically correct, is intuitively recognized as not producing a meaningful whole.

Ricoeur believes that humans possess a competence or preunderstanding of the world of action that is similar to their competence to recognize which groups of words can produce meaningful sentences. With sentences, this competence draws on a recognition of what kind of organization produces an acceptable sentence, what words can be linked together in a meaningful manner, and how order affects understanding. The recognition and composition of meaningful plots require a corresponding understanding of the kinds of activity that compose human action, the kind of events that can be gathered together into a plot, and the importance of temporal order in configuring events into a plot.

This means that the composition of plots draws on the human competence to distinguish the domain of action from the domain of physical movement.[45] The competence to know which bodily movements are human actions is called practical understanding and provides the basic unit for composing and understanding narration. Ricoeur identifies six notions that form part of this competence. (1) Actions imply goals, that is, they are carried out to achieve results or to accomplish an end. (2) Actions refer to motives which explain why someone did or does something. This explanation is clearly different from that used to show how one physical event causes another. (3) Actions are carried out by agents. A person performs or is the author of an action, and thus actions are taken as the work or deed of someone who can be held responsible. The question, "Who did it?", can be answered within the competence of practical understanding. (4) Actions take place in situations that consist of closed physical systems, and an agent recognizes that the circumstances in which the action is to occur places limits on what can be done and sets the favorable and unfavorable conditions that will affect the outcome of the action.[46] (5) Actions take place in interaction with other persons, whether as cooperation, competition, or struggle. Cohorts can either help or hinder the accomplishment of an act. (6) The outcome of an action may bring about a change in one's fortunes or feelings. In short, we are competent to recognize that such questions as "what?", "why?", "who?", "how?", "with whom?", and "against whom?" are appropriate to ask in regard to human actions, but not in regard to plain physical movement.

Narrative assumes practical understanding on the part of the narrator and the listeners, and competence to understand and use such terms as "agent," "goal," "means," "success," "failure," and so on. Narrative adds to simple action statements the structure of a plot. The rules for narrative composition determine how to order action sentences into the total action sequence of a story. Because of the sequential linking of sentences into a plot, the agents, their deeds, and their sufferings receive a deepened meaning.

Human action occurs within cultural settings that maintain symbolic narrative forms for use in the articulation of action. These symbolic forms have a public character and are not the private understandings of a particular actor. Thus, an act is undertaken with the knowledge of what it will mean to the community in which it takes place. The actor in a particular culture realizes that the act of bowing before another is a means of expressing contrition within the community and will be understood by others in it as such an expression. The communal significance of actions confers an initial "readability" on them. The manners, customs, and other social agreements also supply an evaluation of actions in terms of their conformity to moral norms, and they define which actions are good or bad, better or worse. The tellers of tales assume that their audiences understand the appropriate evaluation of the actions in a story. According to Ricoeur: "There is no action [in the narrative] which does not give rise to approbation or reprobation, to however small a degree, as a function of a hierarchy of values for which goodness and wickedness are the poles.[47] Likewise, Aristotle held that it is the ethical quality of the characters in a story that gives rise to the hearer's emotional response, for example, pity for the good character who has experienced unmerited misfortune.

In addition to the competence to understand action sentences and the ability to recognize the culturally given meaningfulness and valuation of actions, the narrative assumes the audience's understanding of human temporality. Time, rather than being a series of instant nows passing through the slit of a present moment, includes an understanding that (1) action projects have to do with the future and with intended and unintended consequences, (2) motivation for action is closely related to the capacity to retrieve, in the present, experience inherited from the past, and (3) statements such as "I feel," "I suffer," "I can," and "I do" contribute to a sense of the present.

Narrative is the form of hermeneutic expression in which human action is understood and made meaningful. Action itself is the living narrative expression of a personal and social life. The competence to understand a series of episodes as part of our story informs our own decisions to engage in actions that move us toward a desired ending. The length of storied actions can range from a short adventure to the time between our own birth and death, or even to the length of all the generations of humankind. To define a narrative as a linked series of episodes contributing to a single adventure with a beginning, a middle, and an end—or as the presentation of a problem that is followed by actions that result in a resolution—is to describe in simple terms what is already included in our ordinary understanding of action.

The recognition of the connection between action and narrative has been part of the Western tradition at least since Aristotle.[48] In *The Poetics*, Aristotle identified narrative[49] as the imitation (mimesis) or representation of human action.[50] The plot *(muthos)* of narrative is the organization of events, not as a static structure but as an operation or construction of synthesis. (Ricoeur prefers to use the term "emplotment" to signify the active character of gathering up or configuring the events into a whole.) *The Poetics*, then, is about the composition of narratives, identified as a hermeneutic activity in which the relationship between parts is made apparent.

In Aristotle's conception, plot has the features of wholeness and completeness. As he put it: "Now a thing is a whole if it has a beginning, a middle, and an end." The poet locates the beginning, not as the place where nothing has happened before it, but as the place where the events begin that are of importance for what follows. The middle is the succession of events, and the end is the poet's determination that the sequence of events contributing to the resolution of the adventure is complete. The plot must also have the appropriate magnitude, which is determined by the author. Narrative is concerned with creating a dramatic or hermeneutic unity, not merely with recording all of the events that have happened over a period of time. Emplotment is concerned with drawing out from the flow of events those that significantly contribute to the story under construction. In Aristotle's words again:

> It is evident . . . that the poet must be more the poet of his stories or plots than of his verses, inasmuch as he is a poet by virtue of the imitative element in his work, and it is actions that he imitates. And if he should come to take a subject from actual his-

tory, he is none the less a poet for that, since some historic occurrences may very well be in the probable and possible order of things; and it is in that aspect of them that he is their poet.[51]

The poet makes plots and represents action. By the same token, the human actor expresses his or her existence through action, and understands it to be part of a larger configuration of meaning. Action is the poetic expression of human existence as it moves toward valued ends. These ends are not simply the fulfillment of personal desires; they also include commitments to ethical standards and the fulfillment of promises. When action is studied as movement caused by the force of other physical or mental events and determined by logically structured, unchanging laws, or when it is studied as an enactment of a rule system, the richness and fullness of its meaning as an expression of a narrative existence is missing. The programs that force human action into formal frameworks have not produced valid statements of logically ordered and mathematically described behavior, on even statements that capture the human experience of acting. A hermeneutically based understanding of human behavior as a narrative expression of existence can produce far more authentic and useful descriptions for a science of the human realm.

Narrative and the self

This chapter has thus far been concerned with descriptions of aspects of human existence when the linguistic realm and narrative expression are understood to be primary. This final section continues this by concentrating on the issues that surround the problem of personal identity—what distinguishes one person from all others—and the role narrative plays in the creation of identity.

Self as a substance

The question, "Who am I?" ("What is it that gives me my identity as this particular person who is different from all others?"), has been variously answered. The term "self-identity" is composed of two countering notions: "self" (ipse), that which is the opposite of otherness and strangeness; and "identity" (idem), that which remains the same, the extreme singular, the opposite of change. The idea of self-identity holds the two notions of difference and sameness in tension. The Enlightenment maintained the concept of substance for that which remains the same, for that which underlies the changes in the qualities of a thing and provides a continuity for the thing throughout whatever changes it undergoes over time. Within a metaphysics of substance, the question of self-identity seeks to understand the basic substance or substratum that remains the same and confers individuality on a person.

There have been two primary, although competing, recent answers to this question: the identity of the body and the identity of memory. The first position can be paraphrased in this way: "I know that I am myself because my substance is this particular body that has continued through time." The advent of plastic surgery and the transplanting of body organs has created a new puzzle: "If this body contains parts of someone else or has been artificially altered, is it really me?" Moreover, if personal identity is necessarily connected with the continuance of one's body through time, then it is logically impossible for a person to survive the death of his or her body. The Hebrew notion of resurrection, which provides the support for our burial practices and our concern with the remains of those who have died, is connected to the notion that a person is primarily identified by his or her body. The Hebrew idea is that life after death does not take the form of a detached spirit; the idea requires the resurrection of the body which will be brought back to life.

The notion that "I am uniquely myself because I have this particular body" has undergone some amendments in recent decades. The realization that the body is not static and that it undergoes constant change by discarding old cells and making new ones has meant that body identity has had to change from an emphasis on appearance to an emphasis on structure. Only a few physical features— fingerprints, for instance—remain unchanged throughout one's life. The focus of the question, "What is the substance or distinctiveness of a person?", is now being placed on the individual's particular genetic configuration, with the fantasy of cloning a part of one's body to produce an identical copy being merely a backward recognition of this idea.

The second position concerning what a person's unique substance is and what provides his or her identity is that each person has a unique set of memories about his or her experiences. This position can be paraphrased in this way: "I am myself because no one else has the particular memory I have of my personal experiences. Even if my body dies and I survive in a disembodied state, I will know that it is myself because I will continue to have my unique memories." People sometimes use this notion to identify each other. A childhood friend, although physically changed beyond recognition, will retain the same memories.

Beyond these two recent answers to the question, there is a third, historically significant, answer. This position is based on the idea that ultimately each of us is an incorporeal self or mental substance, rather than a mere body. As a consequence, personal identity must be related to the mental subject that experiences and remembers, not to experience itself. The substratum that underlies the series of mental or psychological states is a soul, a unique self, and each of us has absolutely certain, although private, knowledge of this self and its states whenever they occur.

Descartes developed this theory, and it was his position that personal identity was to be found in the unique mental substance or self of each person. According to Descartes, we know this self directly, and there is no need to identify our individuality with a continuous body or with the contents of memory. He came to this position from his investigation of human experience and all its various mental processes and states, which he called forms of thinking (*cogitationes*). When we feel chilled, experience disappointment, engage in imaginative fantasies, doubt something, apparently perceive something—either when objects are actually there or when we are dreaming or hallucinating—we are engaged in "thinking." Descartes was concerned that he could be mistaken about the existence of any material thing, including the unique body he called "his." However, he could not be wrong in supposing he has thoughts, even though these thoughts might be erroneous or muddled. From this line of argument he thought that a person could draw four conclusions: (1) I know that this particular "I," or self, exists and thinks. (2) Specifically, I have some kind of direct experience or introspective knowledge of my self and its operations. (3) Because I may be deluded about everything else, I do not know whether this "I" has any characteristics besides thinking, and the safe conclusion is that the self only thinks. (4) I could be mistaken regarding the existence of my body, and because I cannot know that my body exists, but I do know that my self exists, the self and the body must be distinct; the self must therefore be nonbody.

Descarte's notion that a person can know directly the unique self that is his or her personal identity was taken over by others and given certain additions. One was that a person manages to remain one and the same individual because his or her self endures uninterrupted and unaltered throughout that person's life. Another was that a person knows that he or she remains the same because that person periodically reflects on his or her self. A description of this concept of the self was given by Bishop Butler in 1736:

> Our ... bodies are no more ourselves, or part of ourselves, than any other matter around us. ... Upon comparing the consciousness of one's self ... in any two moments, there ... immediately arises to the mind the idea of personal identity. ... Reflecting upon my self now, and ... my self ... years ago, I discern they are ... the same self.[52]

Thus the self was conceived of as a noncorporeal substance that remains the same throughout our existence and to which thought belongs. Although Descartes held that we know with certainty that the unique self we are exists, he did not believe that we could describe its properties.

This idea that our personal identity is linked to a self was attacked by Hume. He held that there is no "thing" or "substance" within which thoughts are maintained, that the mind or self is nothing but a bundle of different perceptions. There is no ghost in the bodily machine which is the real, unique me. The self then becomes understood as simply the sum of all one's experiences without a stable something behind them, and such a self is unsuitable for maintaining the unity of a personal identity.

Self as a construction

William James offered an alternative to the notion that self-identity is based in a mental or self substance. Personal identity is, he said, an idea that a person constructs; it is not an underlying substance to be discovered. He believed that development of a personal identity or self is an ongoing effort that involves the synthesis of many different ideas about oneself and its multiple facets into a single idea of self. He delineated three constituents of the whole self: (1) the "material self," which is derived from an awareness of one's body at large, including one's clothing, one's family, one's home, and one's property; (2) the "social self," which includes, on the one hand, the perceptions or images of one's person that one assumes are held by other, personally significant individuals or groups of individuals and, on the other hand, the social values and norms shared by the person with others; and (3) the "spiritual self," which is the awareness of one's own frailties, dispositions, self-understanding, and judgment.[53]

During the past few decades, ordinary-language philosophers have also criticized the traditional understanding by which personal identity has been tied to the idea of an immaterial self that has received and retained the impressions of experience. They hold that this definition is artificial and has ignored many of the everyday uses of the word "self." They have replaced the immaterial thoughtful self as the seat of personal identity with the notion of a fully embodied person who is engaged in physical actions and speaks to others. The "that by which I am myself" is a fully functioning person who often uses language with self-references and speaks of a unique "I" that acts, thinks, and feels. "I recognize my own identity when I speak about myself and when I hear other people speak about me as a particular person."

The concept of self had been little investigated by the human sciences because of their adoption of the formal science model. That model is committed to the notion that scientific knowledge is possible in regard to a flattened reality that consists of physical objects in time and space along with their relations. Even when this commitment is expanded to include mental objects, it is difficult to include the self as a clearly researchable mental object. In recent years, however, the concept of self has reemerged in research programs in the human disciplines,[54] a "rediscovery" due largely to the inability of formal science research to account for the unexplained variability in human behavior that has shown up in research using experimental designs.

The concept of self that has recently emerged in the human disciplines is closer to the self of the ordinary-language philosophers and James than to

Descarte's incorporeal substance. The human disciplines attribute the development of the notion of personal identity and the self to symbolic and bodily interaction within the social environment. The concept of self is not the discovery or release of some innate "I"; it is a construction built on other people's responses and attitudes toward a person and is subject to change as these responses, inherently variable and inconsistent, change in their character. In order to come to a unified and concordant self concept and personal identity, then, the person needs to synthesize and integrate the diverse social responses he or she experiences.

Self as narrative

The self concept is synthesized out of a myriad of interactions across the life span, and at any given time its contents of internalized roles, statuses, norms, and values are bound to be contradictory and mutually exclusive. The self concept may be vague and disintegrated at times, and the force with which it can operate as a guide to behavior and a criterion for conduct can be scattered. It appears that for the major part of daily life a person's self concept is raised, edited, and implemented preconsciously, at the prelinguistic level of emotion and "felt" dispositions. The attempts in the human disciplines to raise these emotions and dispositions to consciousness and translate them into a language of precise categories are problematic. They are seeking to render manifest something which for the most part is enacted outside of awareness and which is ambiguous and incongruous.[55]

Moreover, the tools being used by the human disciplines to gain access to the self concept are, in general, the traditional research implements designed by formal science to locate and measure objects and things. The position taken in this study is that we achieve our personal identities and self concept through the use of the narrative configuration, and make our existence into a whole by understanding it as an expression of a single unfolding and developing story. We are in the middle of our stories and cannot be sure how they will end; we are constantly having to revise the plot as new events are added to our lives. Self, then, is not a static thing nor a substance, but a configuring of personal events into a historical unity which includes not only what one has been but also anticipations of what one will be.

David Carr has explored the operations of narrative in a person's self-story.[56] His position is similar to the one presented in this book, that "narration, far from being a distortion of, denial of, or escape from "reality," is in fact an extension and confirmation of its primary features." He notes that everything that happens to a person is part of his or her life; however, in one's self-stories the extraneous details are pushed into the background through the capacity of selection. A self-story requires a storyteller as well as an audience. Carr identifies ourselves as the authors as well as part of the audience :

In planning our days and our lives we are composing the stories or the dramas we will act out and which will determine the focus of our attention and our endeavors, which will provide the principles for distinguishing foreground from background.... We are constantly explaining ourselves to others. And finally each of us must count himself among his own audience since in explaining ourselves to others we are often trying to convince ourselves as well.[57]

If the unity and uniqueness of the self is achieved through the process of narrativity and if one conceives of one's own particular existence as a special story and not as a physical or mental thing, then more adequate, hermeneutically oriented research tools will be needed to study personal identity. These tools will seek to understand the self as an expression, and will be modeled on the processes a person uses to understand the meaning of a sentence, not on procedures for identifying characteristics or qualities. Our language creates an expectation that the answer to the question, "What is that?", will be given in terms of some thing or object. Using these questions as models, the answer to the question, "What am I?", is expected to be a substance—for example, "You are your soul" or "You are your body." The answer proposed here is that the self is a concept defined as the expressive process of human existence, whose form is narrativity.

The approach to the self as a story is developed from a metaphysics of potentiality and actuality focused on the changes that occur in organic life, rather than from a metaphysics of substance.[58] From this perspective the focus of one's identity is not centered on the sameness of an underlying substance but on one's process of actualizing what is potentially possible in one's life. The emphasis changes from "What am I?" to "Who am I?" This "who" is found in the person's actions—those actions that are first interpreted by a preunderstanding and competence which distinguishes actions from simple physical movements. As described in the previous section, this preunderstanding of movement as human action is transformed and refigured by narrative. Narrative presupposes and draws on the human competence to understand action. Self identity becomes linked to a person's life story, which connects up the actions into an integrating plot.

Sir Peter Strawson advocates a position which views the self as a personal life narrative.[59] He recognizes the concept of "person" as a logically primitive concept which cannot be further reduced—to, for example, material and mental properties. Ordinary language usage identifies the person—both one's own self and other persons—as an elementary datum in the life-world. In the use of the concept of person, it is "a necessary condition of ascribing states of consciousness, experiences, to oneself, in the way that one does, that one should also ascribe them, or be prepared to ascribe them to others who are not oneself."[60] In the special characteristic or "persona" that an individual has, he or she occupies a particular position in time and space, and so provides a reference point which individuates the network of personal attributes and relationships that is the particular individual. Strawson sees his "individuation" as accentuating the location of a person in a story and, further, in a history. Consequently, words such as "here," "now," "I," and "you" not only belong to the personal sphere but also provide an intersubjective and public reference point of individuality that extends beyond the person's own subjectivity.

The question of "Who am I?" is not answered simply by assigning a predicate to the subject "I," as in such phrases as "I am an American," "I am a male," and "I am a farmer." The everyday answer is given as a narration of the sort, "I was born in St. Louis, and then I went to school, which got me interested in these things," and so on. The experience of self is organized along the temporal dimension in the same manner that the events of a narrative are organized by the plot into a unified story. The self is that temporal order of human existence whose story begins with birth, has as its middle the episodes of a lifespan, and ends with death. It is the plot that gathers together these events into a coherent and meaningful unity, and thereby gives context and significance to the contribution that the individual episodes make toward the overall configuration that is the person. The whole of an individual human existence is articulated in the narrative plot; it is much more than a simple chronicle listing of life occurrences. The self, then, is a meaning rather than a substance or a thing. To look for it in the objective plane is to make a mistake similar to that of examining the substance of the ink on a piece of paper in order to find the meaning of the word it prints.

The plot of the normal self is bound by the episodes and the environment in which a person expresses himself or herself as well as the projects of the imagination that appear as possibilities extending out from the person's actual history. The emplotment is like the work of the historian rather than that of a writer of fiction. One does not simply act out a story of one's own choosing; the events that the self-plot needs to gather into significance are the result of accidents, organic or social givens, and unintended consequences as well as personal motivation.

One kind of event the self-plot integrates is fixed to the stratum of the organic given of human existence. The person interacts with the physical environment and uses his/her body to interfere in the course of natural events and effect changes in the environment. The body supports the psychological states of the person and expresses itself in emotional responses. This organic stratum is not a static given; it is a historically changing stratum that passes from the helplessness of infancy through growth to adulthood and, over time, to physical degeneration. The self-plot attends to genetically established physical dimensions and personal qualities and to organically generated changes in desire. It pays attention to the social and cultural setting in which life events occur, and to responses and requests from other persons. Injury and illness, good fortune, successes, and accomplishments, and defeats and failures are all made meaningful in relation to the whole plot.

One bundle of dispositions and tendencies toward action in one's plot contains the roles one characteristically plays. Because of its connection to the metaphor of drama, the playing of social roles can be confused with the development of a personal plot. Just as the actor on the stage plays a role, acting as if he were someone else and presenting himself to the audience as the character in the play, so the social settings in which people live provide predefined roles that can be adopted as the means for guiding behavior. People borrow aspects of their self-stories from fictive narratives and dramas, learning from the characters such ideas as the depth of jealousy and the consequences of breaking promises. Maurice Natanson points to the stock of social roles provided by each culture for personal adoption: "From the vast storehouse of schemata for interpreting experience and acting in the world, the self mechanically or impishly chooses those patterns which will define its situation and its placement in the social world."[61] A person can assume multiple roles which provide scripts for one's clothing, gestures, and even speech patterns. By taking on a particular role, a person can put on a "show" in order to impress and manage another person's responses. Erving Goffman has developed a series of studies based on the notion of "life as theater" in which we give performances to impute to the audience of cohorts contrived impressions. Goffman, describing his approach, writes:

> The perspective employed in this report is that of the theatrical performance; the principles derived are dramaturgical ones. I shall consider the way in which the individual . . . presents himself and his activity to others, the ways in which he guides and controls the impressions they form of him, and the kinds of things he may and may not do while sustaining his performance before them.[62]

To play a social role is not the same as configuring one's life into a plot that is one's personal identity. Performing a social role is a way in which a person manages and animates his or her actions, but playing a character—of which there are many over a life span—represents only one of the episodes that make up the content of a life story. One may play many different characters which give temporary periods of identity during one's life span. But these various roles—"the precocious child," "the good student," "the fast tracker," and so on—all take on meaning from the perspective of the single adventure that is one person, as defined by the life plot.[63]

Alasdair MacIntyre has said about the relationship between plots and life: "Surely . . . human life has a determinate form, the form of a certain kind of story. It is not just that poems and sagas narrate what happens to men and women, but that in their narrative form poems and sagas capture a form that was already present in the lives which they relate."[64] Cultures do provide specific types of plots for adoption by its members in their configurations of self. These plot outlines are carried and transmitted in the culture by mythic stories and fairy tales, by tales of heroes, and by dramatic constructions. In North American culture, they are conveyed by motion pictures, television dramas, comic books, and novels. Although the content of each life plot is unique to a person, it can share the characteristics of a general plot outline. For example, personal life stories can be emplotted according to the outline of the tragic tale in which a person of good will and innocence is overcome by much pain and suffering, or according to a general heroic tale in which the person understands himself or herself to be engaged in a struggle for principles.[65]

That which differentiates a person from all other persons is a construction as well as a discovery, for the person's story is open-ended, not finished. The realization of self as a narrative in process serves to gather together what one has been, in order to imagine what one will be, and to judge whether this is what one wants to become. Life is not merely a story text: life is lived, and the story is told. The life story is a redescription of the lived life and a means to integrate the aspects of the self. Because life is not a substance, because it is made up of actions that bring into actuality what was once potential, the story about life is open to editing and revision. It can be changed. Nietzsche thought that the kind of story one generated from his or her life events had a moral quality and could be judged as more or less worthy. According to Nietzsche, the self is not a constant, stable entity. Rather, it is something one becomes, something one constructs. The self does not know itself directly; it knows itself only indirectly through signs and symbols of self-interpretation. The self, then, is a figured or represented ego, and it comes into being through the configuration it gives itself.

Without an authentic substance that remains the same, the process of configuring one's actions into a self story is open to two dangers. The first has been identified by the hermeneutics of suspicion, and involves constructing a story of self-deception that is a projection of desires rather than a configuration of real actions.[66] The second danger involves an aimless wandering among imaginative variations supplied by the fictional narratives of the culture and a refusal to construct a self-story. This danger involves a failure to be a self, a lack of self-understanding and identification. The consistency of one's life story is created by one's promises to be constant in one's future actions. The commitments to others to act toward them in a certain way and the contracts one makes with partners and groups presuppose the maintenance of some continuity of actions and the narrative description formed by them. Some psychotherapy can be understood to be the work designed to help a client construct a meaningful story out of the unintegrated fragments of action he or she brings.[67]

Nietzsche believe that a person worthy of admiration is one whose thoughts, desires, and actions are not haphazard but are connected to one another in "the intimate way that indicates in all cases the presence of style.[68] Nietzsche held that an admirable self consists of a large number of powerful and conflicting tendencies that are controlled and harmonized. Although these can be made to cohere because of weakness and imitation, the admirable person gives them harmony through the creation of their own style of coherence. Nietzsche's model for life was literature, and he emphasized the idea that life is something to be fashioned in the way a work of literature is shaped. He held that although past events cannot be changed, one can alter the narrative that is used to connect them to the present, and in this way even the accidents in our past can be turned into actions—that is, into events for which we are willing to accept responsibility. The events of one's life can be read from different perspectives, and they are amenable to various kinds of emplotment. The number of different readings is limited and must fit the given events (as different readings of a sentence must fit the given words). Nietzsche's concern is that people will simply adopt a culturally given plot line—for example, the Christian plot line of gaining salvation through good works or faith, or the Freudian plot line which "begins with the infant and young child as a beast, otherwise known as the id, and ends with the beast domesticated, tamed by frustration in the course of development in a civilization hostile to its nature."[69] Nietzsche wanted the plot of personal identity to be a creative work of quality and style.

This chapter has attempted to draw out implications of narrative for a description of human experience, the subject matter of the human sciences, based on the notion that human existence stands not only within but also out from the plane of objective space and time. To sever the portion of human existence that is hermeneutically expressive in order to fit it into a formal science grid is to misunderstand and distort the subject matter that the human disciplines seek to know. Human existence takes place in and is figured by a linguistic milieu, with narrative being the primary form through which humans construct the dimension of their life's meaningfulness and understand it as significant.

CHAPTER VII

Practice and Narrative

F ROM narrative what do we learn about the practice of the human sciences? There are two interrelated levels of practice in the human sciences. The first level is the study or investigation of a situation through diagnosis and understanding; this is usually followed by the second level, the treatment or restoration of the situation to wholeness through intervention or therapy. On occasion, the first-level investigation leads to the conclusion that the situation does not need correction, that it is sound as it is. Members of the human sciences have divided themselves into first-level workers (scientists or academics) and second-level workers (practitioners), but such a division disregards the obvious fact that those engaged in treatment need to assess and understand a given situation in order to be informed about appropriate methods of intervention.

Human experience as narrative

Figurative language

The practice of the human disciplines is concerned with groups of various sizes. Work is done with individuals, couples, families, organizations, and political units that range in size and complexity from towns to international configurations. The implications of the understanding of narrative are important for work with all of these various human organizations. The case history and the life story of an individual, the story of a marriage, the history of a corporation, and national and world histories are all subjects of the human disciplines. To set the context for the explicit applications of narrative understanding, I will summarize the findings on narrative so far developed in this study.

Human existence is composed of various orders of reality: material reality, organic reality, and the reality that we call meaning. The Enlightenment view of the order of meaning was that it was composed primarily of ideas that were representations of an external reality. Language had no epistemological role; it was a secondary component of the realm of meaning. Ideas and their combinations were understood to exist in the mind, and language functioned to manage the complex of ideas and to transmit ideas when communication to others was needed. This dislocation of language from a role in epistemology was maintained by both empiricism and phenomenology. The difference between the two positions concerned the role that consciousness played in the production of the pure ideas. For empiricism, ideas were passively received from the environment; for phenomenology, the transcendent ego was actively involved in the production of the ideas that appeared. Language was a secondary element of meaning; it was not at all engaged in the production of meaning.

The position taken in this study is that language does not have an innocent and transparent function in knowledge creation, that its grammatical, rhetorical, and narrative structures constitute (that is, impose form upon) the subjects and objects that appear in the order of meaning. Linguistic forms have as much reality as the material objects of the physical realm. For human existence, linguistic forms are paramount, for they filter and organize information from the physical and cultural realms and transform it into the meanings that make up human knowledge and experience. On the basis of this constructed experience, we understand ourselves and the world, and we make decisions and plans regarding how we will act.

The Enlightenment question, "Is it really a box?", assumes that the epistemological problem is to match the idea that a word stands for with an object that exists independently of us. When the inquiry is changed to make it a hermeneutic question about the realm of meaning, it comes closer to being the kind of query appropriate to ask about narrative. For example, the question, "Does the word really mean that?", does not have an external object as a referent. The meaning of a word is socially constructed and can be personally interpreted. The meaning of a word is given by its place in a language system rather than by a set of extralinguistic objects.

The failure to appreciate the ability of language to create meaning and value is related to the Enlightenment view of the role that language plays in understanding and inquiry. Traditionally in the human disciplines, learning how to understand has been construed as learning how to speak more perspicuously about some reality. Locke expressed the Enlightenment notion that language is a conduit between us and things in themselves. Figures of speech, including metaphors and narratives, were distinguished from literal speech. Figurative speech, in which words were used to create nonliteral images and to adorn reality in a forceful and dramatic manner that went beyond what was contained in ideas themselves, was understood to contribute nothing to a person's cognitive understanding. For some, it was believed, figurative speech was acceptable for embellishing statements and making them more pleasing, but for others it could detract from the purpose of knowing things as they are and so should be avoided.

The recognition that human experience is a construction involving the use of figurative linguistic powers leads to several problems. One concerns the attempt to overcome the power of language and to develop a picture of the world as it is in itself before language appears and can influence understanding. This problem is at origin ontological, concerning the nature of reality. The Enlightenment view was that reality was a closed material system organized according to rules that could be expressed in terms of formal logic and mathematics. Heidegger suggested an alternative approach to ontology, in which the most significant order of reality is meaning, not matter, and in which meaning is organized according to aesthetic principles instead of the principles of formal logic. For Heidegger, knowledge of the contents of the realm of meaning (a poem, for example) is not correlated with knowledge of the material that transmits meaning (the sound waves by which the poem is communicated). Thus, there is no relation between the meaning of a word and the sounds that signify it or the number of letters required to represent it. Because the realm of meaning exists in a different ontological mode from the physical reality through which it can be represented, we cannot know it using the same procedures we use to know the physical realm. Knowledge of the realm of meaning is gained through interpretive or hermeneutic procedures, exemplified by the procedures used to understand the meaning of a poem.

The object of inquiry for the human sciences is the reality of human experience, both that present in and that hidden from awareness. Human experience is hermeneutically organized according to the figures of linguistic production. A function of the human sciences is to read or hear and then interpret the texts of human experience. These disciplines do not produce knowledge that leads to the prediction and control of human experience; they produce, instead, knowledge that deepens and enlarges the understanding of human existence. This kind of knowledge of the texts of experience is derived from a whole set of skills, such as an awareness of how texts create and carry meaning, how structures and prototypes organize the parts of expression into meaningful statements and discourse, and how transformative principles relate meaning to different types of discourse. Knowledge of human experience requires the use of interpretive or hermeneutic approaches, approaches that resemble the techniques and rational procedures used by history and literary theory.

Narrative discourse

The basic figuration process that produces the human experience of one's own life and action and the lives and actions of others is the narrative. Through the action of emplotment, the narrative form constitutes human reality into wholes, manifests human values, and bestows meaning on life. Emplotment composes meaning out of events by a process similar to the process that grammar employs to develop meaning from words. To ask of a narrative, "What really happened?", is to assume that plots are simply representations of extralinguistic realities and that they can be investigated empirically by recapturing those extralinguistic realities.

When organizing real past events into meaningful stories, narrative configuration is not simply a personal projection that has no relation to worldly events. When the acknowledged task of a narrative is to organize and make actual past events meaningful, it is required to attend to the accepted reality of those events. Nevertheless, narrative meaning consists of more than the events alone; it consists also of the significance these events have for the narrator in relation to a particular theme. For example, the death of one's mother in a personal narrative cannot be represented as if it did not happen; however, the interpretation and significance of one's mother's death may vary, depending on its placement within a narrative scheme.

Plots are meaning expressions, and the appropriate question to ask of them is what the events have meant to someone. Because plot is the logic or syntax of narrative discourse, it is a linguistic expression that produces meaning through temporal sequence and progression. Narrative discourse is one of the large categories or systems of understanding that we use in our negotiations with reality, most particularly in our negotiation with time. Narrative constructs meaning out of our time-boundedness and our awareness that human existence occurs within the limits of mortality. The emplotment of events into narrative form is so much a part of our ordinary experience that we are usually not aware of its operation, but only of the experience of reality that it produces. We inherently accept that certain kinds of knowledge and truth can be understood only sequentially, in a temporal narrative unfolding.

Plotting is an activity in which temporal happenings are shaped into meaningful units. It manifests itself not only in the construction of experience but also in conversations between people and their literary creations (primarily oral, but also written) that rely on experience: myths, fairy tales, stories, novels, and histories. When we are in the role of hearers or readers of the narrative experiences—the creations—of others, we understand the stories through the linguistic processes we use in constructing our own narratives. We call this kind of understanding—of hearing the meaning of a story—hermeneutic understanding.

Our lives are ceaselessly intertwined with narrative, with the stories that we tell and hear told, with the stories that we dream or imagine or would like to tell. All these stories are reworked in that story of our own lives which we narrate to ourselves in an episodic, sometimes semiconscious, virtually uninterrupted monologue. We live immersed in narrative, recounting and reassessing the meanings of our past actions, anticipating the outcomes of our future projects, situating ourselves at the intersection of several stories not yet completed. We explain our actions in terms of plots, and often no other form of explanation can produce sensible statements. Narrative competence appears at about the age of three, when we are able to recognize narratives and to judge how well formed they are. We can translate and recognize the same plot as it appears in various media. Narrative appears to be a subset of the general language code that we use to summarize and retransmit stories into other words and other languages.

If one accepts the significance of narrative in the construction of human experience, how does one approach the study of human beings? What do the results of these studies look like, and of what use are they? The next section examines the possibilities and limits involved in research undertaken by the human sciences when a person is understood to be a constructor of narrative meaning.

Research with narrative

One of the difficulties in discussing research from a human science perspective is that many of the concepts related to epistemology have been given technical meanings by the logical positivist revisions of formal science. Concepts such as "cause," "validity," "justification," and "explanation" were redefined as part of the effort to limit knowledge to whatever could pass the test of certainty. If investigative criteria are to be effective for research aimed at understanding aspects of the realm of meaning and its linguistic structures, the basic definitions of the concepts concerning the generation of knowledge must be reclaimed. One of the tasks of a more inclusive human science is to point out how the reclaimed concepts apply in a more open research model. Human science can no longer only seek mathematical and logical certainty. Instead, it should also aim at producing results that are believable and verisimilar.[1]

Human science investigations related to narrative can be distinguished according to whether the purpose of the research is (1) to describe the narratives already held by individuals and groups or (2) to explain through narrative why something happened. The first kind of narrative research is *descriptive*; its aim is to render the narrative accounts already in place which are used by individuals or groups as their means for ordering and making temporal events meaningful. The criterion for evaluating this kind of narrative research is the accuracy of the researcher's description in relationship to the operating narrative scheme. The second kind of investigation is *explanatory*; its aim is to construct a narrative account explaining "why" a situation or event involving human actions has happened. The narrative account that is constructed ties together and orders events so as to make apparent the way they "caused" the happening under investigation. Because the research issues in these two kinds of investigations are different, they will be treated separately.

Descriptive narrative research

The purpose of descriptive narrative research is to produce an accurate description of the interpretive narrative accounts individuals or groups use to make sequences of events in their lives or organizations meaningful. This research produces a document describing the narratives held in or below awareness that make up the interpretive schemes a people or community uses to establish the significance of past events and to anticipate the consequences of possible future actions. The research does not construct a new narrative; it merely reports already existing ones.

Most often, the researcher is not presented with a sample situation in which someone can clearly articulate the narrative scheme on which he or she operates. Sometimes several conflicting narratives are at work simultaneously, and these produce confusion among the participants about the meaning of an event and make decisions about future actions uncertain. Narrative schemes are often layered and include socially acceptable surface schemes that operate in unstressed situations along with schemes that exert influence in pressured situations. For example, a person may believe in a narrative plot based on the story of Jesus, in which unselfish and forgiving people, even though temporarily defeated, win out in the end. This is the story he or she uses to interpret others' actions and which functions to inform the understanding of his or her own action in normal contexts. However, he or she may also harbor a narrative scheme in which reward follows when one looks out for one's own self-interests, even when this requires actions which are hurtful to others. This second narrative may override the first in pressured or threatening circumstances. Descriptive narrative research, then, attends to the collection of narrative schemes that operate for a person or group and to the situations that trigger or draw the particular narratives into interpretive expression.

In some situations, the researcher begins with a personal expression or action which is the outcome of an unarticulated narrative scheme. For example, a researcher could undertake to describe the interpretive narrative that informs the experience of a person who continues to grieve several years after a daughter has been killed in an automobile accident. It may be that the underlying narrative scheme expressed in the person's depression is one in which God has used the daughter's death as punishment for the parent's own premarital promiscuity. In the person's story, then, the earlier "bad" actions are the cause of the daughter's death, even though the person was not in the auto at the time. Consequently, the feelings of guilt persist. The research is able to account for the continued depression by showing that it is an expression of the guilt derived from the narrative scheme that the person is using to account for the daughter's death.

Descriptive narrative research is also used by organizational analysts who seek to describe the stories that underlie the values and assumptions of an organization and link the members into a group. For example, the examination of references to an organization in memos, letters and manuals can uncover, together with interviews, the various understandings of the organization's story as it is carried in a narrative scheme. Do the members of the organization hold to a single story and acknowledge the roles they are performing as part of a coherent organizational narrative? One issue for the researcher is whether the interpretations of episodes in the organization's history are taken to support or contradict the organization's "official" narrative. The organizational story might be one that emphasizes the notion of a "family" that has struggled from meager beginnings to become successful but has always protected and treated its employees fairly. A past episode used to support and give credence to the story might be the refusal to dismiss any employees during the Depression, even though this resulted in large financial losses for the owners of the company. Some employees, however, recall more recent episodes in which the company dismissed people who tried to organize the workers into a collective bargaining unit. They have used these recollections to reorganize the organizational plot, which they now believe to be the story of unfeeling ogres who are exploiting the workers. The two different plot lines, by producing two different interpretations of the same set of events, are leading to misunderstanding and conflict between management and employees.

Interviews. Often the operative narrative of a person or group is not immediately apparent to the investigator. It may be that the description has to be reconstructed from fragments of the story or from its operation in the interpretation of specific events. The premise the researcher works from is that people strive to organize their temporal experience into meaningful wholes and to use the narrative form as a pattern for uniting the events of their lives into unfolding themes. For a researcher, the basic source of evidence about the narratives is the interview. Questions such as, "Why did it happen?", elicit narrative explanations. Often the narrative is similar in form to a modern novel, with flashbacks and with portions of the story out of chronological order. The researcher needs to move from the specific stories a person uses to account for particular episodes to more general life stories that provide self-identity and give unity to the person's whole existence.

Elliot Mishler notes that soliciting stories from respondents is not a problem for the interviewer. He reports that interviewers seeking merely short answers from respondents often receive long, storied responses. Because the story frequently is a digression from the answer sought by survey interviewers, only the portions of the response considered relevant are usually recorded. According to Mishler: "There is a cumulative suppression of stories through the several stages of a typical study: interviewers cut off accounts that might develop into stories, they do not record them when they appear, and analysts either discard them as too difficult to interpret or select pieces that will fit their coding systems."[2] Narratives are a recurrent and prominent feature of accounts offered in all types of interviews. If respondents are allowed to continue in their own way until they indicate that they have completed their answers, they are likely to relate stories.[3]

The oral stories produced by respondents in an interview are dynamically different from the written texts of history or fictional narratives, which have been the focus of attention in previous studies of narrative. The insights of discourse theory can help us to understand the dynamics that are involved in the production of narratives in the interview context. In discourse theory, the story is the result of the total situation—the teller of the story, the codes of the story, and the hearer of the story. The interviewee is the teller of the story, the interviewer the hearer. In this context, the story selected to be told can function to present a particular image of the teller; and the kind of interview the hearer undertakes can affect the kind of story told. Paget describes a series of in-depth, unstructured interviews in which control of each interview is given to the interviewee. She proposes that solidarity should be established between the interviewer and the interviewee and that a context should be built in which both people are engaged in a process of trying to understand important aspects of their lives. By describing similarities between her own and an interviewee's experiences, by asking searching and open-ended questions, and by supporting extended responses, Paget builds a context in which the interviewee feels less need to tell stories that are primarily designed to present the self in socially valued images.[4] Narratives are context-sensitive, both in their telling and in the meaning they give to events, and their form and content are responsive to the aims and conditions of the interview situation. Mishler comments, "If we wish to hear respondents' stories, then we must invite them into our work as collaborators, sharing control with them, so that together we try to understand what their stories are about."[5] This context is different from the typical survey interview context, in which the interview is controlled by the interviewer who asks specific questions and intervenes when the answers are "off-track."

Because of the dynamics of the interview situation, understood as a specific discourse situation, the gathering of narrative statements through interviews needs to be followed by an analysis that includes not only the answers of the respondents but also the characteristics of the interview situation. Transcripts of an interview can be broken down and particular statements identified according to the functions they serve in the narrative account. Several models for analyzing interview materials for their narrative content have been proposed recently. One provided by William Labov functions to abstract from the particular content of the interview a core story, which can then be compared to other stories with a similar structure but told in other contexts. Labov's analytical process distinguishes those parts of the interview that contain narrative accounts from those parts that do not. He defines narrative as a "recapitulation of experience that maintains the strict temporal ordering of events as they occurred in the real world."[6] The object of the analysis is to abstract the plot (the theme or point of the story) from the total response of the interviewee. The interview material contains, in addition to the core narrative, such elements as flashbacks, comments on the action, and descriptions of characters and setting. These elements serve to orient the listener within the story, bring the narrator and the listener back to the present, and so on.

Labov uses themes drawn from generalized social meaning and action as the means for analyzing stories. He proposes, for example, that narratives of unexpected violence contained in interviews can be understood as instances of social intercourse involving requests and their responses. By reducing the particular content of the stories to a general structure, he can identify a request by an actor, followed by a second actor's denial of the request, and finally a violent response by the first actor to the denial of his or her request. Thus the stories are inferred to be individual examples of the more abstract and generalizable social interaction pattern of the "request, denial, violence" plot. This formal statement of the plot can be generalized to other contexts with other characters, and stories exemplifying this plot can be sought in these other contexts.

Labov has also suggested that the analytic work of interview narratives requires the procedure of "expansion," whereby knowledge about the speakers and their personal and general circumstances needs to be introduced before the proper inferences can be made about the text. This knowledge is not included in the text itself; it is what must have been presupposed by the narrator in order for the interviewer to understand the story. The analysts must recognize these presuppositions if they are accurately to interpret the story.[7]

Agar and Hobbs offer a second model of analysis of narrative interviews that gives more attention to the particular content of a story than does Labov's method.[8] They also do not make the sharp distinction between plot and auxiliary elements of the interviewee's responses that Labov does. The analysis suggested by Agar and Hobbs emphasizes the question of how an episode in the story is related to the general story, that is, how it coheres with the rest of the account. They propose three levels of coherence: local, in which the succession of statements is connected to prior statements by syntactic, temporal or causal relations; global, in which the statements cohere with the overall theme or intent of the story; and themal, in which general culture themes or values are expressed. Global coherence is achieved through the repetition of examples that relate to the theme uniting the whole story, such as the teller's general honesty in his or her business dealings.

In his analysis of interview narratives, Mishler proposes that the analyst can assume two notions about the story. First, that whatever else the story is about, it is also a form of self-presentation in which the teller is claiming a particular kind of self-identity. The analysis can be directed to the content of this self-identity and to the various episodes and themes that interviewees selected in support of their identity and to the cultural values presupposed by it. Second, because "everything said functions to express, confirm, and validate this claimed identity,"[9] the narrative analyst can search for statements and references related to the teller's identity throughout the account.

Mishler holds that the analysis of interview narratives provides the human sciences with a means for a more appropriate theory construction, one that incorporates an understanding of complex relationships that change through time. He states:

> Theorizing about the structure, forms, and rules of social action requires either this type of narrative analysis or an equivalent that preserves the complex ordering of actions and reactions that constitute social reality ... This cannot be done through standard approaches where each step in the naturally ordered sequence is isolated from its context, coded within the framework of a standard code-category system, and then aggregated across populations of respondents and subjected to statistical analysis. This is the signal contribution of methods of narrative analysis: the story contains a sequence of socially meaningful acts without which it would not be a story; its analysis therefore provides the basis for a direct interpretation of a complex unit of social interaction, in comparison to the standard approach where such inferences are based on decontextualized bits and pieces.[10]

Descriptive narrative investigations most often examine stories retained in the fluid oral form rather than in the more stable written form. This is certainly the case with personal narratives, which must usually be drawn out through the use of interview methods. And even though organizational stories may appear in written form, as in a statement of mission, they function primarily through their individual interpretations and reconstructions by the members of the organization. These investigations, then, draw on the principles underlying anthropological descriptions of operative cultural narratives and values.[11] In these, the researcher has to penetrate behind the fragmented information and a variety of sources to locate the primary story (or stories) that informs the practices and interpretation of community events.

Researchers seeking to describe the operating narratives for groups are confronted by a continuum from complete consensus on a single group story to no agreement at all on any. The researcher first tries to discern if there is a single, overriding story that gives a unity and wholeness to the events of that organization. If none can be identified, the group is without a single direction and must operate by making use of various stories drawn from the common stock of organizational narratives. In this situation, the organization operates in a fragmented or conflicting manner, borrowing interpretive schemes from a multitude of different stories. If, instead of no commitment to a narrative scheme, there is strong commitment by different members of an organization to stories with different themes—such as "making it big in the marketplace" and "serving the public interest"—misunderstanding arises, and there will likely be lack of agreement on the meaning of the same events, and periods of conflict, crisis, and disruption.

Types of plot. A full description of a story should include both the elements that are unique to that particular story and those that can be found, at least in essence, in other stories. The researcher's experience with many narratives allows him or her to produce a description that includes comparisons and contrasts within the story under consideration and between this and other stories. Such comparisons can serve as a means for pointing to the story's special figurational aspects in relation to the cultural stock of stories available to the teller of the tale. Before describing some categorical narrative schemes, a warning must given about their use.

The natural and biological sciences have made use of categorization and typologies as the basis for formal explanation. In the human realm of meaning, however, categorizing does not produce the same power of explanation. Narratives, like sentences, although they conform to the rules of linguistic generation, produce new and context-dependent meanings. To know that a sentence is "declarative" or that a story is "tragic" does not provide its particular and essential meaning. The generation of stories requires using the plots of the past, but as these plots are enlarged and varied by eliminating some elements and adding others, the stories produced become increasingly dissimilar to the exemplar. Thus the stories emerge as something other than mere instances of the exemplar type.

The researcher investigating the order of meaning cannot simply use the principles of categorization and typology that researchers concerned with the natural realm use. The identification of a narrative as a member of a category does not identify its effect and its relationship to other narratives in the same way the categorical identification of a physical object does. In the linguistic order, elements are related primarily according to their similarities and dissimilarities rather than according to their inclusion in or exclusion from a category. The typologies of plots should be considered as statements of similar events that are shared by various stories. They should not be viewed as descriptions of species of stories. Only in fields like biology and botany can differences between species and individuals be clearly found. In the organic realm, types have substantial supports—namely, living organisms—and because these reproduce almost identically one can objectively distinguish the typical and individual peculiarities among them. In the realm of meaning, not everything is typical, and understanding does not reproduce itself exactly. Typologies of narrative function in a very weak sense, and are only useful if seen as an inventory of abstractions and concepts.

The researcher who aims at describing the stories held by people or organizations brings to the interview and written documents experience with a wide variety of narrative plots and an understanding of the various types of plots by means of which events are organized into followable stories. There is no single typology or system of categories to describe plots. The way in which an array of plots is divided appears to depend on the particular perspective of the researcher or the interest of the discipline. For example, as mentioned in Chapter 2, social psychologists Kenneth and Mary Gergen propose that "there are only three prototypical or primitive narrative forms":[12] the progressive narrative, the regressive narrative, and the stability narrative. In the progressive narrative, progress toward the goal is enhanced; in the regressive narrative, it is impeded; and in the stability narrative, there is no change. The three forms represent the logical possibilities of change toward a goal—that is, getting closer to achieving the goal, getting further away, or staying the same. Actual plots are constructed by combining the three rudimentary narrative forms in various ways. For example, the tragic plot begins with the progressive narrative in which the protagonist moves toward the goal and achieves a high position, but then there comes a regressive episode in which there is a rapid fall. This combination of rudimentary forms is contrasted with the comedy, which is the reverse of the tragic plot. In the comedy plot, the story begins with a regressive narrative in which life events are problematic and move the character away from happiness, but then a progressive moment develops in which happiness is restored.[13]

Northrup Frye proposed that four basic narrative structures give form to human experience: (1) the romantic, in which an aspect of life is configured as a quest or a pilgrimage to some desired end, (2) the comic, in which progress toward the goal occurs through evolution or revolution, (3) the tragic, in which one falls away or declines from some achieved goal, and (4) the ironic, in which events overwhelm the person.[14]

Nevertheless, attempts to create a definitive typology of plots have not been successful. The variety and combination of plot structures means that they do not conform to a categorical structure without intense abstraction of the specific features that give an individual story the power to supply a meaningful interpretation of experience. The repertoire of different plot arrays can function only heuristically for the researcher as a first-level attempt to describe the story operating in the situations being studied.

It is possible that plot types might be used for making diagnostic descriptions of life stories. Some of the psychiatric diagnostic categories, for example, especially those relating to personality disorders, could be understood as narrative types. Ernest Keen has provided an illustration of the use of narrative type for describing a self-identifying story.[15] He investigates the notion of paranoia as a "pattern that repeats itself, is reliably discriminable and describable." Keen proposes that, instead of trying to place paranoia according to disease categories, as is most commonly done, we think about paranoia in terms of a kind of narrative that a person uses to give order and coherence to his or her life. In the paranoid narrative, nothing new is allowed for in the story: "Unlike ordinary experience, new events, that have never happened before, are not plotted in my experience; the possibility of a future in the usual sense does not exist."[16] The paranoid narrative tells of the slipping away of life toward an inevitable approach of "cataclysm." Keen compares this story to the depressive story, where the future remains open and the present is unsatisfactory compared to a possibility that can still be envisioned. In the depressive narrative, the person, although pessimistic about what will happen, is not fighting against time and resisting the coming of the future.

Describing a narrative by assigning it to a type is of limited usefulness for researchers studying narratives. When a plot is set up as a type and given a name, the tendency is to forget the definite, to cling to the definition. Merely to locate a plot in a category is to forget that the type is simply the summary of a prefabricated plot. Paul Veyne, writing about the use of types by historians, says:

> In history the type is what one causes it to be; it is subjective, it is what is chosen as typical in the eventworthy field. Because the type is set up, instead of being found ready-made, because the type is what one chooses it to be, it follows that invoking the type adds nothing to the explanation and also that, formulated thus, the idea of "using a typology" is only a scientist myth ... Now faced with the typical, the historian cannot have the same attitude as the naturalist.[17]

In some sciences, Veyne adds, like medicine or botany, in which a type can be clearly described in several pages, "they are lucky that two corn poppies or even two cases of varicella are much more like each other than two wars or even two enlightened despotisms are."[18] There are plot structures that reappear simply because the number of possible combinations of crucial plot forms is finite and because humans imitate and draw on the cultural stock of stories, and the researcher can be guided by the similarities that narratives share with other stories. Yet the uniqueness of the particular narrative being described by the researcher is as important as the features it has in common with other stories.

Results. The research report itself is not simply the presentation of the story of some person or organization. It is an argued essay that conforms to the rules of a scholarly presentation. Alternative narratives and interpretations are recognized, and evidence from the interview text is used to argue for the conclusion the researcher has reached. The theme or point of the story is not usually directly presented by the text, for it requires inference and interpretation on the researcher's part. Like formal science research, descriptive narrative research involves detection, selection, and interpretation of the data, which in narrative is the text of the interview (and the common cultural presuppositions necessary for understanding it). The transcripts of interview materials must be available to other researchers so that they can follow the researcher's move from data to interpretation.

The purpose of descriptive research is to present the narrative schemes the storyteller has intended. Information about actions that were undertaken on the basis of the story supports the researcher's claim that the story allows the person to order and organize his/her experience. The elimination of other possible narrative plots that are less effective than the proposed story in accounting for the person's actions supports the correctness of the researcher's account. The thesis of the research report is that the offered description accurately represents the operating stories that people or groups use to understand the temporal connections between the events they have experienced and to account for their own and others' motives, reasons, expectations, and memories. The report also recognizes how these stories have functioned (or failed to function) to order the events under consideration into a coherent and unified experience.

Explanatory narrative research

The result of a research program aiming to give a narrative explanation is the same as one of the answers to the question of why something that has involved human actions happened. The research can address such questions as, "Why did a person crash his/her auto into a sign post?", "Why did the student become a merit scholar?", "Why did the company go bankrupt?" "Why did the Challenger space shuttle explode?", or "Why did the United States go to war in Vietnam?" Seeking to give a narrative account of why something has happened is not a new form of inquiry; it is already used in many studies undertaken to explain why a project has succeeded or failed. Investigative reports often take the form of narrative accounts that link together the events and actions that have led up to the outcome under investigation. In ordinary conversation we often provide explanations of our own or others' behavior by telling narratives. In answer to such a question as, "Why are you interested in classical literature?", we are apt to tell a story that provides a sequence of critical events accounting for the interest. In research of this type, the researcher is charged to provide an explanation for why an outcome has occured.

It is the narrative explanation, as opposed to an explanation by law or correlation, that makes narrative research different from the research ordinarily undertaken in the human sciences. For example, the explanations of why the Challenger exploded can be given in terms of the physical properties of the o-rings that malfunctioned during the launch, in terms of the probabilities that a launch will fail, or in terms of the probabilities that equipment will malfunction. Although the knowledge of the laws that relate temperature and plasticity are important to include in a narrative explanation, they do not in themselves satisfy the need to know why, in this particular instance and in this context, the space shuttle exploded. A satisfactory answer to this question requires a narrative explanation. Narrative explanations are retrospective. They sort out the multitude of events and decisions that are connected to the launch, and they select those which are significant in light of the fatal conclusion. They draw together the various episodes and actions into a story that leads through a sequence of events to an ending. The story highlights the significance of particular decisions and events and their roles in the final outcome. The researcher's final report reads more like a historical account of why a country has lost a war or why an election has come out in a particular way than like a research report giving the correlations between scores on measuring instruments.

The results draw on all the evidence that is relevant to the outcome, including individuals' interpretations of information, the personal and social forces operating in the context, the individual stories of ambition and pressure, the lack of procedures to insure that appropriate and timely information has reached decision makers, and so on. The narrative research report recreates the history or narrative that has led to the story's end, and draws from it the significant factors that have "caused" the final event. The report does not develop generalizable laws that are supposed to hold whenever the initial conditions are repeated; it does locate the decision points at which a different action could have produced a different ending. The report is retrodictive rather than predictive, that is, it is a retrospective gathering of events into an account that makes the ending reasonable and believable. It is more than a mere chronicling or listing of the events along a time line: it configures the events in such a way that their parts in the whole story become clear.

We use the skill of constructing narrative explanations in our own lives to understand why we and others act in a particular way. The skill is part of our competence to understand the meaning of sentences or the facial expressions of others. The narrative research report differs from this everyday use of narrative explanation in its reflectiveness and consciousness: it seeks out information and calls on the investigator's enlarged experience of prototypical narrative explanations, which may make sense of the complex of events that contribute to explaining the ending.

Historians often use this type of research to give accounts of why small- or large-scale events have occurred, organizing natural occurrences and human actions into a linked and unified story. This is also the type of explanation therapists give in response to such questions as, "Why is the client afraid of taking a new job?" Their answers often take the form of case histories that describe the context in which past events have significantly affected the patients to bring about their present fearful condition.

Historians and therapists use narratives to explain states or events by recounting significant and critical past episodes. Yet the approach has not been generally adopted by the other human disciplines as an acceptable alternate model for research.[19]

Explanation. This study holds that narrative explanations are genuinely explanatory, for they can answer the question of why something has happened. As described in the chapter on history, this position has been challenged on the grounds that because narrative explanation does not derive from universal laws, it cannot provide a basis for prediction. Nevertheless, narratives can be explanatory, if they meet several conditions. Atkinson has addressed these conditions and concluded:

> The question is, then, what conditions have to be satisfied before "mere" narrative (writing about the past) can be counted explanatory. There would, I believe, be common consent that the truth of the individual assertions made is not enough, and that reporting events in chronological order is neither necessary nor sufficient. These are negative points. Positively what is required is some species of coherence–comprehensiveness with unity, nothing relevant omitted, everything irrelevant excluded–a coherence which carries with it intelligibility and explanatory power.[20]

Atkinson gives three characteristics of the kind of coherence required of a narrative account in order for it to be explanatory: it should be intelligible in human terms, it should have an appropriately unified subject matter, and it should be causally related.[21] Narrative explanation is also question-relative, that is, narratives are explanatory when they provide meaningful and complete answers to questions which are worth asking.

Explanation by narrative has the structure, "one because of the other." It includes rational explanation, in which the reasons a person gives for doing something—that is, his or her intentions—are acknowledged as the impetus for the performance. This type of explanation derives from the competence people possess for recognizing that an event is a human action and not a simple physical occurence; that is, it recognizes that people can make something happen by intervening in the course of natural events, by setting a sequence of events in motion. It also involves the notion of teleological inference, in which something is done in order to accomplish a preconceived end: "Why did he enroll in a French class?" "He wanted to learn to speak French." But perhaps he wanted to learn to speak French specifically in order to be offered a new position in his company that required knowledge of French. Ricoeur calls explanations using teleological inference "intentional understanding," and practical inference (a knowledge of the practical consequences of intended actions) "singular causal imputation."[22]

Max Weber has described the logic of singular causal imputation in his work, "Critical Studies in the Logic of the Cultural Sciences."[23] This kind of logic consists essentially of a "what if" procedure: constructing by imagination a different course of events, weighing the probable consequences of the imagined course of events, and then comparing these consequences with the real course of events. As Weber puts it: "In order to penetrate the real causal interrelationships, *we construct unreal ones.* (Emphasis in original)"[24] For example, the researcher imagines that a participant in a narrative did not decide to write a particular letter, and then asks if this changed event would have produced a different outcome. If yes, then the actual event probably has a causal significance in relation to the actual outcome; if no, then it does not. The kind of events that can be submitted to the test for causal implication can be natural and chance events as well as human actions: for example, "What if the other driver had not lost control of the car at that specific moment?", or "What if it had not rained on that day?"

The test for causal significance suggested by Weber actually involves the testing of different plot schemes tried on the actual events. The procedure is a reportable thought experiment, and the reasons for accepting or rejecting particular events as causally significant can be defended through argument. The logical structure of the thought experiment is based on the notion that "things would have been different" if this particular event or combination of events had been different. In order to carry out the thought experiment, the researcher uses knowledge based on rules that describe how humans are prone to react under given situations. The consequences of the imagined, changed past are developed through the application of these rules to the imagined situation. These rules usually are not at the level of formal scientific physical laws; rather they cover knowledge of dispositions to act in certain ways. Ricoeur understands that this use of the rules of behavioral responses in the imaginative reconstruction of a changed past is "sufficient to show ... how laws can be used in history, even though they are not established by history."[25]

In explanatory narrative research, the point is to provide a narrative account that supplies the events necessary or causal for the outcome under investigation to have occured. The term "cause" is another of those concepts that has acquired a technical meaning through formal science, now being limited to the effects of general laws on particular events; for example, gravity "causes" the rock to fall. Cause is defined as the "constant antecedent." In general usage, however, "cause" means whatever produces an effect, result, or consequence, and it can include events, people's actions, or other conditions. Because narrative cause can relate to the antecedents of a peculiar sequence that may never be repeated, its meaning is different from that meaning of cause in formal science.[26] Gareth Williams, to avoid the confusion brought about by these two meanings, has suggested that narrative cause be designated by the word "genesis." Williams writes:

> Given the teleological form of narrative reconstruction, I employ the concept of "genesis" not for stylistic or rhetorical purposes, but in order to liberate myself from the semantic straitjacket imposed by the term "cause" as it has been generally understood since Hume, and so as to establish a connexion with the Greek tradition of reflection on origins of things which attained its apogee in Aristotle's doctrine of the four causes.... It [cause] is an analytic construct through which the respondent can be seen to situate a variety of causal connexions as reference points within a narrative reconstruction of the changing relationships between the self and the world.[27]

In spite of Williams's use of the term "genesis," I believe that the term "cause" should be maintained in explanatory narrative research, with cause by law acknowledged as only one of the broader range of types of causes—laws, rules,

events, and actions. By recounting the connections between events and actions
that have led to a particular occurrence, the researcher arrives at an appropriate
statement of the reasons for the event.

Data collection. A narrative researcher's data—interviews, documents, and other
sources—are the traces of past events; they help uncover the events leading up to
the phenomenon under investigation. Of course, the kind of data collected depends
on the kind of ending to be explained. An analysis of why negotiations over nuclear
arms have broken down requires data from a great many sources covering a long
historical period compared to data for an explanation of why a child has stayed
home from school.

Narrative explanations are based on past facts. These are then organized into
a unified story in which the links between the events are developed, and the
significance provided. Because past "facts" are not open to direct, present observation, they must be established on the basis of traces, for instance, documents,
memos, and personal memory. As described in an earlier chapter, events retained
in memory as aspects of a narrative account are often reshaped by later happenings and by the plot line. The reconstruction of past facts thus frequently resembles detective work, with several personal accounts together with partial written
records needed to infer what actually has happened.[28] For example, to establish
whether or not a person received certain information before deciding to launch
the Challenger, several types of evidence may be required. In some instances, the
researcher may have cause to suspect that a person's story is false and cannot be
relied on for establishing the event. Noting from the daily log that the message
was received in the office at a certain time, that the person was in the office at the
time the message arrived, and that the person has a habit of reading messages at
the time they arrive, the researcher can deduce (but not with certainty) that the
person probably read the message.

Courts of law have established procedures for arriving at an authentic story.
The prosecutor and defendant bring conflicting stories before the bar; various
witnesses are called to give evidence in support of one or the other stories. Rules
of evidence and standards of argument have been designed to assist in deciding
which of the stories is an accurate statement; for example, evidence based on
hearsay or personal conclusions are not acceptable.[29] Thomas Seebohm has
explored the relation between jurisprudence and hermeneutics.[30] Seebohm understands that jurists and historians use similar methods to determine the "facts" of
what happened, including the intentions of the actors. The courts, however, have
means for determining what "really happened" that are sometimes not available
to human science researchers. They have direct communication with witnesses,
testimonies of present persons, and often extensive circumstantial evidence and

pleas. The court investigates present or almost present episodes. In Seebohm's view the interpretive problem is not determining "beyond reasonable doubt" the facts of the case (what I called narrative first-order referents in Chapter 3). It is, rather, determining the plot or kind of story (second-order referents) that connects the facts and how the "original intention of the lawgiver" applies to a particular narrative.

Collecting past "facts" and placing them in correct chronological order, although necessary for a narrative explanation, is not sufficient. The researcher has to select from the multitude of past facts related to an incident, and the selection is made on the basis of the narrative that is under construction. The narrative may show gaps in the information base and may lead the researcher to search for the missing information. A narrative explanation draws the gathered past facts together into a whole account in which the significance of the facts in relation to the outcome to be explained is made clear. For example, that someone received a memo before making a decision may be a simple fact, but it is not an explanatory fact. In the narrative account, however, the meaning of the fact is described in relation to the sequence of events, and the fact becomes significant in light of the subsequent events. It becomes clear in the narrative account that the cause of the failure was the person's refusal to believe or act on the information, not that the information was not received.

Validity, significance, and reliability. As has happened with the concept of "cause" the general concept of "validity" has been redefined by formal science. It has become confused by the narrowing of the concept to refer to tests or measuring instruments. In narrative research, "valid" retains its ordinary meaning of well-grounded and supportable.[31] This ordinary meaning is distinguished from two more limited meanings. The first comes from the context of formal logic, where "valid" describes a conclusion that follows the rules of logic and is correctly drawn from the premises. The second is used in measurement theory, where "validity" refers to the relationship between the measuring instrument and the concept it is attempting to measure. A valid finding in narrative research, however, although it might include conclusions based on formal logic and measurement data, is based on the more general understanding of validity as a well-grounded conclusion.

Conclusions of narrative research are most often defended by the use of "informal" reasoning.[32] The researcher presents evidence to support the conclusions and shows why alternative conclusions are not as likely, presenting the reasoning by means of which the results have been derived. The argument does not produce certainty; it produces likelihood. In this context, an argument is valid when it is strong and has the capacity to resist challenge or attack. Narrative research does not produce conclusions of certainty, the ideal of formal science with its closed systems of mathematics and formal logic.[33] Narrative research, by retaining an emphasis on the linguistic reality of human existence, operates in an area that is not limited by formal systems and their particular type of rigor. The results of narrative research cannot claim to correspond exactly with what has actually occurred—that is, they are not "true," if "truth" is taken to mean exact correspondence or conformity to actuality. Research investigating the realm of meaning aims rather for verisimilitude, or results that have the appearance of truth or reality. Karl Popper has proposed that verisimilitude is the limit on all knowledge and that, at best, we can demonstrate only the falsity of statements, not their truth.[34] The conclusions of narrative research remain open-ended. New information or argument may convince scholars that the conclusion is in error or that another conclusion is more likely. Narrative research, then, uses the ideal of a scholarly consensus as the test of verisimilitude rather than the test of logical or mathematical validity.[35]

The concept of "significance" has also been redefined by formal science to designate a technical, statistical definition of the extent to which a correlation found among variables is probably due to the chance of random sampling. In general usage, the term "significance" points to the notion of meaningfulness or importance. But because the same word is used to designate both the broad and the limited concept, the more limited technical meaning has gathered to it the values of the general usage. Thus, people often interpret statistical significance to mean that the finding is important, without considering the limited idea that the finding probably resulted from the chance drawing of sample elements from the population. In narrative research "significance" retains its more general meaning. A finding is significant if it is important. Finding out that the Challenger accident was caused by a faulty decisioning-making strategy would be significant.

The ordinary meaning of "reliable" refers to the quality of dependability. To rely on someone is to have complete confidence and trust that she or he will do what is asked or that what he or she says can be trusted. Used in the context of quantitative research, "reliability" refers to the consistency and stability of measuring instruments. Reliable instruments continually yield the same score when the variable itself remains stable. If in taking a second measurement the score differs, one can trust that the difference is because of an actual change in the variable, not simply an artifact of a "loose" instrument.

Reliability in narrative study usually refers to the dependability of the data,[36] and validity to the strength of the analysis of the data. Attention has been directed to the trustworthiness of field notes and transcriptions of interviews. Mishler has reviewed the problems that arise in going from tape recordings to written texts.[37] He recommends researchers keep returning to the original recordings and devise explicit transcription rules and a well-specified notation system, including codes for pauses, talk-over, and voice tone. Mishler notes that present interview theory is based on a stimulus-response model. The interviewer's questions are treated as a standard research stimulus and are expected to remain a constant so that any variance in the response can be attributed to factors in the interview population. Mishler argues that interviewing needs to be understood as a discourse, not a constant stimulus provoking a measurable response.[38] Data generation in narrative studies is affected by the context and sequence in which interviews are given. Researchers undergo changes as they gather data, and the people interviewed affect those doing the interviewing. Yet interviewers do generate stories and gather information. It is the responsibility of researchers to establish a free flow of information from participants in their studies and to describe fully how it was accomplished. Narrative studies do not have formal proofs of reliability, relying instead on the details of their procedures to evoke an acceptance of the trustworthiness of the data.

Data analysis. Data collection results in a collection of stories. The goal of analysis is to uncover the common themes or plots in the data. Analysis is carried out using hermeneutic techniques for noting underlying patterns across examples of stories. A simple example of the use of these techniques can illustrate the process. Comparing two reports, "I approached the phone to call her for a date, but my stomach became so tense I couldn't pick up the phone, so I ended up not making the call and went back and watched TV for the evening," and "I saw this job advertised that really looked exciting, I was going to apply but I thought they would probably get a lot of better applications and it wouldn't be worth the effort," yields a number of possible themes. For example, both include initial attraction to a goal, followed by a retreat from pursuing the goal. Perhaps they experienced the debilitating thought that they might be rejected if they exposed themselves by asking for what they wanted. One reported physical symptoms as part of his fear. These notions would have to be held as possible descriptions until further information was given.

A test of the results of this type of linguistic analysis is asking if the identified general pattern would produce the specific stories given in the original data. Furthermore, adequate analysis does not produce idiosyncratic results; other researchers, given the data from which the results were drawn, can agree that the results follow.[39] The analysis of narrative data does not follow an algorithmic outline, but moves between the original data and the emerging description of the pattern (the hermeneutic circle). Amedeo Giorgi has developed a more formal, six-stage process for the analysis of linguistic data.[40] Two recent exemplar studies by Robert Bellah and associates and by Erik and Joan Erikson and Helen Kivnick demonstrate the responsible manner in which linguistic analysis can be carried out systematically and rigorously.[41] Linguistic analysis has a rich tradition as a research approach in literary criticism, providing the behavioral and social sciences a reservoir of principles and guidelines for use in narrative analysis.[42]

Psychotherapy

Although I have separated the process of research from the process of practice, most often these are not completely separate. The interview process itself can help the client or members of an organization bring to awareness the narrative scheme they are using to interpret events. The practitioners of the human sciences are involved in the descriptive research process when they attempt to uncover and understand the narratives used to construct their clients' schemes of meaning. This information is used for diagnosis which continues throughout the intervention process as a means to assess and correct the progress of the case. The goal of practice varies: it can make the latent narrative manifest, it can help construct a unifying narrative, or it can reconstruct a more useful and coherent interpretation of past events and future projects than the client's present narrative.

The recognition that humans use narrative structure as a way to organize the events of their lives and to provide a scheme for their own self-identity is of importance for the practice of psychotherapy and for personal change. Self-help groups, such as Alcoholics Anonymous, stress the telling of "one's story" to the group as a means of publicly acknowledging that one is someone whose story has lacked the element of self-control. The telling of the story in itself is held to have therapeutic value, and sharing one's own narrative with others helps bring cohesion to the support group. In emerging friendships, a person chooses to reveal to another person his or her personal story.

Psychotherapeutic work with individual clients is also centered in narrative statements. This narrative tradition in psychotherapy extends back to Freud. Donald Spence begins his book, *Narrative Truth and Historical Truth*, with a chapter on the narrative tradition in psychoanalysis. He writes:

> Freud made us aware of the persuasive power of a coherent narrative—in particular, of the ways in which an aptly chosen reconstruction can fill the gap between two apparently unrelated events, and in the process, make sense out of non-sense. There seems no doubt but that a well-constructed story possesses a kind of narrative truth that is real and immediate and carries an important significance for the process of therapeutic change.[43]

Freud's case histories are narrative in form, and in their writing he encountered all the problems of narrative design that writers of history and novels face.

A recent movement in psychoanalysis has sought to emphasize the analyst's role as a collaborator in a narrative, as the editor of a living text. Spence and Roy Schafer, both psychoanalysts, propose that analysts understand themselves as interpreters of narrative accounts rather than as positivist natural scientists.[44] Schafer describes psychoanalytic work:

People going through psychoanalysis—analysands—tell the analyst about themselves and others in the past and present. In making interpretations, the analyst retells these stories. In the retelling, certain features are related to others in new ways or for the first time; some features are developed further, perhaps at great length.... The analyst's retellings progressively influence the what and how of the stories told by analysands.... The end product of this interweaving of texts is a radically new, jointly authored work or way of working.[45]

The therapist is working with a patient's narrative constructions rather than with descriptions of actual past events. Literary critic Peter Brooks finds in Freud's case histories an underlying assumption that psychic health corresponds to a coherent narrative account of one's life;[46] and Steven Marcus, in discussing Freud's case history of Dora, writes:

Human life is, ideally, a connected and coherent story, with all the details in explanatory place, and with everything (or close to everything as is practically possible) accounted for, in its proper causal or other sequence. And inversely illness amounts at least in part to suffering from an incoherent story or an inadequate narrative account of oneself.[47]

The patient comes to the analyst with a story to tell, a story that is not so much false—since it does in some manner signify the truth—as incomplete and untherapeutic. Psychoanalysis is not merely the listening to an analysand's story, however. It is a dialogue through which the story is transformed. The plot brought by the analysand lacks the dynamic necessary to create a sequence, or design, that integrates and explains. The fuller plot constructed by the analytic work leads to a more dynamic, and thus more useful, plot which serves as a more powerful shaping and connective force. The new story must above all be hermeneutically forceful and must carry the power of conviction for both its tellers and its listeners.

The point of the analytic work is not to lead the analysand to create a literal description of or to recover the past. Instead, the past is to be reconstructed in the light of the client's present awareness. According to the narrative understanding of the psychoanalytic process, therapy does not consist in the healing effect of the recovery of the repressed but in the reconstruction of a person's authentic psychoanalytic story. Frederick Wyatt describes the essentials of psychoanalytic listening; these provide the interchange in which an approximately authentic personal history emerges out of the groping and defensive story elements.[48]

Wyatt proposes six elements for the psychoanalytic "set-to-listen-and-organize." (1) The analyst listens with an ear for the distinction between latent and manifest significance. In the context of the narrative this means that the story is not merely accepted as it is told: the analyst looks for the subtext of the story, those aspects of the story that point beyond themselves to something the storyteller has not intended to say. (2) The analyst listens to hear what is in transformation, to discover the unending process of coping and experiencing. The story is not a static tale of the past: it is a psychological report that continues to change as the person changes. (3) The analyst is aware that, in the process of coping with experience, there is a tendency to be repetitive, to do the same thing over and over, and so the story will reconstruct what has worked for the person before. (4) The analyst knows that the story testifies to the person's state of identity. "As he strains for order, continuity and coherence of what he has experienced, so will he strive for coherence in his own self, between his subjective past, his present and a possible and desirable future."[49] (5) The analyst listens with the awareness that the self strives to achieve unity and consistency, and uses fantasy and reflection to process what has been experienced so that the self will not be too troubled by conflicts and contrary impulses. (6) The analyst knows that the person strives for multiple goals and gratifications, and is required to maintain a balance and integration of the various wants and desires.

Wyatt believes that psychoanalytic listening helps the person to articulate his or her story with as little constraint and hindrance as possible. The function of the psychoanalytic setting is "to provide the basis and ambience for the kind of listening that will facilitate the telling of stories, as well as invite and evoke them in preparation for the ensuing psychoanalytic conversation."[50] As the person lets out the emerging story, it becomes recognizable as his or her own story. The person comes to know through telling, through hearing her or his own authentic story out loud for the first time.

In a reply to Donald Spence, Morris Eagle focuses on the importance of the therapeutic narrative's relationship to "historical facts."[51] Spence has made the distinction between "historical truth"—what has actually happened—and "narrative truth"—a story about what has happened. Eagle raises a question as to which of these two "truths" has priority in therapeutic work. If it is the persuasiveness of the narrative truth that matters, and if the construction of narrative truth depends on its mixture of form and content, rather than on the number of brute facts it happens to include, then the effectiveness of narrative truth is linked more to its persuasiveness than to its truth. Eagle asks: "Why should the analyst not disregard those factual truths that do not fit in with or that disturb the elegance, coherence, and persuasiveness of the narrative," if the primary considerations are effectiveness and persuasiveness rather than veridicality?[52] Eagle recognizes that facts do not "speak for themselves," which is Spence's reason for proposing that a need exists for an enabling narrative to organize the facts. Although Spence does not argue for the construction of a narrative that neglects the "facts," Eagle believes that the logic of the distinction between "historical truth" and "narrative truth" does not preclude such constructions.

For both Spence and Eagle, the therapeutic narrative needs to include those factual events that do exist. A personal story that neglects or denies the events in one's life in order to be more pleasing or coherent—that is, a fictional account of one's self—is counter to the therapeutic commitment to truth. The commitment to a true historical narrative of oneself is a value commitment. Although facts take on meaning when they are placed in an organizing scheme, whether it be categorical or narrative, the organizing scheme must "fit the facts." Facts only partly determine the particular scheme to be used in their organization, and more than one scheme can fit the same facts: several narratives can organize the same facts into stories and thereby give the facts different significance and meaning. But there is a difference between acknowledging that a variety of organization schemes can fit the same set of facts and denying the existence of facts. If a client has been fired from a job, for example, the significance of this event can vary, depending on whether it is included in a narrative of opportunity or a narrative of tragedy. However, if the client wants to deny having been fired in order to retain a narrative that supports a positive self-image, that person is overstepping the value commitment of therapy to recognize and accept the "factual" happenings.

In addition to the psychoanalytic writers, James Hillman, a Jungian psychologist, and Bradford Keeney, a "cybernetic" family therapist in the Bateson tradition, have also recognized the importance of narrative for therapy. Hillman's book, *Healing Fiction,* depicts Freud as a figure oscillating between two traditions, science and the humanities, and struggling for a suitable form for "telling" the story of the human psyche.[53] Hillman examines Freud's development of the case history as a form of narrative. He understands that Freud's case history is a new genre of writing that combines historical and fictional elements. Writing about Freud's attempt to hold together the stories of empirical outer events (the case) and inner events (the soul) in the case study, Hillman says: "Despite showing his awareness of the requirements of empiricism, our author [Freud] begs off that method of writing in which he was thoroughly competent from his earlier work in brain pathology and cocaine experiments."[54] Hillman quotes the French writer Alain to illustrate the human dichotomy that Freud was trying to include in his psychological narratives:

> The human being has two sides, appropriate to history and fiction. All that is observable in a man falls into the domain of history. But his romanceful or romantic side (*roman* as fiction) includes "the pure passions, that is to say the dreams, joys, sorrows and self-communings which politeness or shame prevent him from mentioning"; and to express this side of human nature is one of the chief functions of the novel.[55]

Hillman holds that it was Freud's development of the psychoanalytic case history that took medical empiricism out of psychotherapy and brought stories into it.

In his *Aesthetics of Change,* Bradford Keeney says that what emerges in therapy is stories and stories about stories.[56] Keeney holds that therapy is a process of therapist and client weaving stories in collaboration, and thus it is a conversation or an exchange of stories. Cybernetic epistemology approaches the person as a system that achieves stability through the process of change. Systems are recursively connected as parts of a whole ecology and are structured by patterns of organization. A person's story reveals how that person punctuates or organizes his or her world, and it therefore provides a clue for discovering the basic premises that underlie the person's actions and cognitions.

Psychotherapy and narrative have in common the construction of a meaningful human existence. When they come to the therapeutic situation, clients already have life narratives, of which they are both the protagonist and author. The life narrative is open-ended: future actions and occurrences will have to be incorporated into the present plot. One's past events cannot be changed. The situation in which one lived one's childhood, the broken arm that kept one out of school when seven years old, and the decision not to attend college after high school are events that have already happened. However, the interpretation and significance of these events can change if a different plot is used to configure them. Recent events may be such that the person's plot line cannot be adapted to include them. The life plot must then itself be altered or replaced.

The rewriting of one's story involves a major life change—both in one's identity and in one's interpretation of the world—and is usually undertaken with difficulty. Such a change is resisted, and people try to maintain their past plots even if doing so requires distorting new evidence. For some, the life plot is an adaptation of a script having cultural value, or it is a role assigned a person as part of a socially constructed drama.

Therapists can assist clients in the reconstruction of life narratives that have been too restrictive. Questions can be asked about the quality of existence and the freedom of choice that a client's narrative allows. Therapists can draw attention to events and attributes not accounted for by the client's narrative, which can challenge and test the story as told. Therapists also serve to offer alternative narratives that more fully incorporate a client's life events in a more coherent and powerful narrative. The constrictions of a personal narrative can be removed by helping the client to reorganize his or her experience and develop a new life plot.

Although each client's personal narrative uniquely integrates his or her own life events, individuals also adopt basic themes provided by the cultural repertoire. These themes can be understood as integrations of personality types, the outlines of which therapists recognize in a client's personal narrative. The culturally given plot lines function as exemplars for the individually adapted and modified personal narratives.

The therapist helps clients articulate and bring to language and awareness the narratives they have developed to give meaning to their lives. The clients are then able to examine and reflect on the themes they are using to organize their lives, and to interpret their own actions and the actions of others. The reflective awareness of one's personal narrative provides the realization that past events are not meaningful in themselves but are given significance by the configuration of one's narrative. This realization can release people from the control of past interpretations they have attached to events and open up the possibility of renewal and freedom for change.

By being aware of the narrative's importance as a structure that people use to organize their own life events into personal stories, therapists can understand the type of coherence that configures a person's existence into a unity.[57]

Conclusion

I have argued that human beings exist in three realms—the material realm, the organic realm, and the realm of meaning. The realm of meaning is structured according to linguistic forms, and one of the most important forms for creating meaning in human existence is the narrative. The narrative attends to the temporal dimension of human existence and configures events into a unity. The events become meaningful in relation to the theme or point of the narrative. Narratives organize events into wholes that have beginnings, middles, and ends.

Although most human sciences have modeled themselves on the physical sciences—which were developed to study structures of reality outside the realm of meaning—several disciplines have come to be concerned with the understanding configured through narrative forms. These disciplines—history, literature, and particular areas of psychology—can provide models for the investigation of narrative by all of the human disciplines.

A fuller appreciation of the importance of the realm of meaning for understanding human beings will require a different kind of training for scholars in the human sciences. This training will need to include study of the structures and relations of a linguistically organized reality. It will also require a redefinition of the human sciences: instead of conceiving themselves as natural sciences, the human sciences need to conceive of themselves as multiple sciences. The object of their inquiry, the human being, exists in multiple strata of reality, which, although interrelated, are organized in different ways. The stratum unique to human beings is organized linguistically, and the human disciplines need to hone the tools for working with linguistic data much as they have done for physical data. The kind of knowledge that can be obtained from the realm of meaning with its linguistic structures is different from that obtainable from the material and organic realms. This knowledge is developed through hermeneutic techniques, and consists of descriptions of meaning. Knowledge of the realm of meaning cannot be organized into covering laws, and it does not provide information for the prediction and control of future linguistic events.

The exploration of the narrative form is still in its early stages. Because it includes the temporal dimension in its organizational structure, it is very different from the formal organization that puts "facts" into categories. The significance of the time order for self-understanding is not yet clearly understood. Although narratives are ubiquitous, we are just beginning to appreciate their significance for creating and organizing our experience. An awareness of the role of narrative in constructing human experience, in giving significance to events in our lives and form to the actions we plan, has only recently surfaced in the human sciences. This awareness can redirect these sciences to the realm of meaning and provide a focus for future investigations. The point of this book has been to give the reader an initial understanding of narrative, so that the exploration of human lives can be expanded to include the recognition of their narrative structures.

Notes

Chapter I: Introduction

1. Peter Checkland, *Systems Thinking, Systems Practice* (New York: John Wiley & Sons, 1981), 74-82.

2. F. Jacob, *The Logic of Living Systems* (London: Allen Lane, 1974).

3. For example, Maurice Merleau-Ponty, *The Structure of Behavior,* 1942, trans. Alden L. Fisher (Boston: Beacon Press, 1963).

4. James Grier Miller, *Living Systems* (New York: McGraw-Hill, 1978).

5. Jason Brown, *Mind, Brain, and Consciousness: The Neuropsychology of Cognition* (New York: Academic Press, 1977), 10-24.

6. Stephan Strasser, *Phenomenology of Feeling: An Essay of the Phenomena of the Heart,* trans. Robert E. Wood (Pittsburgh: Duquesne University Press, 1977), 149-177.

7. See Jerome A. Shaffer, *Philosophy of Mind* (Englewood Cliffs, N.J.: Prentice-Hall, 1968) for a description of the debates about mind and matter in the history of philosophy. See Paul M. Churchman, *Matter and Consciousness: A Contemporary Introduction to the Philosophy of Mind* (Cambridge, Mass.: MIT Press, 1984) and Joseph Margolis, *Philosophy of Psychology* (Englewood Cliffs, N.J.: Prentice-Hall, 1984) for the contemporary discussion of the mind-body problem.

8. Much has been written in the philosophy of meaning without consensus being achieved. C. K. Ogden and J. A. Richards, *The Meaning of Meaning,* 1923 (reprint, New York: Harcourt, Brace and Co., 1952), distinguished sixteen different senses for "meaning." Justin Leiber, in the article "Meaning" in Rom Harre and Roger Lamb, *The Encyclopedic Dictionary of Psychology* (Cambridge, Mass.: MIT Press, 1983), 374, writes, "Some have argued that meaning is not a unitary notion or perhaps not a distinguishable notion at all." I hold that the notion of meaning represents a common mental action, the drawing of connections between the contents of awareness. The paragraphs that follow provide a brief outline of the application of this general description to the meaning of language, symbols, and discourse.

9. This list is not meant to be an exhaustive description of the kinds of relationship noted by the activity of the realm of meaning. The notion that knowledge consists of two elements—an experiential element (a concrete set of sense data, perceptions, and feelings) and a structural or relational element—comes from Kant and is often reiterated in cognitive science. Kant's categories of judgment or kinds of relationship followed those described in Aristotle's logic. Kant also held that his concepts of relationship were a priori. I am not

arguing that the sensitivity to these relationships are "hard wired"; they may be part of our cultural heritage passed on through the structures of language.

The process of producing meaning by recording relationships among rudimentary perceptual experiences is distinct from the original perceptual processes that provide awareness with whole perceptions. Rudimentary experience is not given as atoms of primitive sense data, but as organized wholes. The experiments of the gestalt psychologists Max Wertheimer, Wolfgang Köhler, and Kurt Koffka demonstrated that a perceptual whole (Gestalt) is given immediately to consciousness.

10. For an excellent collection of writings on the importance of the meanings of similarity in human experience, see Andrew Ortony, ed., *Metaphor and Thought* (Cambridge: Cambridge University Press, 1979).

11. Edmund Husserl, *Ideas: A General Introduction to Pure Phenomenology*, 1913, trans. W. R. Boyce Gibson (New York: Humanities Press, 1931).

12. Charles S. Peirce, *Philosophical Writings of Peirce*, ed. Justus Buchler (New York: Dover, 1955), 98-119.

13. Anthony Giddens, *New Rules of Sociological Method: A Positive Critique of Interpretative Sociologies* (New York: Basic Books, 1976), 93-129.

14. Robert D. Romanyshyn, *Psychological Life: From Science to Metaphor* (Austin: University of Texas Press, 1982), 4-20.

15. See Ray Jackendorf, *Semantics and Cognition* (Cambridge, Mass.: MIT Press, 1983).

16. "Revolutionary" Howard Gardner's term, in *The Mind's New Science: A History of the Cognitive Revolution* (New York: Basic Books, 1985).

17. See Hubert L. Dreyfus, *What Computers Can't Do: The Limits of Artificial Intelligence*, rev. ed. (New York: Harper & Row, 1979) for a critical review of the use of computers as analogues for understanding human intelligence.

18. Gardner.

There have been several other recent approaches to the study of consciousness; for example, the examination of brain waves. Changes registered on instruments to measure brain wave activity were supposed to correlate with types of mental activity. In addition, split-brain research has studied patients who had their corpus callosum surgically severed. This research program attempted to correlate types of conscious activity with brain hemispheres (the right and left brain). Despite wide attention and initial excitement, it has also proved of limited value in comprehending the structures and contents of consciousness. All these mainstream research programs to investigate consciousness have retained a commitment to the epistemological principles of the unified science movement. After initial successes, these programs have confronted serious problems as they moved to study the more complex activities of consciousness.

19. Edmund Husserl, *The Crisis of European Sciences and Transcendental Phenomenology*, 1936, trans. David Carr (Evanston, Ill.: Northwestern University Press, 1970).

20. George S. Howard and Christine G. Conway, "Can There Be an Empirical Science of Volitional Action?" *American Psychologist* 41 (1986): 1250.

21. See Donald E. Polkinghorne, "Phenomenological Research Methods," in *Existential-Phenomenological Perspectives in Psychology,* ed. R. S. Valle and S. Halling (New York: Plenum, in press) for a description of a linguistic-based research process.

22. Margolis, 90.

23. For example, Jerome Bruner, *Actual Minds, Possible Worlds* (Cambridge, Mass.: Harvard University Press, 1986), and Theodore R. Sarbin, ed., *Narrative Psychology: The Storied Nature of Human Conduct* (New York: Praeger, 1986), are two recent studies.

Chapter II: Narrative Expression

1. The *Oxford English Dictionary* (1971 edition) traces the etymology of "narrative" to the Latin *narrare,* to relate, to recount, which is supposed to be for *gnarare,* related to *gnarus,* knowing, skilled, and thus ultimately related to "know."

2. Roland Barthes, "Introduction to the Structural Analysis of the Narrative." Occasional Paper, Centre for Contemporary Cultural Studies, University of Birmingham, 1966, stencilled.

3. See Alasdair MacIntyre, *After Virtue: A Study in Moral Theory* (Notre Dame, Ind.: Notre Dame University Press, 1981).

4. The narrative structure can produce stories of complexity and richness—such as "Oedipus Rex"—which neither allow a simple interpretation nor provide an easy moral. But narrative structure is flexible enough to allow overly simple stories, such as Aesop's fables, whose purpose is to demonstrate a clear moral.

5. Kenneth J. Gergen and Mary M. Gergen, "Narrative Form and the Construction of Psychological Science," in *Narrative Psychology: The Storied Nature of Human Conduct,* ed. Theodore R. Sarbin (New York: Praeger, 1986), 22-44.

6. Northrup Frye, *The Anatomy of Criticism* (Princeton, N.J.: Princeton University Press, 1957).

7. See Paul M. Churchland, *Matter and Consciousness: A Contemporary Introduction to the Philosophy of Mind* (Cambridge, Mass.: MIT Press, 1984), for a current statement of the relation between the mind and body. I do not support the dualism (two substances) that has haunted Western philosophy as the ghost in the machine since Descartes, nor do I support the reduction of mind to materialism. I am advocating a version of the "emerged property" position.

8. Arthur W. Combes, Anne Cohen Richards, and Fred Richards, *Perceptual Psychology: A Humanistic Approach to the Study of Persons,* 1949 (rev. ed., New York: Harper & Row, 1976), 17-26.

9. See Kenneth J. Gergen, "The Social Constructionist Movement in Modern Psychology," *American Psychologist* 40 (1985):266-275.

10. Paul Ricoeur, *Time and Narrative 1,* trans. Kathleen McLaughlin and David Pellauer (Chicago: University of Chicago Press, 1984), 53. Ricoeur understands that narrative prefigures human action into narrative form. For an opposing position, that narrative is a reflective experience, see John A. Robinson and Linda Hawpe, "Narrative Thinking as a Heuristic Process," in Sarbin, 111. See also David Carr, *Time, Narrative, and History* (Bloomington: Indiana University Press, 1986) for an excellwnt study of the relation of narrative to experience.

11. See Ilya Prigogine and Isabelle Stengers, *Order out of Chaos: Man's New Dialogue with Nature* (Toronto: Bantam Books, 1984), 7, for a challenge to the model of the materially real as "simple and . . . governed by time-reversible fundamental laws."

12. Calvin O. Schrag, *Communicative Praxis and the Space of Subjectivity* (Bloomington,: Indiana University Press, 1986).

13. Ibid., p. 30.

14. Jerome Bruner, *Actual Minds, Possible Worlds,* (Cambridge, Mass.: Harvard University Press, 1986), 11.

15. "Narrative" in the singular is used to refer to the general narrative process or form. "Narratives" as a plural refers to the diverse individual stories, which differ in content and plot line.

16. A. E. Michotte, *The Perception of Causality,* 1946, trans. T.R. Miles and E. Miles (London: Methuen, 1963).

17. Henry A. Murray, *Explorations in Personality* (New York: Oxford University Press, 1938).

18. For example, see Eric Berne, *Games People Play* (New York: Grove Press, 1964).

19. Susan Kemper, "The Development of Narrative Skills: Explanations and Entertainments," in *Discourse Development: Progress in Cognitive Developmental Research,* ed. Stan A. Kuczaj II (New York: Springer-Verlag, 1984), 99-124.

20. Noam Chomsky, *Cartesian Linguistics* (New York: Harper & Row, 1966).

21. James C. Mancuso, "The Acquisition and Use of Narrative Grammar Structure," in Sarbin, 92.

22. Ricoeur 1:52-87. Ricoeur refers to these three presentations as mimesis$_1$, mimesis$_2$, and mimesis$_3$.

23. Louis O. Mink, "The Autonomy of Historical Understanding," in *Philosophical Analysis and History,* ed. William H. Dray (New York: Harper & Row, 1966), 188.

24. Ibid., 191.

25. For a position that understands personal existence primarily to be an expression of the human genetic code, see Edward O. Wilson, *Sociobiology: The New Synthesis* (Cambridge, Mass.: Harvard University Press, 1975).

26. See Victoria Fromkin and Robert Rodman, *An Introduction to Language,* 3rd Ed. (New York: Holt, Rinehart and Winston, 1983), 325-345.

27. See Hans Jonas, "Image-Making and the Freedom of Man," in *The Phenomenon of Life: Toward a Philosophical Biology,* 1966 (reprint, Westport, Conn.: Greenwood Press, 1979), 157-181.

28. See Arnold L. Glass, Keith J. Holyoak, and John L. Santa, *Cognition* (Reading, Mass.: Addison-Wesley, 1979), 181-229, for a review of the research on attention.

29. This was a homework assignment given to my son in his high school chemistry class.

30. See Charles Taylor, "Language and Human Nature," 1978, reprinted in Charles Taylor, *Human Agency and Language,* vol.1 of *Philosophical Papers* (Cambridge: Cambridge University Press, 1985).

31. Oswald Hanfling, *Logical Positivism* (New York: Columbia University Press, 1981).

32. See Richard Rorty, *Philosophy and the Mirror of Nature,* (Princeton, N.J.: Princeton University Press, 1979), 165-212, for a historical description of the development of this critique.

33. Mary Hesse, "Is There an Independent Observation Language?" 1970, reprinted as "Theory and Observation," in Mary Hesse, *Revolutions and Reconstruction in the Philosophy of Science* (Bloomington: Indiana University Press, 1980), 63-110.

34. See Paul Watzlawick, Janet Helmick Beavin, and Don. D. Jackson, *Pragmatics of Human Communication* (New York: W.W. Norton, 1967), 54-59.

35. Ferdinand de Saussure, *Course in General Linguistics,* 1907-1911, ed. Charles Bally and Albert Sechehaye, trans. Wade Baskin (New York: McGraw-Hill, 1966).

36. Ludwig Wittgenstein, *Philosophical Investigations,* 3rd. ed., trans. G.E.M. Anscombe (New York: Macmillan, 1968).

37. Rorty, 378.

38. Kenneth Baynes, James Bohman, and Thomas McCarthy, eds., *After Philosophy: End or Transformation?* (Cambridge, Mass.: MIT Press, 1987) in their "General Introduction,"4, describe the skeptical argument; "To [reason's] universality they oppose the irreducible plurality of incommensurable language games and forms of life, the irremediably 'local' character of all truth, argument, and validity—to the a priori [of Kant] the empirical, to certainty fallibility, to invariance historical and cultural invariability, to unity heterogeneity, to totality the fragmentary, to self-evident giveness ('presence') universal mediation by differential systems of signs, to the unconditioned a rejection of ultimate foundations in any form".

39. Maurice Merleau-Ponty, *Phenomenology of Perception*, 1945, trans. Colin Smith (New York: Humanities Press, 1962).

40. Although he was critical of Martin Heidegger's neglect of the idea of human embodiment, Merleau-Ponty drew heavily on Heidegger's analysis of language. The idea that language has a primary function in the display of reality is a central theme in Heidegger, *Being and Time*, 1927, trans. John Macquarrie and Edward Robinson (New York: Harper & Row, 1962), and "The Origin of the Work of Art," 1936, in *Poetry, Language, Thought*, trans. and intro. Albert Hofstadter (New York: Harper & Row, 1971).

41. Maurice Merleau-Ponty, *The Prose of the World*, 1969, trans. John O'Neill (Evanston, Ill.: Northwestern University Press, 1973), 3.

42. The extended analysis of prepredicative experience can be found in Edmund Husserl, *Experience and Judgment: Investigation in a Genealogy of Logic*, 1939, trans. James S. Churchill and Karl Ameriks (Evanston, Ill.: Northwestern University Press, 1973), a posthumous publication edited by Ludwig Landgrebe that dates to 1948.

43. Edmund Husserl, *Formal and Transcendental Logic*, 1929, trans. Dorion Cairns (The Hague: Martinus Nijhoff, 1969), 19. In this book Husserl addresses the structure of formal thought as it is expressed through the grammatical structure of language.

44. See Ross Harrison, "The Concept of Prepredicative Experience," in *Phenomenology and Philosophical Understanding*, ed. Edo Pivcevic (Cambridge: Cambridge University Press, 1975), 93-107, for a comparison of Husserl's project with language-game theory.

45. Merleau-Ponty, *Perception*, 182.

46. Ibid., 188.

47. Merleau-Ponty, *Signs*, 1960, trans. Richard C. McCleary (Evanston, Ill.: Northwestern University Press, 1964), 19.

48. Ibid., 44.

49. James L. Kinneavy, *A Theory of Discourse* (New York: W.W. Norton, 1971).

50. See Ian Hacking, *Why Does Language Matter to Philosophy?* (Cambridge: Cambridge University Press, 1975), for a description of the investigation of words and sentences.

51. Alan Garnham, *Psycholinguistics: Central Topics* (New York: Methuen, 1985).

52. Roman Jakobson, "Linguistics and Poetry," in *Style and Language*, ed. T.A. Sebeok (Cambridge, Mass.: MIT Press, 1960), 350-377.

53. Ibid., 353.

54. Bruner, *Actual Minds*, 11.

Chapter III: History and Narrative

1. Kenneth J. Gergen, "Social Psychology as History," *Journal of Personality and Social Psychology* 26 (1973): 309.

2. Ibid., 319.

3. Ernst Breisach, *Historiography: Ancient, Medieval, and Modern* (Chicago: University of Chicago Press, 1983), 12-21.

4. Harry Elmer Barnes, *A History of Historical Writing*, 2nd rev. ed. (New York: Dover, 1962), 3-25.

5. The term "history" allows for confusion in its usage because it refers to both the branch of knowledge that records and analyzes past events and to the events that form the subject matter of that branch of knowledge.

6. An example of this attempt to urge the traditional studies of the human realm to use the methods of formal science was John Stuart Mill's *Logic* in 1843.

7. Johann Gustav Droysen, *Grundrisse de Historik*, 1868, quoted in Karl-Otto Apel, *Understanding and Explanation: A Transcendental-Pragmatic Perspective*, 1979, trans. Georgia Warnke (Cambridge, Mass.: MIT Press, 1984), 1.

8. See Michael Ermarth, *Wilhelm Dilthey: The Critique of Historical Reason* (Chicago: University of Chicago Press, 1978), 94-108. Dilthey's 1883 publication was the *Introduction to the Human Sciences*.

9. Wilhelm Dilthey, *Ideas Concerning a Descriptive and Analytic Psychology*, 1894, in Dilthey's *Descriptive Psychology and Historical Understanding*, trans. Richard M. Zaner and Kenneth L. Heiges (The Hague: Martinus Nijhoff, 1977), 27-28.

10. Wilhelm Dilthey, *The Constitution of the Historical World in the Human Sciences*, 1906, in *W. Dilthey: Selected Writings*, trans. H. P. Rickman (Cambridge: Cambridge University Press, 1976), 174.

11. Alasdair MacIntyre, *After Virtue: A Study in Moral Theory* (Notre Dame, Ind.: University of Notre Dame Press, 1981), 103.

12. Frederick J. Teggart, *The Processes of History*, 1918, in *Theory and Processes of History* (Berkeley and Los Angeles: University of California Press, 1977), 223, bound with "Is History a Science?"

13. Ibid., 243.

14. Frederick J. Teggart, *Theory of History*, 1925, in *Theory and Processes of History*, 57-58.

15. Ibid., 63.

16. Ibid., 18.

17. See Richard Rorty, ed., *The Linguistic Turn: Recent Essays in Philosophical Method* (Chicago: University of Chicago Press, 1967), 1-39.

18. Carl G. Hempel, "The Function of General Laws in History," 1942, reprinted in *Theories of History,* ed. Patrick Gardiner (New York: Free Press of Glencoe, 1959), 344-356.

19. Maurice Mandelbaum, "Historical Explanation: The Problem of Covering Laws," 1961, in Mandelbaum, *Philosophy, History, and the Sciences* (Baltimore: The Johns Hopkins University Press, 1984), 84, identifies Karl Popper, Patrick Gardner, and Carl Hempel as the group of theorists who argued that the deductive-nomological explanation was appropriate for history.

20. Carl G. Hempel, "Explanation in Science and History," 1962, in *Philosophical Analysis and History,* ed. William H. Dray (New York: Harper and Row, 1966), 104-107.

21. Patrick Gardiner, *The Nature of Historical Explanation* (Oxford: Clarendon Press, 1952), 83-99.

22. Charles Frankel, "Explanation and Interpretation in History," *Philosophy of Science* 24 (1957): 137-155.

23. Ibid., 142.

24. William H. Dray, *Laws and Explanations in History* (London: Oxford University Press, 1957).

25. When analyzing the cause for an event, two types of conditions are considered. The sufficient condition is that which is sufficient always to cause the event. But there may be other conditions that will also cause the same event. To use a morbid example, being shot in the heart will cause a person's death, but there are other conditions that will cause death, such as a severe traumatic injury to a person's head. A necessary condition is that condition without which an event could not have occurred at all. To take another example: Without oxygen there can be no fire. However, the presence of oxygen is not enough in itself to cause a fire. When looking back for the causes of an event, one knows that the necessary condition must have been present, or the event would not have happened.

26. Dray, *Laws and Explanations,* 121-122.

27. Georg Henrik von Wright, *Explanation and Understanding* (Ithaca, N.Y.: Cornell University Press, 1971).

28. Paul Ricoeur, *Time and Narrative 1,* 1983, trans. Kathleen McLaughlin and David Pellauer (Chicago: University of Chicago Press, 1984), 142.

29. Arthur C. Danto, *Analytic Philosophy of History* (Cambridge: Cambridge University Press, 1965).

30. In the introductory chapter, distinctions were made between analysis of words, sentences, and discourse, the combination of sentences. Just as a new kind of meaning is gener-

ated as one moves from individual words to their combinations in sentences, so also is another kind of meaning generated when one moves from individual sentences to their combination in discourse.

31. Danto, *Narration and Knowledge* (New York: Columbia University Press, 1985), Xiii.

32. Karl R. Popper, *The Poverty of Historicism,* 1957, (New York: Harper and Row, 1964).

33. W. B. Gallie, *Philosophy and the Historical Understanding* (New York: Schocken Books, 1968), 22.

34. Ibid., 33.

35. Louis O. Mink, "The Autonomy of Historical Understanding," 1965, in *Philosophical Analysis and History,* ed. William H. Dray (New York: Harper and Row, 1966), 160-192, and "History and Fiction as Modes of Comprehension," in *New Directions in Literacy History,* ed. Ralph Cohen (Baltimore: Johns Hopkins University Press, 1974), 107-124.

36. Mink, "Autonomy," 185.

37. Ibid., 187.

38. Ibid., 184.

39. Mink, "History and Fiction."

40. Ibid., 113.

41. See Chapter 5, "Psychology and Narrative," below, for a similar breakdown of the modes of comprehension. There Jean Mandler's fourfold division of categorical, matrix, serial, and schematic knowledge structures is presented.

42. Mink, "History and Fiction," 117.

43. Hayden White, *Metahistory: The Historical Imagination in Nineteenth-Century Europe* (Baltimore: Johns Hopkins University Press, 1973.

44. Ibid., 30.

45. Ibid., 8.

46. Stephen C. Pepper, *World Hypotheses: A Study in Evidence* (Berkeley and Los Angeles: University of California Press, 1948).

47. Leon J. Goldstein, *Historical Knowing* (Austin: University of Texas Press, 1976), 182.

48. See R. F. Atkinson, *Knowledge and Explanation in History: An Introduction to the Philosophy of History* (Ithaca, N.Y.: Cornell University Press, 1978), and Frederick A. Olafson, *The Dialectic of Action: A Philosophical Interpretation of History and the Humanities* (Chicago: University of Chicago Press, 1979), for two recent surveys of the literature in the philosophy of history.

49. Although the last portion of this discussion has focused on Anglo-American contributions, in France Paul Veyne provided an early response (1971) to debate. See Paul Veyne, *Writing History: Essay on Epistemology,* 1971, trans. Mina Moore-Rinvolucri (Middletown,

Conn.: Wesleyan University Press, 1984). Veyne writes: "It is not that we have the least nostalgia for the contrast advanced by Dilthey between the natural sciences that "explain" and the human sciences that would only make us "understand", which is one of the most memorable blind alleys in the history of sciences. Whether it concerns falling bodies or human action, the scientific explanation is the same, it is deductive and nomological; we deny only that history is a science. The frontier passes between the nomological explanation of the sciences, be they natural or human, and the everyday and historical explanation, which is causal and too confused to be generalizable in laws" (161). Also: The choice of plot decides supremely what will or will not be causally relevent; science can make all the progress it wants, but history clings to its fundamental option, according to which the cause exists only through the plot" (169).

50. Raymond Aron, *Introduction to the Philosophy of History: An Essay on the Limits of Historical Objectivity* (Boston: Beacon Press, 1961).

51. Ibid., 118.

52. Fernand Braudel, *The Mediterranean and the Mediterranean World in the Age of Philip II*, 2 vols, trans. Sian Reynolds (New York: Harper and Row, 1972-1974).

53. See Roman Jakobson, "Linguistics and Poetics," in *Styles in Language*, ed. Thomas A. Sebeok (Cambridge, Mass.: MIT Press, 1960).

54. See the section "Narrative and Temporality" in Chapter 6 for the distinction to be made between objective time and historical time.

55. The term *sapienza poetica*, "poetic logic," comes from Giambattista Vico, *The New Science*, 1725, trans. Thomas Goddard Bergin and Max Harold Fisch (Ithaca, N.Y.: Cornell University Press, 1968), 127. Vico was an early proponent of a human science based on an understanding that humans shaped their experience of the world according to myths or stories. He believed that the one genuinely distinctive and permanent human characteristic was the capacity to generate myths and to use language metaphorically—that is, to deal with the world not directly but from a distance. This capacity was possible because of the faculty of poetic wisdom that allowed humans to engage the world poetically rather than literally.

56. "Poiesis" has a twofold meaning of "to make" and "to make poetry." "Noesis" refers to "thinking." I am using the terms along the lines developed by Hayden White, *Tropics of Discourse: Essays in Cultural Criticism* (Baltimore: The Johns Hopkins University Press, 1978), 7, to designate two contrasting types of discourse.

57. This phrase is taken from a treatment by R. F. Atkinson, *Knowledge and Explanation in History: An Introduction to the Philosophy of History*, (Ithaca, N.Y.: Cornell University Press, 1978), 39-45.

58. See Marc Bloch, *The Historian's Craft*, 1941, trans. Peter Putnam (New York: Knopf, 1953). The kind of techniques discussed here still inform historians'¹ methods for establishing "what happened in the past."

59. Louis O. Mink, "Narrative Form as a Cognitive Instrument," in *The Writing of History: Literary Form and Historical Understanding,* ed. Robert H. Canary and Henry Kozicki (Madison: University of Wisconsin Press, 1978), 143-144.

60. Louis O. Mink, "The Autonomy of Historical Understanding," 1965, in *Philosophical Analysis and History,* ed. William H. Dray (New York: Harper and Row, 1966), 183-187.

61. See Hans-Georg Gadamer, "Hermeneutics as a Theoretical and Practical Task," 1978, in *Reason in the Age of Science,* trans. Frederick G. Lawrence (Cambridge, Mass.: MIT Press, 1981), 113-138, for a discussion of the similarity of the use of "integrative reasoning" in practical wisdom, art, and hermeneutics.

62. Hayden White, "The Question of Narrative in Contemporary Historical Theory," *History and Theory* 23 (1984): 24.

63. See Josef Bleicher, *Contemporary Hermeneutics as Method, Philosophy and Critique* (London: Routledge & Kegan Paul, 1980).

64. Ricoeur, *Time and Narrative,* 1:177.

65. Ibid., 182-192.

66. Ibid., 193-206.

67. Ibid., 206-225.

68. Ricoeur has been interested in hidden meaning since he wrote *The Symbolism of Evil,* 1967, trans. Emerson Buchanan (Boston: Beacon Press, 1969).

69. Paul Ricoeur, *The Rule of Metaphor: Multidisciplinary Studies of the Creation of Meaning in Language,* 1975, trans. Robert Czerny (Toronto: University of Toronto Press, 1977).

70. Ricoeur, *Time and Narrative,* 1:ix.

71. Ibid.

72. Hayden White, "The Value of Narrativity in the Representation of Reality, in *On Narrative,* ed. W. J. T. Mitchell (Chicago: The University of Chicago Press, 1981), 23.

73. David Carr, "Review Essay," *History and Theory* 23 (1984): 364.

74. Ibid., 366.

75. White, "Validity of Narrativity," 23.

76. Mink, "History and Fiction," 557.

77. Ricoeur, *Time and Narrative* 1:74.

78. Carr, "Review Essay," 366.

79. Ricoeur, *Time and Narrative* 1:xi.

80. See Aron Gurwitsch, *The Field of Consciousness* (Pittsburgh: Duquesne University Press, 1964) for an early argument against the idea of perception as a two-step process in which the atoms of sense data are organized by a second-step process into objects. On page 101, Gurwitsch writes: "The object thus present itself in sense-perception is itself, with no special organizing, assimilating, or interpreting activity intervening."

81. See Susan Kemper, "The Development of Narrative Skills: Explanations and Entertainments," in *Discourse Development: Progress in Cognitive Development Research,* ed. Stan A. Kuczaj II (New York: Springer-Verlag, 1984), 99-124.

Chapter IV: Literature and Narrative

1. Jonathan Culler, *On Deconstruction: Theory and Criticism after Structuralism* (Ithaca, N.Y.: Cornell University Press, 1982), 7-11, suggests that this domain be called "textual theory" and given the nickname "theory." He makes the point that it is not literary theory, because many of its most interesting works do not explicitly address literature. He would include Nietzsche, Freud, Erving Goffman, Lacan, and Gadamer among its practitioners. In describing the domain he quotes Richard Rorty's description: "A kind of writing has developed which is neither the evaluation of the relative merits of literary productions, nor intellectual history, nor moral philosophy, nor epistemology, nor social prophecy, but all of them mingled together in a new genre" (8). He holds that this new domain "takes up the most original thinking of what the French call *les sciences humaines*" (9).

Two books give an overview of the work on narrative that has been carried out in literary theory. W. J. T. Mitchell, ed., *Un Narrative* (Chicago: University of Chicago Press, 1981) contains a selection of articles dealing with narrative that appeared in the journal *Critical Inquiry,* and Wallace Martin, *Recent Theories of Narrative* (Ithaca, N.Y.: Cornell University Press, 1986) has presented a survey of the various developments in narrative theory.

In history the number of publications about narrative has decreased considerably after the extensive efforts of the 1960s, while in psychology interest in narrative is in a beginning stage.

2. Martin, *Recent Theories,* 30.

3. Ibid., 28-29: "What appears to be new [in recent fiction and narrative theory] may simply be something that has been forgotten .... Historical studies .... have shown that theories of narrative are not as recent a phenomenon as many critics previously thought."

4. Seymour Chatman, *Story and Discourse: Narrative Structure in Fiction and Film* (Ithaca, N.Y.: Cornell University Press, 1978), 227.

5. See Jonathan Culler, *The Pursuit of Signs: Semiotics, Literature, Deconstruction* (Ithaca, N.Y.: Cornell University Press, 1981), 3-8.

6. Joseph Frank, "Spatial Form in Modern Literature," 1945, in *The Widening Gyre* (Bloomington: Indiana University Press, 1963), 3-62.

7. In spite of Frank's work mentioned in the previous paragraph, early narrative expressions were not considered works of art.

8. Northrup Frye, *The Anatomy of Criticism* (Princeton, N.J.: Princeton University Press, 1957).

9. In this classification, Frye calls attention to the transforming effect that writing and printing have on stories previously limited to oral presentation. This theme was to assume great significance for later poststructuralist theorists, for example, Jacques Derrida, *Of Grammatology*, trans. Gayatri Chakravorty Spivak (Baltimore: The Johns Hopkins University Press, 1974), 18-26. Derrida proposes the development of a science of the written word, which he terms "grammatology."

10. Paul Ricoeur, *Time and Narrative*, 2, trans. Kathleen McLaughlin and David Pellauer (Chicago: University of Chicago Press, 1986), 20.

11. Robert Scholes and Robert Kellogg. *The Nature of Narrative* (London: Oxford University Press, 1966).

12. Joseph Campbell, *The Hero With a Thousand Faces* (New York: Pantheon, 1949), 245-246.

13. In Lord Raglan's version of the primary story, the hero is a person of royal birth, conceived in some unusual manner, who is reputed to be the son of a god; his birth is followed by attempts to kill him, and he escapes to another country where he is raised by foster parents; when he is of age, he goes on a journey to a new country where he is forced to engage in some form of combat; he wins, marries a princess, and becomes a king of the new country; in the end, however, he must flee from his new kingdom. See Lord Raglan, *The Hero: A Study in Tradition, Myth, and Drama*, 1936 (New York: Vintage, 1956).

14. Robert McAndrews: "Journeys: An Inquiry into Meaning and Value." (PhD diss., Saybrook Institute, 1979), 1.

15. See Marthe Robert, *Origins of the Novel*, 1971 (Bloomington: Indiana University Press, 1980). See also the section on "Psychotherapy" in Chapter 7 "Practice and Narrative," below.

16. J. Hollis Miller, "The Problematic of Ending in Narrative," *Nineteenth-Century Fiction* 33 (1978): 3-7.

17. Frank Kermode, *The Sense of an Ending: Studies in the Theory of Fiction* (New York: Oxford University Press, 1967).

18. Ricoeur, *Time and Narrative* 2:26, says that Kermode held that the narrative productions of dramatic episodes in human existence are impositions of meaning. The function of these productions is to console us about the ultimate meaninglessness of death. Frye, on the other hand, believed that human existence is actually meaningful at its core and that the function of narrative is to give this meaning form.

19. The desire in literary criticism to find a logical structural order beneath the ordinary and everyday operations of discourse performance was akin to the desire in history to

find a logical, nomological order underneath the ordinary understanding of history as human actions.

20. Roland Barthes, "Introduction to the Structural Analysis of the Narrative." Occasional Paper. Centre for Contemporary Cultural Studies, University of Birmingham, 1966. Stencilled 3.

21. Dorothy Lee, "Lineal and Nonlineal Codifications of Reality," in *Explorations in Communication,* ed. Edmund Carpenter and Marshall McLuhan (Boston: Beacon Press, 1960), 136-154.

22. Ricoeur, *Time and Narrative* 2:32.

23. Claude Levi-Strauss, *Structural Anthropology,* 1958, trans. Claire Jacobson and Brooke G. Schoepf (London: Penguin Books, 1972), 203-204.

24. Propp's work was first translated into English in 1958; Vladimir Propp, *The Morphology of the Folktale,* 1928, trans. Laurence Scott, 2nd ed. revised by Louis A. Wagner (Austin: University of Texas Press, 1968). He abstracted from Russian fairy tales a universal plot with some similarities to the plots of Campbell and Raglan: a villain brings harm to a family member, and the hero is approached to do something about it; the hero leaves home and is tested; receiving help from a magical agent or helper, the hero then engages and defeats the villain in combat; the original harm is undone, and the hero returns home where he has to perform another difficult task; when he has accomplished this task and the villain is punished, the hero marries and ascends the throne.

25. Ibid., 14.

26. Ibid., 20.

27. Ricoeur, *Time and Narrative,* 2:38.

28. Claude Bremond, "Le message narratif," quoted in Jonathan Culler, *Structuralist Poetics* (Ithaca, N.Y.: Cornell University Press, 1975), 209.

29. Robert Scholes, *Structuralism in Literature: An Introduction* (New Haven, Conn.: Yale University Press, 1974), 111.

30. Tzvetan Todorov, *Grammaire du Décamréron,* quoted in Scholes, *Structuralism,* 111.

31. Roland Barthes, *SZ,* 1970, trans. Richard Miller (New York: Hill and Wang, 1974), 9.

32. Martin, *Recent Theories,* 121-122.

33. Walter Benjamin, *Illuminations: Essays and Reflections,* 1955, ed. Hannah Arendt (New York: Schocken Books, 1968), 83-109.

34. Jonathan Culler, *Structuralist Poetics: Structuralism, Linguistics, and the Study of Literature* (Ithaca, N.Y.: Cornell University Press, 1975).

35. The Russian formalists use the term "fabula" in a somewhat equivalent way to "story" and "syuzhet" for "discourse." Other theorists propose different terms for this difference, for example "récit" sometimes refers to the story (Bremond) and sometimes to discourse (Genette).

36. Seymour Chatman, "What Novels Can Do That Films Can't," In *On Narrative,* ed. W. J. T. Mitchell (Chicago: University of Chicago Press, 1980), 117-136.

37. Mieke Bal, *Narratologie: essai sur la signification narrative dans quatre romans moderns,* quoted in Culler, *Pursuit of Signs,* 171.

38. See the section on "Freudian Psychoanalysis and Narrative" in the following chapter for Freud's use of those two logics. Freud changed from an earlier understanding in which effects must be dependent on earlier causes to an understanding in which the effects of an interpretation can project into the past an event which did not happen (for instance, seeing one's parents having intercourse).

39. See E. M. Forster, *Aspects of the Novel* (London: Arnold, 1927).

40. See Culler, *On Deconstruction,* 85-89.

41. This use of discourse logic appears similar to William James's interpretation of emotion where he holds that physiological changes are experienced and then attributed to an emotional cause. Instead of "I am angry and therefore I strike," James proposes "I strike, therefore I must be angry."

42. Culler, *Pursuit of Signs,* 186.

43. Ricoeur, *Time and Narrative,* 2:61-99.

44. Gérard Genette, *Narrative Discourse: An Essay in Method,* 1972, trans. Jane E. Lewin (Ithaca, N.Y.: Cornell University Press, 1980).

45. Martin, *Recent Theories,* 126.

46. Ricoeur, "Narrative Time," in *On Narrative,* ed. W. J. T. Mitchell (Chicago: University of Chicago Press, 1981), 180.

47. Martin, *Theories of Narrative,* 137-138.

48. Mikhail Bakhtin, *Problems of Dostoevsky's Poetics,* 1929 (Minneapolis: University of Minnesota Press, 1984).

49. See Robert C. Holub, *Reception Theory: A Critical Introduction* (London: Methuen, 1984) for a review of the literature in reception theory with an emphasis on the work of Hans Robert Jauss and Wolfgang Iser.

50. Wolfgang Iser, *The Act of Reading: A Theory of Aesthetic Response,* 1976, (Baltimore: The Johns Hopkins University Press, 1978), 3.

51. Ibid., 37.

52. Norman Holland, "Unity Identity Text Self, in *Reader-Response Criticism: From Formalism to Post Structuralism,* ed. Jane P. Tompkins (Baltimore: The Johns Hopkins University Press, 1980), 118-133.

53. For an example, see Marthe Robert's work as described in the first part of this chapter.

54. See Paul Ricoeur, *Le temps raconte,* vol. 3 of *Temps et récit* (Paris: Seuil, 1985), 244-245.

55. Hans-Georg Gadamer, *Truth and Method*, 1960, trans. Garrett Barden and John Cumming (New York: Seabury, 1975).

56. Hans Robert Jauss, "Literary History as a Challenge to Literary Theory," 1967, in *Toward an Aesthetic Reception*, trans. Timothy Bahti (Minneapolis: University of Minnesota Press, 1982).

57. Gadamer, *Truth and Method*, 269.

58. See Ricoeur, *Le temps raconte*, 250-259.

59. Barthes, *SZ*.

60. Ibid., 92.

61. Terry Eagleton, *Literary Theory: An Introduction* (Minneapolis, University of Minnesota Press, 1983), 82.

Chapter V: Psychology and Narrative

1. See Donald E. Polkinghorne, *Methodology for the Human Sciences* (Albany: State University of New York Press, 1983), 15-57.

2. See *The Encyclopedic Dictionary of Psychology*, s.v. "Individual Psychology: History of," by Jean-Pierre de Waele, for a short history of individual psychology.

3. Alfred Adler, quoted in de Waele. See Alfred Adler, *The Individual Psychology of Alfred Adler*, ed. and annotated by Heinz L. Ansbacher and Rowena R. Ansbacher (New York: Harper Torchbooks, 1956) for a systematic presentation of Adler's position and his influence on psychology. the Ansbachers report that the psychological system with which Adler was most in sympathy was that of William Stern (10).

4. Henry A. Murray, *Explorations in Personality* (New York: Oxford University Press, 1938). See Calvin S. Hall and Gardner Lindzey, "Murray's Personology," Chap. 6 in *Theories of Personality*, 3rd ed. (New York: John Wiley & Sons, 1978) for a summary of Murray's theory and research.

5. Gordon Allport, *The Person in Psychology: Selected Essays* (Boston: Beacon Press, 1968). See also Joseph P. Ghougassian, *Gordon W. Allport's Ontopsychology of the Person* (New York: Philosophical Library, 1972) for a description of Allport's contribution to a psychology of the individual.

6. Hall and Lindzey, 458.

7. Charolotte Bühler, *Der menschliche Lebenslauf als psychologishes Problem* (The human course of life as a psychological problem) (Leipzig: Hirzel, 1933). John Dollard, *Criteria for the Life History* (New Haven: Yale University Press, 1935).

8. William M. Runyan, *Life Histories and Psychobiography*, (New York: Oxford University Press, 1982), 10, lists the contributions in sociology and anthropology.

9. W. I. Thomas and Florian Znaniecki, *The Polish Peasant in Eurpoe and America,* 1920, two volume edition (New York: Knopf, 1927).

10. See Jerome G. Manis and Bernard N. Melter, *Symbolic Interaction: A Reader in Social Psychology,* 3rd ed. (Boston: Allyn and Bacon, 1978) for a description of the methods and procedures used by the symbolic interactionist approach. W. I. Thomas and Florian Znaniecki, *The Polish Peasant in Europe and America,* 1920, two volume edition (New York: Knopf, 1927).

11. Runyan, *Life Histories,* pp. 10-11.

12. Although interest in life histories and narrative forms of presentation were far removed from the mainstream of the human disciplines, it should be noted that Alexander and Dorothea Leighton published the study, *Gregorio the Hand-Trembler: A Psychobiologcial Study of a Navaho Indian* in 1949, Robert W. White wrote his important book, *Lives in Progress* in 1952, the first of Erik Erikson's psychobiographical studies, *Young Man Luther,* appeared in 1958, and Oscar Lewis's *The Children of Sanchez: Autobiography of a Mexican Family* was published in 1961.

13. Quoted in de Waele, 301.

14. de Waele, Individual Psychology," 301.

15. Runyan, *Life Histories.*

16. Ibid., p. 12.

17. Ibid., p. 11-13.

18. See Peter Loewenberg, *Decoding the Past: The Psychohistorical Approach,* 1969 (reprint, Berkeley, Cal.: University of California Press, 1985) 9-41.

19. Jerome Bruner, *Actual Minds, Possible Worlds* (Cambridge, Mass.: Harvard University Press, 1986).

20. The concept of self and self-identity is taken up again in a more general way in the next chapter, "Human Existence and Narrative."

21. Karl E. Scheibe, "Self-Narratives and Adventure," in *Narrative Psychology: The Storied Nature of Human Conduct,* ed. Theodore R. Sarbin (New York: Praeger, 1986), 131.

22. Vonegut, Kurt *Dead Eye Dick* (New York: Dell, 1982), 208, in Ibid., 139.

23. Ibid., 143.

24. Stephen Crites, "Storytime: Recollecting the Past and Projecting the Future," in *Narrative Psychology: The Storied Nature of Human Conduct,* ed. Theodore R. Sarbin (New York: Praeger, 1986), 152-173.

25. Ibid., 162.

26. Ibid., 172.

27. See Howard Gardner, *The Mind's New Science* (New York: Basic Books, 1985), 28. Gardner cites George A. Miller's statement that the beginning of cognitive science can be set

in September 1956, when the Symposium on Information Theory was held at the Massachusetts Institute of Technology. Development of the field was already proceeding at a regular pace when the Sloan Foundation decided in 1976 to fund a five-to-seven-year program in cognitive science and committed twenty million dollars for research in the field.

28. For a discussion of this confrontation by the chief proponent of speech-act theory, see John Searle, "Chomsky's Revolution in Linguistics," in *On Noam Chomsky: Critical Essays,* ed. Gilbert Harman (New York: Anchor Books, 1974), 2-33.

29. Kenneth J. Gergen, "The Social Constructionist Movement in Modern Psychology," *American Psychologist* 40 (1985): 266.

30. Ibid., 267.

31. See Stan A. Kuczaj II, ed., *Discourse Development: Progress in Cognitive Development Research* (New York: Springer-Verlag, 1984) for a collection of recent articles on discourse.

32. See James C. Mancuso, The Acquisition and Use of Narrative Grammar Structure," in *Narrative Psychology: The Storied Nature of Human Conduct,* ed. Theodore R. Sarbin (New York: Praeger, 1986), 91-110, for an overview of the psychological literature on narrative structures.

33. N. L. Stein and M. Policastro, "The Concept of Story: A Comparison between Children's and Teacher's Viewpoints," in *Learning and Comprehension of Text,* ed. H. Mandl, N. L. Stein, and T. Trabasso (Hillsdale, N.J.: Lawrence Erlbaum Associates, 1984), 150.

34. Jean Matter Mandler, *Stories, scripts, and scenes: Aspects of a Schema Theory* (Hillsdale, N.J.: Lawrence Erlbaum Associates, 1984).

35. E. Rosch and C. B. Mervis. "Cognitive Reference Points," *Cognitive Psychology* 7 (1975): 532-547.

36. John Ferccero, "Autobiography and Narrative," in *Reconstructing Individualism: Autonomy, Individuality, and the Self in Western Thought,* eds. Thomas C. Heller, Morton Sosna, and David E. Wellbery (Stanford, Cal.: Stanford University Press, 1986), 16-29, says that Augustine, in his *Confessions,* presented "for the first time the literary self-creation of an individual seen both as object and as subject" (16). It is the separation of self as character and self as author that founds the possibility of any self-portraiture or autobiography, a narrative of the self. The narrative form transforms "discontinuous moments into a linear trajectory" (19) and "individualism, with all its contradictions, is inconceivable, in the Augustinian tradition, without its literary expression" (29).

37. I am following Jean Mandler's suggestion that the plural of "schema" be normalized from the exotic "schemata" to the more common English plural form. This follows the convention of using "dogmas" as the plural of "dogma," rather than "dogmata."

38. Mandler, 22.

39. Stein and Policastro 113-155.

40. Mancuso, 94-98.

41. Stein and Policastro, 113-155.

42. Mandler, 50-53.

43. R. Fuller, "The Story as the Engram: Is It Fundamental to Thinking?" *Journal of Mind and Behavior* 3 (1982), 134, quoted in Mancuso, 98-99.

44. Jean Mandler, "Stories: The Function of Structure" (Paper presented at the annual meeting of the American Psychological Association, Anaheim, Cal., August 1983), 6.

45. Mancuso, 101.

46. Susan Kemper, "The Development of Narrative Skills: Explanations and Entertainments," in *Discourse Development: Progress in Cognitive Development Research*, ed. Stan A. Kuczaj, II (New York: Springer-Verlag, 1984), 99-124.

47. Ibid., 99.

48. Ibid., 101-103.

49. Ibid., 113.

50. Gail Sheehy, *Passages: Predictable Crisis in Adult Life* (New York: Bantam, 1977).

51. Daniel Levinson, *The Season's of a Man's Life* (New York: Ballantine Books, 1978); Roger Gould, *Transformations: Growth and Change in Adult Life* (New York: Simon and Schuster, 1978).

52. *The Encyclopedic Dictionary of Psychology*, s.v. "Lifespan Psychology" by Nancy Datan.

53. Erik H. Erikson, *Childhood and Society*, 1950, 2nd and enlarged ed. (New York: Norton, 1963). See Datan, for a review of other early literature concerned with life-span development.

54. Kenneth J. Gergen, "Stability, Change, and Chance in Understanding Human Development," in Life-Span Development Psychology: Dialectical Perspectives in Experimental Research, ed. Nancy Datan and Wayne W. Reese (New York: Academic Press, 1977).

55. Mark Freeman, "History, Narrative, and Life-Span Developmental Knowledge," *Human Development* 27 (1984) 1.

56. Ibid., 2.

57. Ibid., 3.

58. Paul B. Baltes, Hayne W. Reese, and John R. Nesselroade, *Life-Span Developmental Psychology: Introduction to Research Methods* (Monterey, Cal.: Brooks/Cole, 1977) in their textbook on life-span research write: "It's [developmental psychology's] aim, . . . is not only to *describe* these intraindividual changes and interindividual differences but also to *explain* how they come about and to find ways to *modify* them in an optimum way" (1).

59. Freeman, 8. The pool ball model refers to the illustration in which one rolling pool ball strikes a second ball, "causing" the second ball to roll. This is an oversimplification of Hume's psychological explanation of the experience of cause and effect. See Tom L. Beauchamp and Alexander Rosenberg, *Hume and the Problem of Causation* (New York: Oxford University Press, 1981).

60. Freeman, 17.

61. Mary M. Gergen and Kenneth J. Gergen, "The Self in Temporal Perspective," in *Life-Span Social Psychology*, ed. R. Abeles (Hillsdale, N.J.: Lawrence Erlbaum Associates, in press).

62. Kenneth J. Gergen and Mary M. Gergen, "Narrative and the Self as Relationship," in *Advances in Experimental Social Psychology*, ed. L. Berkowitz (New York: Academic Press, in press).

63. Ibid.

64. Donald P. Spence, *Narative Truth and Historical Truth: Meaning and Interpretation in Psychoanalysis* (New York: Norton, 1982), 21.

65. Roy Schafer, *The Analytic Attitude* (New York: Basic Books, 1983), 240.

66. Ibid.

67. Peter Brooks, *reading for the Plot: Design and Intention in Narrative* (New York: Alfred A. Knopf, 1984), 264-285.

68. Sigmund Freud, *The Wolfman and Sigmund Freud*, 1918 (Harmondsworth: Penquin, 1973), 220.

69. Brooks, *Reading for the Plot*, 277.

70. *Ibid.*

71. Linda Smircich, *"Concepts of Culture and Organizational Analysis,"* Administrative Science Quarterly, 28 (1983): 339-358.

72. Linda Smircich, "Studying Organizations as Cultures," in *Beyond Method: Strategies for Social Research*, ed. Gareth Morgan (Beverly Hills, Cal.: Sage, 1983), 160.

73. Edgar H. Schein, *Organizational Culture and Leadership: A Dynamic View* (San Francisco: Jossey-Bass, 1985) says, "There is a possibility . . . that the *only thing of real importance that leaders do is to create and manage culture* and that the unique talent of leaders is their ability to work with culture" (Emphasis in original) 2.

74. Joanne Martin, Martha S. Feldman, Mary J. Hatch, and Sim B. Sim, "The Uniqueness Paradox in Organizational Stories," *Administrative Science Quarterly*, 28 (1983): 438-453.

75. See *Administrative Science Quarterly*, 29 (September 1983). The issue is devoted to articles on Organizational Culture.

76. Ian Mittroff and R. H. Killman, "Stories Managers Tell: A New Tool for Organizational Problem Solving," *Management Review*, 64 (1975) 18-28.

77. See Gareth Morgan, ed. *Beyond Method: Strategies for Social Research* (Beverly Hills, Cal.: Sage, 1983) for a collection of papers on investigating the realm of meaning of organizations.

Chapter VI: Human Existence And Narrative

1. Heidegger's subject was ontology, the understanding of Being itself, and his main purpose was not to give a full description of the human experience of Being. He believed that being itself was structured aesthetically, and showed up or was experienced by humans through linguistic forms. However, human experience was not the product of a separate, knowing subject removed from and observing Being, he said. Human Being was an aspect of Being; it was Being in place (*Dasein*) where the Reality of Being reflected on itself. Human experience was a clearing prepared by a part of Being (*humanness*) in which Being could show itself.

2. Peter K. McInerney, "The Sources of Experienced Temporal Features," in *Descriptions*, eds. Don Ihde and Hugh J. Silverman, 91-109 (Albany: State University of New York Press, 1985), examines Sartre's thesis that temporality is an ontological structure only of human existence. McInerney's investigation focuses on Sartre's *Being and Nothingness* and does not address the role of the narrative scheme in the experience of temporality.

3. Paul Ricoeur, *Time and Narrative*, 2 vols, trans. Kathleen McLaughlin and David Pellauer (Chicago: University of Chicago Press, 1984-1986).

4. Ibid, 1:52.

5. See Brent D. Slife, "Linear Time Reliance in Psychological theorizing: Negative Influence, Proposed Alternative." *Philosophical Psychology* 1 (Summer 1980): 46-58, for a discussion of the effect of the linear analogy of time on psychological theories.

6. William James, *Principles of Psychology,* 1890, (New York:Dover, 1950), ch. 15.

7. Edmund Husserl, *The Phenomenology of Internal Time-Consciousness*, 1928, trans. James S. Churchill (Bloomington: Indiana University Press,1964).

8. Henri Bergson, *Creative Evolution*, 1907, trans. Arthur Mitchell (New York: the Modern Library, 1944), 7.

9. See Chapter 3, "History and Narrative".

10. Martin Heidegger, *Being and Time,* 1927, trans. John Macquarrie and Edward Robinson (New York: Harper & Row, 1971) Division 2.

11. See Eugene Minkowski, *Lived Time: Phenomenological and Psychopathological Studies*, 1933, trans. Nancy Metzel (Evanston, Ill.: Northwestern University Press, 1970), for another analysis of time as it is lived in the normal personality. Minkowski finished his study prior to his acquaintance with Heidegger's work. His position distinguishes clock time from lived time and relates the distortions of normal lived time to psychopathologies.

12. Ricoeur understands that Heidegger is using procedures close to those used in ordinary-language philosophy in his investigation of the level of time organization. Ricoeur, *Time and Narrative* (1:62), writes: "The plane we occupy, at this initial stage of our transversal, is precisely the one where ordinary language is truly what Austin and others have said it is, namely, the storehouse of those expressions that are most appropriate to what is properly human in our experience. It is language, therefore, with its store of meanings, that prevents the description of Care, in the mode of preoccupation, from becoming prey to the description of the things we care about."

13. The German philosopher and mathematician Gottlob Frege proposed the distinction between the *reference* of a word, which is the object designated, and the *sense* of a word, which is the additional meaning. He used for examples the expressions "the evening star" and "the morning star." In both cases the *reference* is to the planet Venus, but the *sense* carried by the words involves more than just reference.

14. Paul Ricoeur, "The Human Experience of Time and Narrative," *Research in Phenomenology* 9 (1979):24.

15. Paul Ricoeur "Narrative Time," in *On Narrative*, ed.W.J.T. Mitchell (Chicago:University of Chicago Press, 1981), 172.

16. This meaning of "the thought of a narrative" is meant to refer to the type of explanation William H. Dray calls "explaining in colligatory terms." The explanation is a synthesis of the parts into a whole, such as "The Renaissance," or "The French Revolution." See William H. Dray, *Philosophy of History* (Englewood Cliffs, N.J.: Prentice Hall, 1964),19-20

17. The term is from Frank Kermode, *The Sense of An Ending: Studies in the Theory of Fiction* (New York: Oxford University Press, 1967).

18. W. Wolfgang Holdheim, *The Hermeneutic Mode* (Ithaca: Cornell University Press, 1984), 250.

19. Ricoeur, "Narrative Time,"184.

20. Hans-Georg Gadamer, *Truth and Method*, 1960, trans. Garrett Barden and John Cumming (New York: Seabury Press, 1975, 235-341, discusses the problematic of the transmission of possibilities in the tradition.

21. Ricoeur, "Narrative Time," 185.

22. Ibid. 185-86.

23. Ricoeur, "Human Experience of Time," 34.

24. Calvin O. Schrag, *Communicative Praxis and the Space of Subjectivity* (Bloomington: Indiana University Press, 1968), 32-47, points out that humans express themselves with both action and speech. He emphasizes that speech is an act, not only when it is commanding or promising, but also when it is used to refer and describe.

25. Martin J.Packer, "Hermeneutic Inquiry in the Study of Human Conduct," *American Psychologist* 40 (October 1985): 1081. The recent writers Packer refers to are A. Blasi and D. Locke.

26. See chapter 1.

27. See Brendan O'Regan, "Inner Mechanisms of the Healing Response," *Saybrook Review* 5 (1985): 10-31, for a review of literature on changes in the medical approach to healing.

28. Using the model of physical cause with the accompanying metaphor of the transmittal of forces, the human disciplines have developed sophisticated models and research programs for the investigation of human action that include concepts of drive, instinct, libido, cognitions, reinforcement, mental states, habits, and so on. But these theories reduce the issue of human action to a play of impersonal forces without an agent. See Patricia H. Miller, *Theories of Developmental Psychology* (New York: H.W.Freeman,1983), 180-246, for an overview of current theories based on the model of physical force as cause.

29. Alvin I. Goldman, *A Theory of Human Action* (Princeton, N.J.: Princeton University Press, 1970), 80.

30. James E. Faulconer and Richard N. Williams, "Temporality in Human Action," *American Psychologist* 40 (November 1985): 1179.

31. See Max Weber, *The Theory of Social and Economic Organization*, 1922, trans. A.M. Henderson and Talcott Parsons (London: Free Press, 1947).

32. Weber divided moral philosophy into the ethics of principle—that is, the absolutizing ethics of Kant's categorical imperative—and the ethics of accomodation—that is, the relativizing ethics of Bentham's ultilarianism. The ethics of accomodation is satisfied with a little step here and a little step there, and it is meant for the world that is inflicted with impurities and limitations. In either case, the ethical end toward which action is aimed cannot be decided by formal science.

33. Kant proposed that human reason acted in two spheres—one in the organization of the things in the sphere of objective space and time, the other in the sphere of rationality itself. Moral worth was thought to be developed in the second sphere of pure rationality. Kant's categorical imperative was a logical derivative that held that a right action was one that a person could will into a universal law to govern not merely this particular action of an individual person but also the actions of all agents in similar circumstances. However, morality could not be concerned with ends, since a moral action was an action that was commanded for its own sake, not with a view to some purpose that it was expected to bring about.

34. Alasdair MacIntyre, *After Virtue: A Study in Moral Theory* (Notre Dame, Ind.: University of Notre Dame Press, 1981), 42-45.

35. See Donald W. Crawford, *Kant's Aesthetic Theory* (Madison, University of Wisconsin Press, 1974), 145-159.

36. Claude Levi-Strauss, *Structural Linguistics* , 1958, trans. Claire Jacobson and Brooke G. Schoepf (New York: Basic Books, 1963).

37. Jean Piaget, *Structuralism*, 1968, trans. Chaninah Maschler (New York: Harper and Row, 1970).

38. Noam Chomsky, *Language and Mind*, enl. ed. (New York: Harcourt Brace Jovanovich, 1972), 115-160.

39. Packer, 1084.

40. See Chapter 4, "Literature and Narrative," for a fuller discussion of the structuralist approach and its treatment of narrative.

41. See Peter Winch, *The Idea of a Social Science and Its Relation to Philosphy* (London: Routledge and Kegan Paul, 1958).

42. Peter Winch, "Understanding a Primitive Society," 1964, in *Understanding and Social Inquiry*, ed. Fred R. Dallmayr and Thomas A. McCarthy (Notre Dame, Ind.: Notre Dame University Press, 1977), 174-179.

43. See Mario von Cranach and Rom Harre, eds., *The Analysis of Action: Recent Theoretical and Empirical Advances* (Cambridge: Cambridge University Press, 1982), for articles which address human action as goal-directed action.

44. See Richard Rorty, *Philosophy and the Mirror of Nature* (Princeton, N.J.: Princeton University Press, 1979), for his proposition that humans keep the conversation within the games going, even though they accept the fact that there is no possibility to ground a game on some foundation that would assure the truth of its propositions.

45. See Lawrence H. Davis, *Theory of Action* (Englewood Cliffs, N.J.: Prentice-Hall, 1979), 27-41.

46. George Henrick von Wright, *Explanation and Understanding*, (Ithaca: Cornell University Press, 1971), 63-64.

47. Ricoeur, *Time and Narrative* 1:59.

48. Aristotle, *The Poetics of Aristotle*, trans. Ingram Bywater, in *The Rhetoric and The Poetics of Aristotle*, (New York: The Modern Library, 1954), 223-266.

49. See Ricoeur, *Time and Narrative*: 32, for the use of "narrative" as the encompassing term for Aristotle's treatment of drama, epic, and history.

50. The imitating or representing of human action is not the same concept that Plato used when he spoke of the imperfect imitations of ideas. Aristotle used the concept of mimesis to describe the practice of the arts of composition, the human making of representation.

51. Aristotle, *Poetics*, 235.

52. Quoted in *The Encyclopedia Dictionary of Psychology*, s.v. "Self Philosophic Usage," by Irving G. Thalberg.

53. James.

54. See Susan Hales, "The Inadvertent Rediscovery of Self in Social Psychology," *Journal for the Theory of Social Behavior* 15 (October 1985) :237-282.

55. *The Encyclopedic Dictionary of Psychology*, s.v. "Self: Psychological Usage," by E. W. Shepherd.

56. David Carr, "Life and the Narrator's Art," in *Hermeneutics and Deconstruction*, eds. Hugh J. Silverman and Don Idhe (Albany: State University of New York Press, 1985), 108-121.

57. Ibid. 117.

58. The metaphysics of potentiality and actuality was suggested by Aristotle in recognizing the changes that occur in organic life, rather than from a metaphysics of substance.

59. Peter F. Strawson, *Individuals: An Essay in Descriptive Metaphysics* (London: Methuen, 1959).

60. Ibid. 99.

61. Maurice Natanson, *The Journeying Self: A Study in Philosophy and Social Role* (Reading, Mass.: Addison-Wesley, 1970), 22.

62. Erving Goffman, *The Presentation of Self in Everyday Life* (Garden City, N.Y.: Doubleday Anchor, 1959), xi.

63. See Theodore R. Sarbin, "The Narrative as a Root Metaphor for Psychology," in *Narrative Psychology,* ed. Theodore R. Sarbin (New York: Praeger, 1986), 7. Sarbin, who has previously published work on role theory, writes: "Drama . . . is a subordinate concept to the superordinate narrative."

64. MacIntyre, 117.

65. Ernest Keen, "Paranoia and Cataclysmic Narratives," in *Narrative Psychology,* ed. Theodore R. Sarbin (New York: Praeger, 1986), 174-190, describes the plot outlines of the paranoic and cataclysmic narratives adopted as the emplotment strategy by some people.

66. See Sarbin, 16-18, for an overview of authors who have described self-deception from a narrative perspective.

67. See chapter 7, "Practice and Narrative."

68. Alexander Nehamas, *Nietzsche: Life as Literature* (Cambridge, Mass.: Harvard University Press, 1985), 7.

69. Roy Schafer, "Narration in the Psychoanalytic Dialogue," in *On Narrative,* ed. W.J.T. Mitchell (Chicago: The University of Chicago Press, 1981), 26.

Chapter VII: Practice and Narrative

1. Jerome Bruner, *Actual Minds, Possible Worlds,* Cambridge, Mass.: Harvard University Press, 1986), 11.

2. Elliot G. Mishler, "The Analysis of Interview-Narratives," in *Narrative Psychology: The Storied Nature of Human Conduct,* ed. Theodore R. Sarbin (New York: Praeger, 1986), 235.

3. Ibid.

4. M.A. PAGET, "Experience and Knowledge." *Human Studies* 6 (1983), 67-90.

5. Mishler, 249.

6. This description is given by Mishler, 236.

7. William Labov, "Speech Actions and Reactions in Personal Narrative," in *Analyzing Discourse: Text and Talk,* ed. D. Tannen (Washington, D.C.: Georgetown University Press, 1977); and William Labov and D. Fanshel, *Therapeutic Discourse: Psychotherapy as Conversation* (New York: Academic Press, 1977).

8. Michael Agar and Jerry R. Hobbs, "Interpreting Discourse: Coherence and the Analysis of Ethnographic Interviews," *Discourse Processes* 5: 1-32.

9. Mishler, 243.

10. Ibid. 240-241.

11. See Clifford Geertz, *The Interpretation of Cultures* (New York: Basic Books, 1973), 3-30.

12. Kenneth J. Gergen and Mary M. Gergen, "Narrative Form and the Construction of Psychological Science," in *Narrative Psychology: The Storied Nature of Human Conduct,* ed. Theodore R. Sarbin (New York: Praeger, 1986), 27.

13. Gergen and Gergen, analyze the three major developmental theories—learning theory, Piagetian theory, and psychoanalytic theory—according to the rudimentary plot forms they pose for human development.

14. Northrup Frye, *Fables of Identity,* (New York: Harcourt, Brace, and World, 1963).

15. Ernst Keen, "Paranoia and Cataclysmic Narratives," in *Narrative Psychology: The Storied Nature of Human Conduct,* ed. Theodore R. Sarbin (New York: Praeger, 1986) 174-190.

16. Ibid. 177.

17. Veyne, Paul. *Writing History,* 1971, trans. M. Moore-Rinvolucri (Middletown, Conn.: Wesleyan University Press, 1984), 118.

18. Ibid. 120.

19. An exception in sociology is Robert N. Bellah, Richard Madison, William M. Sullivan, Ann Swidler, and Steven M. Tipton, *Habits of the Heart: Individualism and Commitment in American Life* (Berkeley and Los Angeles: University of California Press, 1985), and in anthropology the collection of articles in Victor W. Turner and Edward M. Bruner, eds., *The Anthroplogy of Experience* (Urbana: University of Illinois Press, 1986).

20. R.F. Atkinson, *Knowledge and Explanation in History: An Introduction to the Philosophy of History* (Ithaca, N.Y.: Cornell University Press, 1978), 131.

21. Ibid. 133-135.

22. Paul Ricoeur, 1:138.

23. Max Weber, "Critical Studies in the Logic of the Cultural Sciences." In Max Weber, *The Methodology of the Social Sciences,* trans. Edward Shils and Henry A. Finch (Glencoe, Ill.: The Free Press, 1949), 113-188.

24. Weber, 185-186.

25. Paul Ricoeur, *Time and Narrative*, 1, trans. Kathleen McLaughlin and David Pellauer (Chicago, University of Chicago Press, 1984), 185.

26. See Rom Harré and E.H. Madden, *Causal Powers: A Theory of Natural Necessity* (Totowa, N.J.: Rowman and Littlefield, 1975), for a discussion of the move from a classical Humean notion of cause applicable to the assumed closed systems of experimentation to the self-generation found in open systems. Their view of causal explanation does not contradict the notion of free-will or self-determined human actions.

27. Gareth Williams, "The Genesis of Chronic Illness: Narrative Reconstruction," *Sociology of Health and Illness* 6 (1984): 179-180.

28. See William B. Sanders, "The Methods and Evidence of Detectives and Sociologists," in *The Sociologist as Detective: An Introduction to Research Methods*, ed. William B. Sanders (New York: Praeger, 1974), 1-17.

29. See H.L.A. Hart and A.M. Honoré, *Causation in the Law* (Oxford: Oxford University Press, 1959).

30. Thomas M. Seebohm, "Facts, Words, and What Jurisprudence Can Teach Hermeneutics." *Research in Phenomenology* 16 (1986): 25-40.

31. "Valid" is an adjective usually attached to a statement, argument, or reasoning. Its synonyms in ordinary usage are "sound," "convincing," "telling," and "conclusive." The synonyms designate the differences in the power of an argument to convince the hearer. "Valid" and "sound" both refer to the notion that the argument is able to resist attack. A "convincing" argument is slightly stronger than a "valid" one: it not only can withstand attack, it can silence the opposition. A "conclusive" argument is still stronger; it puts an end to doubt or debate.

32. John Eric Nolt, *Informal Logic: Possible Worlds and Imagination* (New York: McGraw-Hill, 1984).

33. See Murray Levine, "Scientific Method and the Adversary Model: Some Preliminary Thoughts," *American Psychologist* 29 (1974): 661-677, for comments on the requirement that the relevance of statistical measures is dependent on the proposition that the mathematical model underlying them is a reasonable approximation of the nature of the effect being studied. It is the position of this study that the appropriate model for the realm of meaning is linguistic and not mathematical.

34. Karl Popper, *The Logic of Scientific Discovery* (London: Hutchinson, 1959), 53.

35. I agree with the criticism leveled at Habermas that he has made a "category mistake" by identifying consensus derived from argument as "truth." A statement is not "true" because after submission to public debate a general consensus in support of the statement is reached. Instead, the statement agreed to is to be understood as the best understanding we can reach at this time—"the best" meaning that which is judged most accurate given the present evidence and the rational considerations of free participants in a discussion. See

Thomas A. McCarthy, "A Theory of Communicative Competence," in *Critical Sociology*, ed. Paul Connerton (Middlesex, England:Penguin Books, 1976), 478-496.

36. Jerome Kirk and Marc L. Miller, *Reliability and Validity in Qualitative Research* (Beverly Hills, Cal.:Sage, 1986), 51.

37. Elliot G. Mishler, *Research Interviewing: Context and Narrative* (Cambridge, Mass.: Harvard University Press, 1986), 47-50.

38. Ibid. 35-51.

39. Donald E. Polkinghorne, "Phenomenological Research Methods," in *Existential-Phenomenological Perspectives in Psychology*, eds. R.S. Valle and S. Halling (New York: Plenum, in press).

40. Amedeo Giorgi, "An Application of Phenomenological Psychology: Vol. 2, eds. by Amedeo Giorgi, Constance T. Fischer, and Edward L. Murray (Pittsburgh: Duquesne University Press, 1975), 82-103. Giorgi's process was developed for the analysis of phenomenological descriptions; however, its principles of linguistic analysis are also applicable to narrative data.

41. Bellah et al; Erik H. Erikson, Joan M. Erikson, and Helen G. Kivnick, *Vital Involvement in Old Age: The Experience of Old Age in Our Time* (New York: W.W. Norton, 1986).

42. See P.D. Juhl, *Interpretation: An Essay in the Philosophy of Literary Criticism* (Princeton, N.J.: Princeton University Press, 1980) for a systematic review of the positions on linguistic analysis by literary critics.

43. Donald P. Spence, *Narrative Truth and Historical Truth: Meaning and Interpretation in Psychoanalysis*, (New York: W.W. Norton, 1982), 21.

44. Roy Schafer, *The Analytic Attitude* (New York: Basic Books, 1983), 212.

45. Ibid. 219.

46. Peter Brooks, *Reading for the Plot: Design and Intention in Narrative*. (New York: Alfred A. Knopf, 1984), 282-283.

47. Steven Marcus, "Freud and Dora: Story, History, Case History," *Partisan Review* 41 (1974): 92.

48. Frederick Wyatt, "The Narrative in Psychoanalysis: Psychoanalytic Notes on Story-telling, Listening, and Interpreting," in *Narrative Psychology: The Storied Nature of Human Conduct*, ed. Theodore R. Sarbin (New York: Praeger, 1986), 201-205.

49. Ibid. 203.

50. Ibid. 204.

51. Morris N. Eagle, "Psychoanalysis and Narrative Truth: A Reply to Spence." *Psychoanalysis and Contemporary Thought* 7 (1984): 629-640.

52. Ibid. 632.

53. James Hillman, *Healing Fiction* (Barrytown, N.Y.: Station Hill, 1983), 3-49.

54. Ibid. 6.

55. Ibid. 6-7.

56. Bradford P. Keeney, *Aesthetics of Change* (New York: The Guilford Press, 1983).

57. Eagle, 633, warns that the efficacy of therapeutic work using coherent narrative schemes has not been demonstrated. He writes: "The main point I was making was that merely claiming that creative myths, coherent meaning schemes, narratives are curative and therapeutically effective does not automatically make them so. Whether or not they are in fact therapeutically effective (and, if they are, what makes them so) is a crucial empirical question."

References

Adler, Alfred. *The Individual Psychology of Alfred Adler.* Edited and annotated by Heinz L. Ansbacher and Rowena R. Ansbacher. New York: Harper Torchbooks, 1956.

Agar, M., and J.R. Hobbs. "Interpreting Discourse: Coherence and the Analysis of Ethnographic Interviews." *Discourse Processes.* 5 (1982): 1-32.

Allport, Gordon. *The Person in Psychology: Selected Essays.* Boston: Beacon Press, 1968.

Apel, Karl-Otto. *Understanding and Explanation: A Transcendental-Pragmatic Perspective,* 1979. Translated by Georgia Warnke. Cambridge, Mass.: MIT Press, 1984.

Aristotle. *The Poetics of Aristotle.* Translated by Ingram Bywater. In *The Rhetoric and The Poetics of Aristotle.* New York: The Modern Library, 1954.

Aron, Raymond. *Introduction to the Philosophy of History: An Essay on the Limits of Historical Objectivity.* Boston: Beacon Press, 1961.

Atkinson, R.F. *Knowledge and Explanation in History: An Introduction to the Philosophy of History.* Ithaca, N.Y.: Cornell University Press, 1978.

Bakhtin, Mikhail. *Problems of Dostoevsky's Poetics.* 1929. Minneapolis: University of Minnesota Press, 1984.

Baltes, Paul B., Hayne W. Reese, and John R. Nesselroade. *Life-Span Developmental Psychology: Introduction to Research Methods.* Monterey, Cal.: Brooks/Cole, 1977.

Barnes, Harry Elmer. *A History of Historical Writing.* 2nd revised ed. New York: Dover, 1962.

Barthes, Roland. "Introduction to the Structural Analysis of the Narrative." Occasional Paper, Centre for Contemporary Cultural Studies, University of Birmingham, 1966. Stencilled. *S/Z,* 1970. Translated by Richard Miller. New York: Hill and Wang, 1974.

Baynes, Kenneth, James Boham, and Thomas McCarthy, eds. *After Philosophy: End or Transformation?.* Cambridge, Mass.: MIT Press, 1987.

Beauchamp, Tom L. and Alexander Rosenberg. *Hume and the Problem of Causation.* New York: Oxford University Press, 1981.

Bellah, Robert N., Richard Madison, William M. Sullivan, Ann Swidler, and Steven M. Tipton. *Habits of the Heart: Individualism and Commitment in American Life.* Berkeley, Cal.: University of California Press, 1985.

Benjamin, Walter. *Illuminations: Essays and Reflections,* 1955. Edited by Hannah Arendt. New York: Schocken Books, 1968.

Bergson, Henri. *Creative Evolution,* 1907. Translated by Arthur Mitchell. New York: The Modern Library, 1944.

Berne, Eric. *Games People Play.* New York: Grove Press, 1964.

Bleicher, Josef. *Contemporary Hermeneutics as Method, Philosophy and Critique.* London: Routledge & Kegan Paul, 1980.

Bloch, Marc. *The Historian's Craft,* 1941. Translated by Peter Putnam. New York: Knopf, 1953.

Braudel, Fernand. *The Mediterranean and the Mediterranean World in the Age of Philip II.* 2 vols. Translated by Sian Reynolds. New York: Harper and Row, 1972-1974.

Breisach, Ernst. *Historiography: Ancient, Medieval, and Modern.* Chicago: University of Chicago Press, 1983.

Brooks, Peter. *Reading for the Plot: Design and Intention in Narrative.* New York: Alfred A. Knopf, 1984.

Brown, Jason. *Mind, Brain, and Consciousness: The Neuropsychology of Cognition.* New York: Academic Press, 1977.

Bruner, Jerome. *Actual Minds, Possible Worlds.* Cambridge, Mass.: Harvard University Press, 1986.

Bühler, Charlotte. *Der menschliche Lebenslauf als psychologishes Problem* The human course of life as a psychological problem. Leipzig: Hirzel, 1933.

Campbell, Joseph. *The Hero with a Thousand Faces.* New York: Pantheon, 1949.

Carr, David. "Review Essay." *History and Theory* 23 (1984): 357-70.
—"Life and the Narrator's Art." In *Hermeneutics and Deconstruction,* edited by Hugh J. Silverman and Don Idhe, 108-21. Albany: State University of New York Press, 1985.
—*Time, Narrative, and History.* Bloomington: Indiana University Press, 1986.

Chatman, Seymour. *Story and Discourse: Narrative Structure in Fiction and Film.* Ithaca, N.Y.: Cornell University Press, 1978.
—"What Novels Can Do That Films Can't." In *On Narrative,* edited by W.J.T. Mitchell, 117-36. Chicago: University of Chicago Press, 1980.

Checkland, Peter. *Systems Thinking, Systems Practice.* New York: John Wiley & Sons, 1981.

Chomsky, Noam. *Cartesian Linguistics: A Chapter in the History of Rationalist Thought.* New York: Harper & Row, 1966.
—*Language and Mind,* enlarged ed. New York: Harcourt Brace Jovanovich, 1972.

Churchman, Paul M. *Matter and Consciousness: A Contemporary Introduction to the Philosophy of Mind.* Cambridge, Mass.: MIT Press, 1984.

Combes, Arthur W., Anne Cohen Richards, and Fred Richards. *Perceptual Psychology: A Humanistic Approach to the Study of Persons,* 1949. Rev. ed. New York: Harper & Row, 1976.

Cranach, Mario von, and Rom Harré, eds. *The Analysis of Action: Recent Theoretical and Empirical Advances.* Cambridge: Cambridge University Press, 1982.

Crawford, Donald W. *Kant's Aesthetic Theory.* Madison: University of Wisconsin Press, 1974.

Crites, Stephen. "Storytime: Recollecting the Past and Projecting the Future." In *Narrative Psychology: The Storied Nature of Human Conduct,* edited by Theodore R. Sarbin, 152-173. New York : Praeger, 1986.

Culler, Jonathan. *Structuralists Poetics: Structuralism, Linguistics, and the Study of Literature.* Ithaca, N.Y.: Cornell University Press, 1975.
  —*The Pursuit of Signs: Semiotics, Literature, Deconstruction.* Ithaca, N.Y.: Cornell University Press, 1981.
  —*On Deconstruction: Theory and Criticism after Structuralism.* Ithaca, N.Y.: Cornell University Press. 1982.

Danto, Arthur C. *Analytic Philosophy of History.* Cambridge: Cambridge University Press, 1965.
  —*Narration and Knowledge.* New York: Columbia University Press, 1985.

Datan, Nancy. "Lifespan Psychology." In *The Encyclopedic Dictionary of Psychology,* edited by Rom Harré and Toger Lamb, 350-351. Cambridge, Mass.: MIT Press, 1983.

Davis, Lawrence H. *Theory of Action.* Englewood Cliffs, N.J.: Prentice-Hall, 1979.

Derrida, Jaques. *Of Grammatology,* 1967. Translated by Gayatri Chakravorty Spivak. Baltimore: The Johns Hopkins University Press, 1974.

Dilthey, Wilhelm. *Ideas Concerning a Descriptive and Analytic Psychology, 1894.* In Wilhelm Dilthy, *Descriptive Psychology and Historical Understanding,* translated by Richard M. Zaner and Kenneth L. Heiges, 23-120. The Hague: Martinus Nijhoff, 1977.
  —"The Constitution of the Historical World in the Human Sciences," 1906. In *W. Dilthey: Selected Writings,* translated by H.P. Rickman. Cambridge: Cambridge University Press, 1976.

Dollard, John. *Criteria for the Life History.* New Haven: Yale University Press, 1935.

Dray, William H. *Laws and Explanations in History.* London: Oxford University Press, 1957.
  —*Philosophy of History.* Englewood Cliffs, N.J.: Prentice-Hall, 1964.
  —(ed.) *Philosophical Analysis and History.* New York: Harper & Row, 1966.

Dreyfus, Hubert L. *What Computers Can't Do: The Limits of Artificial Intelligence,* Rev. ed. New York: Harper & Row, 1979.

Droysen, Johann Gustav. *Grundrisse de Historik,* 1868. Quoted in Karl-Otto Apel. *Understanding and Explanation: A Transcendental-Pragmatic Perspective.* Translated by Georgia Warnke. Cambridge, Mass.: MIT Press, 1984.

Eagle, Morris N. "Psychoanalysis and 'Narrative Truth': A Reply to Spence." *Psychoanalysis and Contemporary Thought* 7 (1984): 629-640.

Eagleton, Terry. *Literary Theory: An Introduction.* Minneapolis: University of Minnesota Press, 1983.

Erikson, Erik H. *Childhood and Society,* 1950. 2nd and enlarged ed. New York: W.W. Norton, 1963.
— *Young Man Luther: A Study in Psychoanalysis and History.* Austen Riggs Center, Monograph No. 4. New York: W.W. Norton, 1958.

Erikson, Erik H., Joan M. Erikson, and Helen Q. Kivnick. *Vital Involvement in Old Age: The Experience of Old Age in Our Time.* New York: W.W. Norton, 1986.

Ermath, Michael. *Wilhelm Dilthey: The Critique of Historical Reason.* Chicago: University of Chicago Press, 1978.

Faulconer, James E., and Richard N. Williams. "Temporality in Human Action." *American Psychologist* 40 (1985): 1179-1188.

Ferccero, John. "Autobiography and Narrative." In *Reconstructing Individualism: Autonomy, Individuality, and the Self in Western Thought,* edited by Thomas C. Heller, Morton Sosna, and David E. Wellbery, 16-29. Stanford, Cal.: Stanford University Press, 1986.

Forster, E.M. *Aspects of the Novel.* London: Arnold, 1927.

Frank, Joseph. "Spatial Form in Modern Literature," 1945. In Joseph Frank, *The Widening Gyre,* 3-62. Bloomington: Indiana University Press, 1963.

Frankel, Charles. "Explanation and Interpretation in History." *Philosophy of Science* 24 (1957): 137-155.

Freeman, Mark. "History, Narrative, and Life-Span Developmental Knowledge." *Human Development* 27 (1984): 1-19.

Freud, Sigmund. *The Wolfman and Sigmund Freud,* 1918. Harmondsworth: Penguin, 1973.

Fromkin, Victoria, and Robert Rodman. *An Introduction to Language,* 3rd ed. New York: Holt, Rinehart and Winston, 1983.

Frye, Northrup. *The Anatomy of Criticism.* Princeton, N.J.: Princeton University Press, 1957. *Fables of Identity.* New York: Harcourt, Brace, and World, 1963

Gadamer, Hans-Georg. *Truth and Method,* 1960. Translated by Garrett Barden and John Cumming (New York: Seabury Press, 1975.)
— "Hermeneutics as a Theoretical and Practical Task," 1978. In *Reason in the Age of Science,* translated by Frederick G. Lawrence, 113-138. Cambridge, Mass.: MIT Press, 1981.

Gallie, W.B. *Philosophy and the Historical Understanding.* New York: Schocken Books, 1968.

Gardiner, Patrick. *The Nature of Historical Explanation.* Oxford: Clarendon Press, 1952.

Gardner, Howard. *The Mind's New Science: A History of the Cognitive Revolution.* New York: Basic Books, 1985.

Garnham, Alan. *Psycholinguistics: Central Topics.* New York: Methuen, 1985.

Geertz, Clifford. *The Interpretation of Cultures.* New York: Basic Books, 1973.

Genette, Gérard. *Narrative Discourse: An Essay in Method,* 1972. Translated by Jane E. Lewin. Ithaca, N.Y.: Cornell University Press, 1980.

Gergen, Kenneth J. "Social Psychology as History." *Journal of Personality and Social Psychology* 26 (1973): 309-320.
—"Stability, Change, and Chance in Understanding Human Development." In *Life-Span Development Psychology: Dialectical Perspectives in Experimental Research,* edited by Nancy Datan and Wayne W. Reese. New York: Academic Press, 1977.
—"The Social Constructionist Movement in Modern Psychology." *American Psychologist* 40 (1985): 266-275.

Gergen, Kenneth J., and Mary M. Gergen. "Narrative Form and the Construction of Psychological Science." In *Narrative Psychology: The Storied Nature of Human Conduct,* edited by Theodore R. Sarbin, 22-44. New York: Praeger, 1986.
—"Narrative and the Self as Relationship." In *Advances in Experimental Social Psychology,* edited by L. Berkowitz. New York: Academic Press, in press.

Gergen, Mary M., and Kenneth J. Gergen, "The Self in Temporal Perspective." In *Life-Span Social Psychology,* edited by R. Abeles. Hillsdale, N.J.: Lawrence Erlbaum Associates, in press.

Ghougassian, Joseph P. *Gordon W. Allport's Ontopsychology of the Person.* New York: Philosophical Library, 1972.

Giddens, Anthony. *New Rules of Sociological Method: A Positive Critique of Interpretative Sociologies.* New York: Basic Books, 1976.

Giorgi, Amedeo. "An Application of Phenomenological Method in Psychology." In *Duquesne Studies in Phenomenological Psychology: Vol. 2,* edited by Amedeo Giorgio, Constance T. Fischer, and Edward L. Murray, 82-103. Pittsburgh: Duquesne University Press, 1975.

Glass, Arnold L., and John L. Santa. *Cognition.* Reading, Mass.: Addison-Wesley, 1979.

Goffman, Erving. *The Presentation of Self in Everyday Life.* Garden City, N.Y.: Doubleday Anchor, 1959.

Goldman, Alvin, I. *A Theory of Human Action.* Princeton, N.J.: Princeton University Press, 1970.

Goldstein, Leon J. *Historical Knowing.* Austin: University of Texas Press, 1976.

Gould, Roger. *Transformations: Growth and Change in Adult Life.* New York: Simon and Schuster, 1978.

Gurwitsch, Aron. *The Field of Consciousness.* Pittsburgh: Duquesne University Press, 1964.

Hacking, Ian. *Why Does Language Matter to Philosophy?* Cambridge: Cambridge University Press, 1975.

Hales, Susan. "The Inadvertant Rediscovery of Self in Social Psychology." *Journal for the Theory of Social Behavior* 15 (October 1985): 237-282.

Hall, Calvin S., and Gardner Lindzey. *Theories of Personality*, 3rd ed. New York: John Wiley & Sons, 1978.

Hanfling, Oswald. *Logical Positivism*. New York: Columbia University Press, 1981.

Harré, Rom, and E.H. Madden. *Causal Powers: A Theory of Natural Necessity*. Totowa, N.J.: Rowman and Littlefield, 1975.

Harrison, Ross. "The Concept of Prepredicative Experience." In *Phenomenology and Philosophical Understanding*, edited by Edo Pivcevic, 93-107. Cambridge: Cambridge University Press, 1975.

Hart, H.L.A., and A.M. Honoré. *Causation in the Law*. Oxford: Oxford University Press, 1959.

Heidegger, Martin. *Being and Time*, 1927. Translated by John Macquarrie and Edward Robinson. New York: Harper & Row, 1962.
—"The Origin of the Work of Art," 1936. In Martin Heidegger, *Poetry, Language, Thought*, translated and introduction by Albert Hofstadter, 17-87. New York: Harper & Row, 1971.

Hempel, Carl G. "The Function of General Laws in History," 1942. Reprinted in *Theories of History*, edited by Patrick Gardiner, 344-356. New York: Free Press of Glencoe, 1959.
—"Explanation in Science and History," 1962. In *Philosophical Analysis and History*, edited by William H. Dray, 95-126. New York: Harper and Row, 1966.

Hesse, Mary. "Is There an Independent Observation Language?" 1970. Reprinted as "Theory and Observation," in Mary Hesse, *Revolutions and Reconstruction in the Philosophy of Science*, 63-110. Bloomington: Indiana University Press, 1980.

Hillman, James. *Healing Fiction*. Barrytown, N.Y.: Station Hill, 1983.

Holdheim, W. Wolfgang. *The Hermeneutic Mode*. Ithaca, N.Y.: Cornell University Press, 1984.

Holland, Norman. "Unity, Identity, Text, Self." In *Reader-Response Criticism: From Formalism to Post Structuralism*, edited by Jane P. Tompkins, 118-133. Baltimore: The Johns Hopkins University Press, 1980.

Holub, Robert C. *Reception Theory: A Critical Introduction*. London: Methuen, 1984.

Howard, George S., and Christine G. Conway. "Can There Be an Empirical Science of Volitional Action?" *American Psychologist* 41 (1986): 1241-1251.

Husserl, Edmund. *Ideas: A General Introduction to Pure Phenomenology*, 1913. Translated by W.R. Boyce Gibson. New York: Humanities Press, 1931.
—*The Phenomenology of Internal Time-consciousness*, 1928. Translated by James S. Churchill. Bloomington: Indiana University Press, 1964.
—*Formal and Transcendental Logic*, 1929. Translated by Dorion Cairns. The Hague: Martinus Nijhoff, 1969.

—*The Crisis of European Sciences and Transcendental Phenomenology,* 1936. Translated by David Carr. Evanston, Ill: Northwestern University Press, 1970.

—*Experience and Judgment: Investigation in a Genealogy of Logic,* 1939. Translated by James S. Churchill and Karl Ameriks. Evanston, Ill.: Northwestern University Press, 1973.

Iser, Wolfgang. *The Act of Reading: A Theory of Aesthetic Response.* 1976. Baltimore: The Johns Hopkins University Press, 1978.

Jackendorf, Ray. *Semantics and Cognition.* Cambridge, Mass.: MIT Press, 1983.

Jacob, F. *The Logic of Living Systems.* London, Allen Lane, 1974.

Jakobson, Roman. "Linguistics and Poetry." In *Style and Language,* edited by Thomas A. Sebeok, 350-377. Cambridge, Mass.: MIT Press, 1960.

James, Williams. *Principles of Psychology.* 1890. New York: Dover, 1950.

Jauss, Hans Robert. "Literary History as a Challenge to Literary Theory," 1967. In *Toward an Aesthetic Reception.* Translated by Timothy Bahti. Minneapolis: University of Minnesota Press, 1982.

Jonas, Hans. *The Phenomenon of Life: Toward a Philosophical Biology.* 1966. Reprint, Westport, Conn.: Greenwood Press, 1979.

Juhl, P.D. *Interpretation: An Essay in the Philosophy of Literary Criticism.* Princeton, N.J.: Princeton University Press, 1980.

Keen, Ernest. "Paranoia and Cataclysmic Narratives." In *Narrative Psychology: The Storied Nature of Human Conduct,* edited by Theodore R. Sarbin, 174-190. New York: Praeger, 1986.

Keeney, Bradford P. *Aesthetics of Change.* New York: The Guilford Press, 1983.

Kemper, Susan. "The Development of Narrative Skills: Explanations and Entertainments." In *Discourse Development: Progress in Cognitive Development Resarch,* edited by Stan A. Kuczaj, II, 99-124. New York: Springer-Verlag, 1984.

Kermode, Frank. *The Sense of an Ending: Studies in the Theory of Fiction.* New York: Oxford University Press, 1967.

Kinneavy, James L. *A Theory of Discourse.* New York: W.W. Norton, 1971.

Kirk, Jerome, and Marc L. Miller. *Reliability and Validity in Qualitative Research.* Beverly Hills, Cal.: Sage, 1986.

Kuczaj, Stan A., II., ed. *Discourse Development: Progress in Cognitive Development Research.* New York: Springer-Verlag, 1984.

Labov, William. "Speech Actions and Reactions in Personal Narrative." In *Analyzing Discourse: Text and Talk,* edited by D. Tannen. Washington, D.C.: Georgetown University Press, 1982.

Labov, William, and D. Fanshel. *Therapeutic Discourse: Psychotherapy As Conversation.* New York: Academic Press, 1977.

Lee, Dorothy. "Lineal and Nonlineal Codifications of Reality." In *Explorations in Communication,* edited by Edmund Carpenter and Marshall McLuhan, 136-154. Boston: Beacon Press, 1960.

Leiber, Justin. "Meaning." In *The Encyclopedic Dictionary of Psychology,* edited by Rom Harré and Toger Lamb, 373-374. Cambridge, Mass.: MIT Press, 1983.

Levine, Murray. "Scientific Method and the Adversary Model: Some Preliminary Thoughts," *American Psychologist* 29 (1974): 661-677.

Levinson, Daniel. *The Season's of a Man's Life.* New York: Ballantine Books, 1978.

Lewis, O. *The Children of Sanchez: Autobiography of a Mexican Family.* New York: Random House, 1961.

Lévi-Strauss, Claude. *Structural Anthropology,* 1958. Translated by Claire Jacobson and Brooke G. Schoepf. New York: Basic Books, 1963.

Lowenberg, Peter. *Decoding the Past: The Psychohistorical Approach.* 1969. Reprint. Berkeley, Cal.: University of California Press, 1985.

MacIntyre, Alasdair. *After Virtue: A Study in Moral Theory.* Notre Dame, Ind.: University of Notre Dame Press, 1981.

Mancuso, James C. "The Acquisition and Use of Narrative Grammar Structure." In Narrative Psychology: The Storied Nature of Human Conduct, edited by Theodore R. Sarbin, 91-110. New York: Praeger, 1986.

Mandelbaum, Maurice. "Historical Explanation: The Problem of Covering Laws," 1961. In Maurice Mandelbaum, *Philosophy, History, and the Sciences: Selected Critical Essays,* 84-96. Baltimore: Johns Hopkins University Press, 1984.

Mandler, Jean Matter. "Stories: The Function of Structure." Paper presented at the annual meeting of the American Psychological Association, Anaheim, Cal., August 1983.
—*Stories, Scripts, and Scenes: Aspects of a Schema Theory.* Hillsdale, N.J.: Lawrence Erlbaum Associates, 1984.

Manis, Jerome G., and Bernard N. Melter. *Symbolic Interaction: A Reader in Social Psychology,* 3rd ed. Boston: Allyn and Bacon, 1978.

Marcus, Steven. "Freud and Dora: Story, History, Case History." *Partisan Review* 41(1):87-102 (1974).

Margolis, Joseph. *Philosophy of Psychology.* Englewood Cliffs, N.J.: Prentice-Hall, 1984.

Martin, Joanne, Martha S. Feldman, Mary Jo Hatch, and Sim B. Sim, "The Uniqueness Paradox in Organizational Stories." *Administrative Science Quarterly* 28 (1983): 438-453.

Martin, Wallace. *Recent Theories of Narrative.* Ithaca, N.Y.: Cornell University Press, 1986.

McAndrews, Robert. "Journeys: An Inquiry into Meaning and Value." Ph.D. diss., Saybrook Institute, 1979.

McCarthy, Thomas A. "A Theory of Communicative Competence." In *Critical Sociology,* edited by Paul Connerton, 478-496. Middlesex, Englans: Penguin Books, 1976.

McInerney, Peter K. "The Sources of Experienced Temporal Features." In *Descriptions,* edited by Don Ihde and Hugh J. Silverman, 91-109. Albany: State University of New York Press, 1985.

Merleau-Ponty, Maurice. *The Structure of Behavior,* 1942. Translated by Alden L. Fisher. Boston: Beacon Press, 1963.
—*Phenomenology of Perception,* 1945. Translated by Colin Smith. New York: Humanities Press, 1962.
—*Signs,* 1960. Translated by Richard C. McCleary. Evanston, Ill.: Northwestern University Press, 1964.
—*The Prose of the World,* 1969. Translated by John O'Neill. Evanston, Ill.: Northwestern University Press, 1973.

Michotte, A.E. *The Perception of Causality,* 1946. Translated by T.R. Miles and E. Miles. London: Methuen, 1963.

Miller, J. Hollis. "The Problematic of Ending in Narrative." *Nineteenth Century Fiction* 33 (1978): 3-7.

Miller, James Grier. *Living Systems.* New York: McGraw-Hill, 1978.

Miller, Patricia H. *Theories of Developmental Psychology.* New York: W.H. Freeman, 1983.

Mink, Louis O. "The Autonomy of Historical Understanding," 1965. In *Philosophical Analysis and History,* edited by William H. Dray, 160-192. New York: Harper & Row, 1966.
—"History and Fiction as Modes of Comprehension." In *New Directions in Literary History* edited by Ralph Cohen, 107-124. Baltimore: The Johns Hopkins University Press, 1974.
—"Narrative Form as a Cognitive Instrument." In *The Writing of History: Literary Form and Historical Understanding,* edited by Robert H. Canary and Henry Kozicki. Madison, Wis.: University of Wisconsin Press, 1978.

Minkowski, Eugene. *Lived Time: Phenomenological and Psychopathological Studies,* 1933. Translated by Nancy Metzel. Evanston, Ill.: Northwestern University Press, 1970.

Mishler, Elliot G. *Research Interviewing: Context and Narrative.* Cambridge, Mass.: Harvard University Press, 1986.
—"The Analysis of Interview-Narratives." In *Narrative Psychology: The Storied Nature of Human Conduct,* edited by Thedore R. Sarbin, 233-255. New York: Praeger, 1986.

Mitchell, W.J.T., ed. *Recent Theories of Narrative.* Chicago: Chicago University Press, 1981.

Mitroff, Ian, and R.H. Killman. "Stories Managers Tell: A New Tool for Organizational Problem Solving." *Management Review,* 64 (1975): 18-28.

Morgan, Gareth, ed. *Beyond Method: Strategies for Social Research.* Beverly Hills, Cal.: Sage, 1983.

Murray, Henry A. *Explorations in Personality.* New York: Oxford University Press, 1938.

Natanson, Maurice. *The Journeying Self: A Study in Philosophy and Social Role.* Reading, Mass.: Addison-Wesley, 1970.

Nehamas, Alexander. *Nietzche: Life as Literature.* Cambridge, Mass.: Harvard University Press, 1985.

Ogden, C.K., and J.A. Richards, *The Meaning of Meaning,* 1923. Reprint. New York: Harcourt, Brace and Co., 1952.

Olafson, Frederick A. *The Dialectic of Action: A Philosophical Interpretation of History and the Humanities.* Chicago: University of Chicago Press, 1979.

O'Regan, Brendan. "Inner Mechanisms of the Healing Response." *Saybrook Review* 5 (1985): 10-31.

Ortony, Andrew, ed. *Metaphor and Thought.* Cambridge: Cambridge University Press, 1979.

Packer, Martin J. "Hermeneutic Inquiry in the Study of Human Conduct." *American Psychologist* 40 (1985): 1081-1093.

Paget, M.A. "Experience and Knowledge." *Human Studies* 7 (1983), 67-90.

Peirce, Charles S. *Philosophical Writings of Peirce,* edited by Justus Buchler. New York: Dover, 1955.

Pepper, Stephen C. *World Hypotheses: A Study in Evidence.* Berkeley and Los Angeles: University of California Press, 1948.

Piaget, Jean. *Structuralism,* 1968. Translated by Chaninah Maschler. New York: Harper and Row, 1970.

Polkinghorne, Donald E. "Phenomenological Research Methods" In *Existential-Phenomenological Perspectives in Psychology,* edited by R.S. Valle and S. Halling. New York: Plenum, in press.
    —*Methodology for the Human Sciences: Systems of Inquiry.* Albany: State University of New York Press, 1983.

Popper, Karl R. *The Poverty of Historicism,* 1957. New York: Harper & Row, 1964.
    —*The Logic of Scientific Discovery.* London: Hutchinson, 1959.

Prigogine, Ilya, and Isabelle Stengers. *Order out of Chaos: Man's New Dialogue with Nature.* Toronto: Bantam Books, 1984.

Propp, Vladimir. *The Morphology of the Folktale.* 1928. Translated by Laurence Scott, 2nd. ed. revised by Louis A. Wagner. Austin: University of Texas Press, 1968.

Raglan, Lord. *The Hero: A Study in Tradition, Myth, and Drama,* 1936. New York: Vintage, 1956.

Ricoeur, Paul. *The Symbolism of Evil,* 1967. Translated by Emerson Buchanan. Boston, Beacon Press, 1969.
    —*The Rule of Metaphor: Multidisciplinary Studies of the Creation of Meaning in Language,* 1975. Translated by Robert Czerny. Toronto: University of Toronto Press, 1977.

—"The Human Experience of Time and Narrative." *Research in Phenomenology* 9 (1979): 25.

—"Narrative Time." In *On Narrative,* edited by W.J.T. Mitchell, 165-186. Chicago: University of Chicago Press, 1981.

—*Time and Narrative.* 2 vols. Translated by Kathleen McLaughlin and David Pellauer. Chicago: University of Chicago Press, 1984-1986.

—*Le temps raconte.* Vol. 3 of *Temps et récit.* Paris: Seuil, 1985.

Robert, Marthe. *Origins of the Novel,* 1971. Bloomington: Indiana University Press, 1980.

Robinson, John A. and Linda Hawpe. "Narrative Thinking as a Heuristic Process." In *Narrative Psychology: The Storied Nature of Human Conduct,* edited by Theodore R. Sarbin, 111-125. New York: Praeger, 1986.

Romanyshyn, Robert D. *Psychological Life: From Science to Metaphor.* Austin: University of Texas Press, 1982.

Rosch, E., and C.B. Mervis. "Cognitive Reference Points." *Cognitive Psychology* 7 (1975): 532-547.

Rorty, Richard, ed. *The Linguistic Turn: Recent Essays in Philosophical Method.* Chicago: University of Chicago Press, 1967.

Rorty, Richard. *Philosophy and the Mirror of Nature.* Princeton, N.J.: Princeton University Press, 1979.

Runyan, William M. *Life Histories and Psychobiography.* New York: Oxford University Press, 1982.

Sanders, William B. "The Methods and Evidence of Detectives and Sociologists." In *The Sociologist as Detective: An Introduction to Research Methods,* edited by William B. Sanders, 1-17. New York: Praeger, 1974.

Sarbin, Theodore R. "The Narrative as a Root Metaphor for Psychology." In *Narrative Psychology: The Storied Nature of Human Conduct,* edited by Theodore R. Sarbin, 3-21. New York: Praeger, 1986.

Sarbin, Theodore R., ed. *Narrative Psychology: The Storied Nature of Human Conduct.* New York: Praeger, 1986.

Saussure, Ferdinand de. *Course in General Linguistics,* 1907-1911, edited by Charles Bally and Albert Sechehaye, translated by Wade Baskin. New York: McGraw-Hill, 1966.

Schafer, Roy. "Narration in the Psychoanalytical Dialogue." In *On Narrative,* edited by W.J.T. Mitchell, 25-49. Chicago: The University of Chicago Press, 1981.

Schafer, Roy. *The Analytic Attitude.* New York: Basic Books, 1983.

Scheibe, Karl E. "Self-Narratives and Adventure." In *Narrative Psychology: The Storied Nature of Human Conduct,* edited by Theodore R. Sarbin, 129-151. New York: Praeger, 1986.

Schein, Edgar H. *Organizational Culture and Leadership: A Dynamic View,* San Francisco: Jossey-Bass, 1985.

Scholes, Robert, and Robert Kellogg. *The Nature of Narrative*. London: Oxford University Press, 1966.

Scholes, Robert. *Structuralism in Literature: An Introduction*. New Haven, Conn.: Yale University Press, 1974.

Schrag, Calvin O. *Communicative Praxis and the Space of Subjectivity*. Bloomington: Indiana University Press, 1986.

Searle, John. "Chomsky's Revolution in Linguistics." In *On Noam Chomsky: Critical Essays*, edited by Gilbert Harman, 2-33. New York: Anchor Books, 1974.

Seebohm, Thomas M. "Facts, Words, and What Jurisprudence Can Teach Hermeneutics." *Research in Phenomenology* 16 (1986): 25-40.

Shaffer, Jerome A. *Philosophy of Mind*. Englewood Cliffs, N.J.: Prentice-Hall, 1968.

Shaw, C.R. *The Jack Roller: A Delinquent Boy's Own Story*. Chicago: The University of Chicago Press, 1930.
    —*The Natural History of a Delinquent Career*. Chicago: University of Chicago Press, 1931.
    —*Brothers in Crime*. Chicago: University of Chicago Press, 1936.

Sheehy, Gail. *Passages: Predictable Crisis in Adult Life*. New York: Bantam, 1977.

Shepherd, E.W. "Self: Psychological Usage;" In *The Encyclopedic Dictionary of Psychology*, edited by Rom Harré and Roger Lamb, 558-559. Cambridge, Mass.: MIT Press, 1983.

Slife, Brent D. "Linear Time Reliance in Psychological Theorizing: Negative Influence, Proposed Alternative." *Philosophical Psychology* 1 (Summer 1980): 46-58.

Smircich, Linda. "Concepts of Culture and Organizational Analysis." *Administrative Science Quarterly* 28 (1983): 339-358.
    —"Studying Organizations as Cultures." In *Beyond Method: Strategies for Social Research*, edited by Gareth Morgan, 160-172. Beverly Hills, Cal.: Sage, 1983.

Spence, Donald P. *Narrative Truth and Historical Truth: Meaning and Interpretation in Psychoanalysis*. New York: W.W. Norton, 1982.

Stein, N.L., and M. Policastro. "The Concept of Story: A Comparison between Children's and Teacher's Viewpoints." In *Learning and Comprehension of Text*, edited by H. Mandl, N.L. Stein, and T. Trabasso, 113-155. Hillsdale, N.J.: Lawrence Erlbaum Associates, 1984.

Strasser, Stephan. *Phenomenology of Feeling: An Essay of the Phenomena of the Heart*, 1977. Translated by Robert E. Wood. Pittsburgh: Duquesne University Press, 1977.

Strawson, Peter F. *Individuals: An Essay in Descriptive Metaphysics*. London: Methuen, 1959.

Thalberg, Irving G. "Self: Philosophical Usage." In *The Encyclopedic Dictionary of Psychology*, edited by Rom Harré and Toger Lamb, 556-557. Cambridge Mass.: MIT Press, 1983.

Taylor, Charles. *Philosophical Papers*. 2 vols. Cambridge: Cambridge University Press, 1985.

Teggart, Frederick, J. *The Processes of History*, 1925. In Frederick J. Teggart, *Theory and Processes of History*. Berkeley and Los Angeles: University of California Press, 1977.
— *Theory of History*, 1925. In Frederick J. Teggart, *Theory and Processes of History*. Berkeley and Los Angeles: University of California Press, 1977.

Thomas, W.I., and Florian Znaniecki. *The Polish Peasant in Europe and America* [Originally, 5 volumes, 1918-1920, Boston: Richard C. Badger]. New York: Alfred A. Knopf, 1927.

Turner, Victor W., and Edward M. Bruner, eds. *The Anthropology of Experience*. Urbana: University of Illinois Press, 1986.

Veyne, Paul. *Writing History: Essay of Epistemology*, 1971. Translated by Mina Moore-Rinvolucri. Middletown, Conn.: Wesleyan University Press, 1984.

Vico, Giambattista. *The New Science*, 1725. Translated by Thomas Goddard Bergin and Max Harold Fisch. Ithaca, N.Y.: Cornell University Press, 1968.

Waele, Jean-Pierre de. "Individual Psychology: History of." In *The Encyclopedic Dictionary of Psychology*, edited by Rom Harré and Toger Lamb, 300-302. Cambridge, Mass.:MIT Press, 1983.

Watzlawick, Paul, Janet Helmick Beavin, and Don D. Jackson. *Pragmatics of Human Communication*. New York: W.W. Norton, 1967.

Weber, Max. "Critical Studies in the Logic of the Cultural Sciences." In Max Weber, *The Methodology of the Social Sciences*, 113-188. Translated by Edward Shils and Henry A. Finch. Glencoe, Ill.: The Free Press, 1949.
— *The Theory of Social and Economic Organization*, 1922. Translated by A.M. Henderson and Talcott Parsons. London: Free Press, 1947.

White, Hayden. *Metahistory: The Historical Imagination in Nineteenth-Century Europe*. Baltimore: The Johns Hopkins University Press, 1973.
— *Topics or Discourse: Essays in Cultural Criticism*. Baltimore: The Johns Hopkins University Press, 1978.
— "The Value of Narrativity in the Representation of Reality." In *On Narrative*, edited by W.J.T. Mitchell, 1-23. Chicago: The University of Chicago Press, 1981.
— "The Question of Narrative in Contemporary Historical Theory." *History and Theory* 23 (1984): 1-33.

White, Robert W. *Lives in Progress*. New York: Holt, Rinehart & Winston, 1952.

Williams, Gareth. "The Genesis of Chronic Illness: Narrative Reconstruction." *Sociology of Health and Illness* 6 (1984): 175-200.

Wilson, Edward O. *Sociobiology: The New Synthesis*. Cambridge, Mass.: Harvard University Press, 1975.

Winch, Peter. *The Idea of a Social Science and Its Relation to Philosophy.* London: Routledge & Kegan Paul, 1958.

—"Understanding a Primitive Society," 1964. In *Understanding and Social Inquiry,* edited by Fred R. Dallmayr and Thomas A. McCarthy, 159-188. Notre Dame, Ind.: Notre Dame University Press, 1977.

Wittgenstein, Ludwig. *Philosophical Investigations.* 3rd. ed. Translated by G.E.M. Anscombe. New York: Macmillan, 1968.

Wright, Georg Henrik von. *Explanation and Understanding.* Ithaca, N.Y.: Cornell University Press, 1971.

Wyatt, Frederick. "The Narrative in Psychoanalysis: Psychoanalytic Notes on Storytelling, Listening, and Interpreting." In *Narrative Psychology: The Storied Nature of Human Conduct,* edited by Theodore R. Sarbin, 193-210. New York: Praeger, 1986.

Index